The Springdale Series—Book One

Glory Be!
A Novel

Martha B. Hook

A Story of Courageous Love in
Post Civil War America

Copyright © 2014 by Martha B. Hook

Glory Be!
A Novel
by Martha B. Hook

Printed in the United States of America

ISBN 9781628713923

All rights reserved solely by the author. The author guarantees all contents are original and do not infringe upon the legal rights of any other person or work. No part of this book may be reproduced in any form without the permission of the author. The views expressed in this book are not necessarily those of the publisher.

Unless otherwise indicated, Bible quotations are taken from The New International Version of the Bible. Copyright © 1973 by International Bible Society.

All characters and places in *Glory Be!* are fictional.

www.xulonpress.com

Dedication

If you have endured abuse or trauma,
this story is for you.

"My God turns my darkness into light."
Psalm 18:28 NIV

PART ONE

"I sought the Lord, and He answered me;
He delivered me from all my fears."
Psalm 34:4 NIV

Chapter 1

August, 1866

God, forgive me—I'm glad he's gone. Clarissa Chambers prayed in silence over her clenched hands. She was thankful beyond the telling for the shield of her black widow's veil, even though it made the oppressive August heat almost unbearable. The Elders nailed her husband's coffin shut and lowered it into its yawning grave as the grieving congregation looked on in silence. Clarissa stepped forward, took a bit of soil and let it slide through her fingers onto the casket. She watched dry-eyed as shovelfuls of dirt landed with soft thuds on Reverend Elliot Chamber's coffin. Armloads of summer flowers were arranged over the mounded raw earth. At last it was over.

When she stumbled away from the graveside, her friends Ida and Tom Lewis rushed to her side. "Lean on us, Clarissa," Ida whispered. Tom offered his arm. Others followed as they walked from the local cemetery to the Trinity Community Church yard. Clarissa knew each and every one, for they had struggled together through the recent War Between the States. The long, weary conflict had left Springdale, Kentucky outwardly intact but demolished in other subtle ways. Many times the community had gathered in those days to honor one of their own fallen warriors. Now the death of Rev. Elliot Chambers, her husband and their young minister, united them again. This time they gathered for her.

Tables covered with food waited in the shade of the churchyard. Scents of the feast wafted toward her. As much as she appreciated the efforts of the church's "Compassion Committee" to feed the hungry crowd, the thought of food sickened her.

How can I eat? How can I not eat? Her legs failed her. "I—I need to sit down."

"Sit here and I'll bring you some water." Ida, at her best with a job to do, bustled off and returned with a cup of water. "Stay right here while I fix you a plate. Don't you dare move."

The new widow's thoughts were clouded by her last glimpse of Elliot's expressionless face at the graveside. *So this is how it ends? Will no one ever know what it was like to be his wife?* Moisture trickled from under the thick auburn braids twisted at the nape of her neck.

People stared and whispered, fanned themselves, and whispered some more.

"Gracious, she's thin as a broomstick," Prudence, wife of Elder Philips, said.

"Bless her heart, she's been through so much with that sick husband," said Aunt Mag, the local source of any necessary sympathy. Clarissa overheard fragments of their remarks, but stared up at the white wooden church where she had been Rev. Chamber's wife since before The War.

"She ain't shed a tear, has she? And at her own dear husband's service," Prudence said.

Only once had Clarissa come close to tears—when her piano students sang a little chorus at the graveside. On an impulse, ignoring Ida's orders, she walked to the children's table.

"Children, your sweet song blessed my heart. I appreciate it more than you'll ever know. I know you worked very hard on it." They surrounded her as she hugged each one. Elliot would have forbidden children's songs at a funeral, most certainly his own. *But he's not here to voice his objections anymore, is he?* Hazel eyes downcast, she returned to her seat. *Clarissa Francine, don't you dare smile*

The whispering continued.

"Now Prudence, don't be so critical. You can't see tears with that veil over her pretty face," Aunt Mag said from behind the paper fan provided by the undertaker.

"Pretty? Not with all those blemishes."

"She's still young. Them spots'll clear up—just takes time."

Ida pushed her way behind the food tables. "You ladies hush talking about our Clarissa. Fix up her plate and I'll take it to her."

Clarissa's throat clamped shut when Ida placed a lavish plate of food in front of her. Out of courtesy she nibbled at a bite or two as she looked over the scene before her. In spite of the crowd, a flood of loneliness swept over her. Ida had left her side to prepare plates for her family. Her parents, who visited while Elliot was still alive, were not present. Elliot's parents arrived at the last minute for the funeral, but she rarely felt any warmth in their presence. And now Elliot, her husband of eight years, was gone—no loss to her but certainly an absence.

When Aunt Mag cozied up to her and said, "Honey, he was a good man," she felt lonelier than ever. She forced a smile and nodded her feigned agreement.

God, help me though this charade. No one will ever understand.

When the midday sun hovered over the sweltering mourners, she joined Elliot's parents in a small spot of shade to murmur goodbyes to friends, church members, and town dignitaries. Her elderly in-laws never faltered in their dull adherence to their role as grieving parents. As the crowd thinned, people had only praise for the man who'd made her life a nightmare behind the closed doors of the parsonage.

Ida, her black dress showing circles of perspiration around the waist and underarms, came alongside. "You must be exhausted. We'll walk with you to the parsonage whenever you're ready. Maybe you can rest before callers start arriving."

"I'm ready."

They said little during the short walk to the parsonage, but Clarissa's mind swirled with her release as Elliot's wife. *Is my nightmare finally over? No more of his tirades? No more of him? Can I be myself again?*

The first waves of relief swept over her.

Chapter 2

"No rest for the weary," Clarissa whispered to Ida as they walked into the parsonage. Several church members swarmed around her to ease the supposed pain of her loss. Their well-meant condolences engulfed her.

Dr. Angus Logan, Springdale's elderly doctor, called later at the parsonage. He and Clarissa had spent long hours together when she volunteered as his nurse during The War. After a generous helping of food from the dinner table, he walked over to her.

"So, Elliot's dreadful struggle with that brain tumor is over. And aren't we all relieved?" The long tendrils of his white moustache twitched. His word "relieved" lingered in Clarissa's mind. *Why would he ask that? Does he suspect the secrets of my marriage?*

"Yes, thank God he's free of pain now." All day she had given this response by rote.

"Now, you be sure to rest. You don't realize how exhausted you are from taking care of our preacher."

"You always worry too much about me. Even if I'm tired, I can't stop now. I must find somewhere to live."

"Aren't you going back to Virginny with your folks?" He peered at her through his perpetually grimy spectacles.

"No, I'll stay here in Springdale where I can make my own way with my sewing customers and music students. My widow's stipend from the church won't last long."

"Don't you come down with something because you're so worn out, and don't be afraid to shed those tears you're holding back."

Why does he or anyone else care whether I cry. . .or not?

He continued, "Next week I'm traveling to Lexington, but when I return I'll stop by to see how you're doing."

"Don't worry a minute about me. You know me—I'll be fine." Their memories of the difficult times they endured during The War surfaced. Exhaustion was never an excuse during those horrific days in the makeshift hospital set up in the Springdale town hall.

"I'll tell you a secret, missy. While I'm in Lexington, I'm meeting with a British doctor, Adam Norcutt, about taking over my clinic. If he's the right one for the job, I'll move back East near my family and let him have at it."

Clarissa stared up at him, surprised.

"Please don't leave us. What'll we do without you and your old horse making house calls? You and Standard are so necessary here." Out of habit, she reached for his spectacles and cleaned them with her handkerchief.

"Standard and I are an old matched pair, aren't we?" He smoothed his whiskers and turned to her guests. "Folks, this young lady could use some peace and quiet, so let's move along. She won't slow down until we leave." He reached for his clean glasses as everyone gathered by the front door.

"Shall I stay with you again tonight?" Ida asked.

"No, I must adjust to being alone, so I might as well start tonight." Saying the words gave her the courage to stand a bit taller.

Elliot's parents assured her they would stop by the next morning to say goodbye. They were staying with a neighbor because the parsonage was still in disarray after Elliot's illness. Clarissa had always puzzled over them. Despite their cordial veneer, their relationship with Elliot had been cool. They rarely corresponded and he had never expressed any affection for them.

Finally, the door closed on the last of her friends. Alone at last, she walked through the silent rooms. The sound of the elders hammering long black nails into Elliot's casket still pounded in her head. When she came to the parlor, the room spun and the horsehair sofa rose up to meet her. She collapsed onto it in a crushed heap of black taffeta, clenched her fists to her temples and cried out in the darkness.

"Is he really gone?" She whispered into the silence of the parsonage. "Sweet Jesus, can You ever forgive me for these feelings?" She pushed away bitter memories and at last she wept—from relief, not sorrow.

As her sobs subsided, a quiet resolve filled her heart and she fell asleep. Awakening past midnight, she stumbled through the darkness into her bedroom, slipped out of her widow's garb and fell into bed.

In her troubled sleep, she dreamed that Elliot was pounding on the front door. When she jumped out of bed in a panic, the sun was barely up and her in-laws were knocking at her front door. After the Chambers' brief farewells, she watched their carriage disappear in a cloud of dust and lingered on the front porch of the parsonage. The sun was rising over the eastern hills to start the first day of her life as a widow. Her thoughts wandered.

I wonder what the rest of my life will be like.

Chapter 3

That night, the nightmares began. They were always the same: Elliot crying out in pain and demanding her help—first a cold pack, then a warm towel; a bigger pillow, then a lighter blanket; a urinal, then a change of sheets. Awake in the night, she wondered if she had done enough. Her conscience rode back and forth over her wounded feelings and memories, the ones she had never shared. She took long walks in an attempt to escape her emotional turmoil.

Why do I feel so guilty? I know I did my best to take care of him.

Ida and her ten-year-old twins, Lester and Lydia, often stopped by the parsonage to visit. Clarissa wished they could simply sit together and say nothing. However, quietude was not in Ida's nature. She always started by filling Clarissa in on all the town gossip, but eventually she would pause with concern in her eyes. Today's visit was no different.

"How are you doing, Clary? Still crying a lot?" The twins also waited for Clarissa's answer, but Ida sent them out to the kitchen. "You children, scoot. See if you can find something in Miss Clarissa's cookie jar."

When the twins were out of earshot, Clarissa replied. "I'm trying to make the best of it." She smoothed the red and white checkered apron she had created with the remnants of a customer's kitchen curtains.

"Aren't you a bit too brave?"

Clarissa almost told Ida the secrets about her marriage, but she balked. Who would believe her if she revealed the true Elliot?

"With God's help I'm holding on." Her voice trembled.

"Good for you. Don't forget, everyone in this town wants to help you get through this." Ida wiped the damp creases in her neck and fanned herself with her moist handkerchief. "I know you must have lots to do. We should go."

"Don't run off." Even though she resisted Ida's chatter, she dreaded an afternoon by herself. She cast about for a new topic of conversation. "I finished reading Elliot's will. There's not much there for me. Without telling me, he gave all our savings to that church mission project up in Minetown."

"Why, that's commendable." Ida, as plump as Clarissa was slender, settled into a rocker that creaked under her size. "Tom and I also gave to that little mission. I wonder what will become of it?"

"Who knows? I suppose our new preacher will have to decide."

"He'll probably latch right onto it—if he doesn't mind going all the way up to Minetown." Ida laughed and called to the twins. "That's enough cookies, children. You go on outside while Miss Clarissa and I visit a bit."

The friends continued chatting over several cups of tea.

"I don't know, Ida, I want to be brave, but I hate being alone."

"In time you'll adjust to this. Remember, dinner with us after church this Sunday."

"You know I won't forget. You're sweet to invite me."

"You never need an invitation with us. You come on over any time." She looked at a tiny gold watch attached to the bar pin on her bodice. "Gracious, look how late it is. Come on, children, I need to start our supper. Your pa is going to wonder where we've gotten off to."

Ida gave Clarissa a hug with many pats on the back and the new widow had the rest of the afternoon to herself.

After dinner on Sunday, Clarissa and the Lewis family lingered around the dining room table. When the children were excused to change out of their church clothes, Tom spoke up.

"So, Clarissa, tell us about your plans for the future."

"Tomorrow I'm reserving a room at the boarding house on the square."

"Surely you don't mean that old broken down place?" Ida was appalled. "Is it safe?"

"It's the best solution for me right now. I'll have to sell my piano, but The Elders have agreed to let me teach my piano students at the church."

Ida went out to the kitchen with their empty dessert plates. After a few moments, she called to Tom.

"Could you come and help me a moment, dear?" From the sound of her voice, she was in a dither.

Tom grimaced, left his unfinished coffee and went to help her. Clarissa could hear serious whispering and wondered what Ida was up to. Why would she and Tom argue over Sunday dinner? Ida marched through the door and plunged right in.

"Clary, you have no business living in that old boarding house—not when you can live in Mama's cottage. It's been standing vacant for months."

Clarissa stared at them in shocked silence. She knew about the small cottage on the outskirts of Springdale. She had often visited Ida's mother there when she was still alive. But she was speechless at this unexpected offer.

"You won't need to pay us a thing," Tom said. They kept describing the small cottage's amenities while Clarissa struggled to accept their offer. She knew they were offering the perfect solution to her dilemma.

"I don't know, Ida. How would I ever repay you?"

Ida stood with her hands on her ample hips.

"Mama's cottage is perfect for what you need and we all know it." Her infectious laughter broke the tension. "Come on, Clary, say 'yes.'"

Looking from one to the other, Clarissa began to weep. Fumbling for her Sunday handkerchief, she nodded her agreement.

As she walked to the parsonage, she thanked God for His amazing provision. "Lord, a cottage of my own? This is too good to be true. And I can keep my piano."

She felt lighter than she had in days.

Over the next few days, Clarissa filled the parsonage dining room with packed crates and luggage. On a Saturday morning some burly churchmen arrived to move everything to her new home.

"Mrs. Chambers? You here?"

"Yes, I'm coming, I'm coming."

Glory Be!

"You ready for us, ma'am?" asked Max Capehart, the boss of the saw mill south of town. Strong as an ox, his muscled arms stretched the limits of his red work shirt. Sporting what he called "my wife's love handles," his britches were buckled below his large belly.

"I'm as ready as I'll ever be."

"It's a crying shame you have to move at a time like this," said Jacob Featherson, who struggled with his brother Luke to make ends meet on a hardscrabble farm north of Springdale.

"It can't be helped," Clarissa replied. "Our new preacher and his family are coming soon."

"Stop the chit-chat," shouted the impatient Luke as he steadied the mules hitched to their sturdy farm wagon. His thirteen-year-old daughter, Rosalie, who would help Clarissa unpack, sat next to him.

Max shouted back, "Just hang on while I see what's s'posed to stay here." He turned back for her instructions.

"I've tied red yarn on all the furniture that is ours—I mean, mine. And that piano in the parlor goes with me." She picked up a basket to carry out, but Jacob stopped her.

"I'll take that. You and Rosalie go on over to the new place. We'll be there directly."

After sweeping out the cottage and making decisions about where to arrange her furniture, Clarissa and Rosalie sat on the steps of the cottage to cool off. When the wagon arrived, she directed the men as they brought in her belongings. They struggled up the front steps with the last item—her piano.

"I'm sorry you have to worry with my heavy piano."

"Shucks," Jacob said, "We're up for this task, ma'am. You tell us where to put this box of ivories and chicken wire and we'll call it a day."

"All we need is a drink from that cold spring of yours and we'll get out of here, Widow Chambers," said Max when the piano was in place.

Am I already Widow Chambers? She shuddered to own her new title.

"Ma'am, you all right?" asked Max. "You need to set yourself down a spell?"

"No, Max, I'm fine—I was a bit distracted for a moment. Come out back by the spring."

She led them outside where a spring bubbled up through the rocks a few steps away from her back door. She handed them the granite ladle that hung on a rusty nail.

"Please, help yourselves."

The men took long gulps of water and Luke splashed the last bit on Jacob's head. Amidst lots of laughter and back slapping, the volunteers walked to their wagon with a heartfelt "thank you" from Clarissa. Luke called to Rosalie.

"Rosie, we're going on out to the river to wet a line. We'll pick you up on our way back. Now, you do whatever Widow Chambers needs."

"Yes sir, I will."

The two worked side by side for the rest of the day. Clarissa's emotions rose and fell as each item with its memories settled into its new place. She appreciated Rosalie's company more than her help. When the men returned from the river, Max brought Clarissa a short string of fish and the Featherson brothers held up their bigger catches for the ladies' approval.

"C'mon, Rosie," shouted Luke. She ran out to the wagon and showed him the coins that had been slipped into the pocket of her apron—the first money she had ever earned.

Clarissa walked out to wave them on their way. Before going back inside, she pulled a wilted blossom off a volunteer zinnia that defied the August heat. The Yankees had ignored the little cottage and its contents when they marched through Springdale. Except for some fencing torn away for firewood, the property was intact and perfect for her needs.

With two bedrooms alongside a parlor and dining room, she had plenty of space. Inside the kitchen door was a pump which brought clear spring water inside. A small room by the front door was large enough for a narrow couch and a bookcase full of Elliot's old theology books. She made a mental note to get rid of them—the sooner the better.

The cottage stood at the intersection of two main roads. Prather Road came in from the north to become the main boulevard through the heart of Springdale. River Road began at Clarissa's cottage and wound east through the hills past several war-torn plantations. It meandered down to the river near a shantytown where freed slaves had built a village.

When Ida came to visit the next day, Clarissa asked, "Did your mother ever have any trouble with the shanty folks who walk back and forth into town?"

"Mama knew most of them from before The War. She always waved to them and sometimes they did odd jobs for her. You're plenty safe out here."

"Ouch," Clarissa cried out when her arm brushed against the edge of the oven. She almost dropped the loaf of hot bread, her first since moving into her new home. She tried to ignore it, but the burn became more painful as the day wore on. She applied compresses of cold spring water, but they did not prevent a large blister. While she was on an errand in town, she stopped by Dr. Logan's clinic.

"Good afternoon, Clarissa, what can I do for you? I hope you aren't ill?"

"No, but I need something for this burn on my arm." He looked at the blister and reached into his cabinet.

"How'd you do this, young lady?"

"Clumsy me, my arm touched the oven while I was baking."

"You caught me in the nick of time. I'm waiting on a rig to take me to the riverboat."

Remembering their conversation after Elliot's funeral, she narrowed her eyes. "You're not leaving for Lexington to visit that new doctor, are you?"

Doctor Logan laughed. "That's right. It's time, Clarissa. I'm getting old." He finished bandaging her arm. "Why don't you visit with me while I wait?" They went out to the wicker chairs on the front porch, and reminisced about caring for the wounded during The War.

"We're lucky those Yankees kept on marching, aren't we?" she said. She looked up and down Prather Boulevard and remembered the hundreds of soldiers who had marched through Springdale during the national conflict. "Thank God no pitched battle ended up around here."

"Springdale looks pretty much the same on the surface, but it will never be like you and I remember it."

He was correct. The brutal war still occupied the minds and hearts of those who had lost so much. Even though Kentucky was a slave state, it had never completely seceded. Feelings were still raw and divided, for many in the state had supported the Union cause. The embers of The War still flared up from time to time. Perhaps it would never be over. No one liked being defeated; nevertheless, they must reinvent themselves and go on.

"Our beautiful plantation homes didn't fare as well as downtown, did they, Dr. Logan? Think they'll ever be restored?" She thought back on the life the stately mansions represented, one that would never flourish again.

"Maybe so, maybe not. Planters can't farm without workers and most of the shanty folks never want to set foot on a plantation again. Can't rebuild without crop income. The blasted carpetbaggers hang around waiting for some poor gentleman to sell even an acre or two. But it's not all gloom and doom. A planter bragged to me just last week that the Yankees missed the heirloom silver and gold coins he hid in their well."

Just then his carriage arrived.

"Have a safe trip. I hope that new doctor is all wrong for your clinic." Clarissa leaned over to kiss his cheek. "Maybe we'll have our new preacher when you return."

"I'm hoping that new doctor is just right," he replied with a wink. "You take good care of that burn now." He jumped into the carriage with an ease that belied his age and waved as it drove away.

Steven and Sophie Jackson with their four children arrived in mid-September to take over the vacant pulpit and parsonage of the Trinity Community Church. Clarissa and several churchwomen helped the new family unpack. Ill at ease in the parsonage, she avoided the bedroom where Elliot died.

Still she tried to look on the bright side—the parsonage, which held so many of her dark secrets, now welcomed a young, happy family. Her mood lightened as she watched the children running about, but she couldn't shake the memories that followed her around as she helped Sophie.

She was happy to agree when Reverend Jackson made a suggestion. "Widow Chambers, you've been through a lot and needn't wear yourself out over here. Please, feel free to go on home and we'll get better acquainted soon."

With a barely disguised sigh of relief, she gathered her things and headed home. Clarissa longed for the day when she would be past the emotional upheaval of Elliot's death, but most days were still a trial. Once after a morning filled with weeping, a new thought occurred to Clarissa.

"I'm grieving over Elliot! What on earth is the matter with me?"

Confused at first, her mind cleared. The loss of her girlhood dream of a happy marriage fueled her grief. She missed the man Elliot could have been, but that man never existed. They met when he was a seminarian who swept her off her feet with love letters and romantic visits. After a brief engagement, they married before he began his ministry as a junior clergyman. She soon realized she was married to a man she barely knew. The man she thought she loved and married disappeared shortly after their honeymoon. Nevertheless, when she found herself brooding over her dark memories, she tried to be thankful for the new, positive things in her present life.

God, You are so faithful. Look at how You've provided for me.

Ida, sensing her friend's grief was far from over, was relentless. "You seem so sad all the time. Clary, you must move on and find some joy. Look at all you have left in your life."

Clarissa tried to smile and brush off Ida's concerns. "Ida, quit your worrying. I'll be fine. There's a passel of things worse than being lonely. Thanks to you, I have this cozy cottage. I'll soon start taking customers and students again, so I'll have plenty to keep me busy. Honestly, I've turned the corner on my old life."

"Next time I catch you looking so sad, I'm going to remind you of what you just said."

Chapter 4

Clarissa greeted the new morning with a need to be busy. She welcomed this unusual surge of energy. Elliot died six weeks ago, and she had only done mending for a few customers since then. Today she looked for a project that would keep her busy for the entire day. Cleaning out the old, dilapidated shed in her backyard suited her mood.

After a quick breakfast, she walked out toward the ramshackle building. The day was cool and soft sunlight filled the scene before her. Willow trees along the distant creek bordering her property tempted her for a walk later in the day. A militant mockingbird flared his wings to distract her from his territory. She stopped to watch the gray, feathered tyrant and his mate tend to their family.

"You don't have to protect your chicks anymore. They're as big as you are now."

Her gaze followed him and she wondered how many generations of his kind had lived in the branches of the weathered oak tree. She opened the door of the shed—and shrieked.

A filthy Union soldier filled the doorway.

"Wha. . .what are you doing here?" Her heart throbbed in her throat. Trying to maintain her composure, she backed away.

"I needed a place to sleep last night, ma'am. That's all."

"Who are you? How long have you been out here?"

"Private George Gary, ma'am. I drank too much yesterday and missed muster when my platoon left, so here I am."

He shoved his filthy blond curls out of his eyes, spat a stream of tobacco juice onto the dirt floor and leered at her. His foul breath covered her like a cloud as he leaned toward her. His clothing smelled as bad as his breath. She trembled with anger and fear.

"It's high time you move on, George Gary. Get off my property. I want you to leave. Now!"

"Not yet, pretty lady. Come on in here with me."

She dodged, but he caught her wrist and pulled her into the darkness of shed. She grabbed a rusty garden spade near the doorway and swung it at him. The spade shattered the window of the shed but was no threat to George Gary. His strength and intentions overpowered her. When she kept screaming, he covered her mouth with his calloused hand.

"I'd as soon slit your little throat, so shut your mouth. Hear? No one can hear you out here anyway." He cursed her with words she'd never heard before. She fell silent and motionless—and prayed for the brutal attack to be over. When the nightmare ended, he tossed her torn clothes at her and sauntered out of the shed. She heard him wash at the spring and rattle around in her kitchen for food. He let her know when he was leaving.

"Thanks for the breakfast, pretty lady. I'll be going now." The screen door slapped shut. He whistled as he walked away.

Pulling herself up to the broken window of the shed, she watched George Gary head north on Prather Boulevard. Waves of revulsion and nausea swept over her. She couldn't stop trembling. Sobbing into her torn, bloody petticoat, she struggled with what to do.

"Dear God in heaven, why this? Am I still alive? What should I do?" She ran to sit by the spring where the water still flowed cold and clear. "Maybe some spring water will help." But the feelings of filthy horror would not wash off.

"Should I tell someone? Maybe Ida or the new preacher? If only Dr. Logan were here, he'd know what to do."

After she gathered enough composure to go inside, she locked all the doors and windows and went to bed for the rest of the day. Even though she knew it was false security, she pulled the pillows and covers over her head. That afternoon, she ate a bite of a stale biscuit and drank some warmed over tea.

The next morning, after writing notes to her piano students to cancel their lessons, she paid a woman walking to Springdale to deliver them. She shut out the world and once again hid under the home made quilt covering her bed.

I need to be alone. I hope Ida doesn't come calling today.

On Sunday, because she was still the church pianist, she dressed for the first time since the assault. She walked to the church where she forced herself to maintain a facade of cheerfulness. The familiar church house and the melodies of the old hymns brought a semblance of quiet into her heart. The hymns were God's gift sent to sing her back to peace.

She turned down several invitations for Sunday dinner. How could she sit down with friends and visit about life's little ups and downs? What would she say if someone asked why she canceled her piano students? She needed to be at home where no one could talk to her.

Memories of what happened in the old shed plagued Clarissa. Her nerves were in such turmoil that often her stomach cramped and caused her to double over. She resumed her normal activities but kept running into inquisitive people who sensed something was troubling her. Her caring friends assumed she still grieved Elliot's death. She kept assuring them that she was fine and was thankful for the curtain of widowhood to hide behind.

One day at The Mercantile she ran into Aunt Mag.

"I know you're still sad. We all miss our pastor, but in time you'll feel better. I promise."

"I hope and pray you're right, Aunt Mag."

"You know I am. Now be sure to get some rest and do some things you enjoy."

"Yes, ma'am, I'll do that." She turned away and made a show of reading her shopping list. As soon as she could, she ran back to her cottage and gave in to the cramps and nausea. She took a long nap to calm her nerves and lectured herself for being so unfriendly.

What's the matter with me? Why can't I let people be nice to me?

Chapter 5

By the end of October, Clarissa knew she was pregnant. The early symptoms of pregnancy, morning sickness and pervasive exhaustion were unmistakable. When she began having severe pain and bleeding, she was torn between wanting to miscarry and wanting to protect the little life inside her. Under the guise of settling into her cottage, she stayed to herself and prayed that somehow God would give her words to explain her condition.

One afternoon when Ida came to call, Clarissa did not answer her knock. Never one to be shy, she pushed on the door and came in.

"Is anyone home? Clary? I thought you were going to start locking your doors."

"I'm back here in bed," Clarissa called to her. "I had a piano student earlier and forgot to lock up behind her. Come on back."

"What's the matter? Are you sick?" Ida hurried into the house and dropped her shopping bag in an empty chair.

"I guess so," she replied as she heard Ida hurrying through the cottage.

"Why, honey, you're as white as a bed sheet."

"I'm feeling a bit better. Let me fix us some tea." When she shoved back the covers, Ida gasped. Blood stained the sheets and Clarissa's nightgown.

"Gracious sakes, Clary! What's this? Are you all right?"

Weeping, Clarissa crumpled back into bed and shook her head.

"You've no business getting out of this bed. You stay right here while I fix our tea. I know where everything is." Ida always knew where everything was. "Then I want you to tell me what's going on."

"I will." She steeled herself to share her shameful story. "I need to talk to someone."

Ida returned with a tray holding two steaming teacups. "You're pregnant, aren't you?" She put down the tray with authority and waited.

Clarissa slowly nodded and put her head in her hands. "Yes, but. . ."

Before she could launch into her confession, Ida squealed and smothered her with a hug.

"Oh, I'm so happy for you! Won't—Wouldn't Elliot be pleased? What a shame you can't tell him your good news."

The thought of passing her baby off as Elliot's had occurred to her, but the timing was off—wasn't it? Now Ida's assumption freed her to keep her dark secret. Waves of relief crept into her heart.

"I hate to be so weepy over this, but I can't face being pregnant right now."

"You poor dear, of course you can't. Don't you worry, everyone will help take care of you and this baby. Everything will work out just fine."

Clarissa said nothing. Her storehouse of comments intended to put everyone at ease was empty.

"I insist you see Dr. Logan when he returns. You can't ignore this bleeding."

"I've decided to have Betsy Capehart, Max's wife, help me when my time comes. She'll let me pay her midwife fees a little bit at a time by sewing for her family."

"I'm still going to tell Dr. Logan when he returns. You know he'll be happy for you."

"I guess I can't keep this a secret any longer. Go ahead and tell him." Finally, one of her secrets was out in the open.

"You don't worry another minute. You've wanted a little one so much, especially after you lost that other baby. It's a crying shame that Elliot will miss holding his firstborn."

By the time Ida left, Clarissa was in a clean nightgown, rested on fresh linens and felt her secret was secure. But did she want it to be? She had been keeping secrets for so long.

Lord, I want to tell the truth, but I can't—can I?

Chapter 6

As Clarissa's news filtered through Springdale, the community rejoiced. To the uninformed, this put a fairy tale ending on the last sad chapter of her marriage to Reverend Chambers. Wherever she went, she was congratulated. Offers to help with the baby were countless. All over town, knitting needles clicked and tiny garments soon filled a drawer at her house.

One day at the Lewis Mercantile as Clarissa browsed among the sewing supplies, some fluffy yellow yarn caught her eye.

"Ida, could you come here a minute?"

"Need some help?"

"I've never crocheted much, but I'm so tempted."

"Do you see something you like?"

"This yellow yarn is so soft. Could I crochet a baby blanket with this weight?"

"It's too light for anything but a baby blanket. Why don't you give it a try? I'll start you out with a crochet hook and the first skein."

"I won't turn you down. I saw this yarn and was so tempted, but I didn't think I could afford it. My baby and I thank you." She patted her still slim waistline.

My baby—the words kept sending a blessing through her shattered nerves. Soon she mastered the skill of crocheting and the yellow blanket began to take shape. However, whenever she felt the excitement of becoming a mother, memories of George Gary would intrude. She tried to rid her mind of his presence with little success. *He was so filthy.*

Another problem plagued her: she no longer felt safe alone at the cottage. She prayed that God would protect her, but to her dismay, she now questioned His ability to do so.

"Where were You that morning when Pvt. Gary showed up? I need more than a mockingbird to guard my back yard. I know You're able, but why doesn't it feel that way?" Doubting God made her even more miserable.

As if this weren't enough, she struggled with the lie she allowed her friends to believe. She agonized over her choice to deceive them.

"I know the Bible says, 'Thou shalt not bear false witness,' but shouldn't I protect this baby from the truth? Doesn't an innocent child deserve a decent life? If I tell the truth, won't my child always feel shamed? Besides, the least the Reverend Chambers can do is give this baby his name."

When Dr. Logan returned from Lexington, he called on Clarissa.

"Welcome back, Dr. Logan. Come in, we missed you." He had no idea how true this was.

"Some bad weather and gracious relatives held me up. What's this I hear about you and a little one?"

"I'll bet Ida told you, bless her. It's true. The midwife says I'm due the end of May. She's letting me pay her fees by sewing for her family."

"I know you're thrilled. Now we must work out a plan of food and rest. No matter who's helping you, I don't want you losing another baby."

"Me neither. I promise to do whatever you say."

He wrote down some notes for her and chuckled. "I reckon that preacher of yours was healthier than I thought."

"I reckon." *Please, please don't ask me any questions.*

"Now you run by my clinic any time you need me. If I'm still here when your time comes, I'll deliver this baby. You won't owe me a penny."

While they lingered on her porch, she changed the subject.

"You haven't mentioned your trip to Lexington. Did you like that new doctor?"

"As a matter of fact, I did. Dr. Adam Norcutt is coming soon to look things over. He was working at that big hospital in Lexington when he found himself smack-dab in the middle of our war. He spent a lot of time caring for our wounded. Now he's looking for a more peaceful place to settle in America."

"He's not returning to England?"

"Nope—says there's nothing there for him."

"I hoped you wouldn't like him. Why can't you stay here with us? You know we'll take care of you."

"Thank you, but I want to retire while I can still enjoy my old hometown. Don't forget, this Dr. Norcutt may not accept my offer."

"If our church can help his family get settled when they arrive, you let us know."

"Norcutt won't come with a family. He's a war-weary bachelor and his stint as a battlefield surgeon left him with only some personal belongings and a crate of medical equipment. I'll tell him the church will help out, but I don't think he's much of a churchgoer."

A warning bell went off in her heart. "Sounds like he's cut from a different cloth than you, Dr. Logan. Are you sure about this?"

"We'll see. His heart for the profession is refreshing. He was at the top of the London medical community when he came to Lexington to partner with my friend, Dr. Hugo Perry. When The War broke out, he didn't hesitate to help our Confederate wounded even though he supported Wilberforce—the man who struggled against slavery in England. Hugo can't say enough about his character and skills with a scalpel."

"Are you sure you asked him enough questions?" She felt protective of her elderly friend.

"Enough to know that we are similar in how we view doctoring. Good skills and a good heart are what I am looking for."

Standard was restless and pawing out at the hitching post. "Looks like Stan is ready for his supper. Now be sure to rest and eat right. We want this baby to be able to handle lots of attention and love."

"And not come down with the epozootics. Right?" She laughed as she used his word to describe any illness he was at a loss to diagnose.

"Most definitely, little mother."

Clarissa waved until he turned toward Springdale. When the door closed behind her, she went straight to bed, exhausted but also a little relieved. If she could deceive Dr. Logan with this trumped up story of Elliot's last stand as her husband, she could fool anyone.

One cold afternoon as Clarissa's last piano student was leaving, Dr. Logan's buggy stopped at her hitching post. She watched the doctor and a tall stranger walk up the path to her front door. An icy fear came over her—she didn't like male strangers. However, if the man was with Dr. Logan, he must be trustworthy.

"Come in, Dr. Logan." She backed away from the doorway.

"Greetings, Miss Clarissa, this is Dr. Norcutt, the English doctor I told you about."

"Yes, I remember," Clarissa tried to be courteous. "How do you do?"

"It's my pleasure to meet you, Widow Chambers." His British accent added a distinguished air to his cordial response. She paused, not quite sure how to welcome an English gentleman. Dr. Logan spoke up.

"I've taken Dr. Norcutt all over Springdale today. We saved our last stop for a cup of your tea. I hope we aren't imposing."

"Of course not, I'm glad you stopped by. Let me take your wraps and I'll find us a pastry. The tea is already steeping." She put their wraps on the couch in her study. "Please have a seat while I pull things together in the kitchen."

She could overhear the doctors' conversation as Dr. Logan explained the medical details of Elliot's death. When he commented on Elliot's excellence as a minister, she clattered the cups and saucers and quit eavesdropping. She returned with a serving tray of tea and pound cake. After a few moments of visiting, Dr. Norcutt turned to Clarissa.

"I barely set my baggage down this morning when we were out and about meeting people." He ran his long fingers through his wind blown black hair. "I'm ready for a break and I'm glad someone in Springdale serves afternoon tea." He sipped his tea again. "Your tea is superb."

"My family came here from England years ago, and I still stop in the afternoon for tea. I have a sinking spell about this time when my piano students leave but I still have sewing to do."

"So you have two occupations?"

"Yes, sir, I teach piano and sew for several ladies. I also do mending."

"Ah, I have some clothing that needs the attention of a seamstress. Fortunately for me, there are no bullet holes. Might you have time for my mending?"

"Certainly, Dr. Norcutt."

Clarissa watched them leave and wondered if Adam Norcutt would pass the test of replacing Dr. Logan. Still she had to agree, this newcomer had a way about him. His easy conversation and impeccable manners had impressed her in spite of her wish to dislike him.

Chapter 7

The next morning Adam Norcutt was up early and ready to go to work with Dr. Logan. But the older doctor had a different plan.

"Why don't you take this morning to unpack and settle in? I didn't give you a chance to catch your breath yesterday. Nothing is happening in the clinic that demands both of us right now. If I have an emergency, I won't hesitate to call you in."

"Splendid. I'll take my mending out to your seamstress and when I return we can sort through my medical equipment to decide what might be useful here—if anything."

With the beautiful fall morning tempting him on a walk and a seamstress willing to do his mending, Adam hurried to unpack. He soon had three mounds of clothing: one to keep, one to discard and one to take to Widow Chambers. Before he left, he puzzled over life in a small town. To be sure he didn't stumble over any invisible local customs, he took his concerns to Dr. Logan.

"I have a question about Springdale etiquette."

"Of course, fire at will."

"Should you accompany me to Widow Chambers' home? I don't want to embarrass myself on my second day in town."

"She won't be offended. Folks take her mending all the time. and you can't go out there a'courting yet because she's still in mourning."

"Great Scott, I hadn't even considered that."

"You go on out there. You won't offend our little widow. We'll have to see which young buck around here wins her heart. He'll have an instant family because the reverend left her pregnant. She's chosen our local midwife for her delivery, but I'm concerned about her because she and the preacher once lost a baby at birth. If you stay, keep an eye on her for me."

"What a hardship to raise their child alone. I'll watch out for her."

Adam gathered up his frayed clothing and breathed in the fresh, crisp air as he left the clinic. The scenery along Prather Boulevard brought him up short. He took in the breathtaking sights that surrounded him. He'd not expected Springdale scenery to be so beautiful. The cattle grazing in the lush meadows impressed him and some exceptional horseflesh caught his eye. He walked up the path to Clarissa's cottage and knocked.

"Good morning, Doctor. Please come in. Late yesterday I received several mending jobs, but I told them that you're in line ahead of them."

"Thank you for saving time for me. Until I unpacked, I hadn't realized my clothing is in such dismal condition." He handed her his armload of mending, but she backed away to avoid touching him.

"Please put it there on my sewing table. I'll have this for you by the end of the week."

"No hurry. I've managed without these for a long time."

"Oh, I try to be prompt. I like to keep my mending moving along. Now if you can wait a moment, I'll send some dinner home with you."

"I won't turn that down. I've been enjoying the scents coming from your kitchen."

As Clarissa walked to the kitchen she could see him looking around her home.

"I'm still settling into my new surroundings," she said over her shoulder. "By God's grace, some dear friends allow me to live here. With The War and now Rev. Chamber's death, I'm barely making do." She handed him a bowl of chicken and dumplings nestled in a basket and covered with an embroidered tea towel.

"Thank you, I haven't had many decent meals lately." He peeked under the towel and made a show of breathing in the fragrance. "Mmmm!"

"I hope you'll be happy here—if you decide to stay."

"So far, I've no complaints. Springdale is a delightful town and the views magnificent."

"We're a far cry from London or Lexington, but we're a lively group with busy lives. We're even holding theater productions in the town hall."

She knew local hostesses would clamber over one another to entertain this new arrival. An unattached, mature gentleman, especially one as handsome as Dr. Norcutt, would be sought after by every Confederate widow in town.

"I'm afraid our southern hostesses may wear you out with invitations."

"I don't need many to fill my social calendar. Doctoring doesn't leave much spare time."

"Dr. Logan told me you don't have a family, so you beware. One of our Dixie Belles may steal your heart." Clarissa cringed, afraid she had spoken too freely.

"Don't worry. Right now my goal is to get acquainted with my new patients."

After he left, Clarissa stood looking at his mending and sighed. The task would take hours, but she welcomed the income. He seemed like a congenial gentleman.

I wonder what attracted him to Springdale?

Chapter 8

Adam walked back to Dr. Logan's clinic lost in a dilemma he had avoided since arriving in America. After Widow Chamber's comments about his social life, he realized that people in Springdale would assume he was single. But that assumption would be false. He was a married man who had lived as a bachelor since leaving London before the American Civil War. Why should anyone know otherwise as long as he never married again?

He grimaced as he remembered the foggy night in London when he found a note from his wife, Josephine. He remembered every word: "Our marriage is over. Nathan and I are staying temporarily with my parents. Please remove your belongings as soon as possible. I will never humiliate myself by seeking a divorce." There was no signature.

His frantic attempts to see Josephine and Nathan were rebuffed. In desperation, he called on her father at his place of business, but the perplexed gentleman only confirmed Josephine's decision. With that single short note, his life had been devastated by an empty marriage and the loss of his son. Nothing had happened in the intervening years to change the sad state of the family he left behind in London.

Lost in his personal struggles, Adam ignored the beautiful scenery on his walk back to the clinic. Since Dr. Logan was nowhere to be seen, he set aside his worries long enough to devour Clarissa's provisions. He was still seated at the kitchen table with an empty bowl before him when the other doctor came in.

"I fear you're a bit late, Dr. Logan."

"Was that Widow Chamber's famous chicken and dumplings?"

"We have something similar in England, but your little widow's recipe far exceeds anything I've ever tasted. Now it's high on my new list of Kentucky favorites."

Doctor Logan served himself from some leftovers he found in the pie safe. No patients arrived at the clinic as the men sat talking at the table.

"Think you'll be able to adjust to our slower pace of life around here?"

"So far Springdale appears to be a charming community. I like the country atmosphere and I've already been invited to a dinner party. A nice lady, Aunt Mag, gave me a loaf of fresh bread. Now I must remember all of these new names and faces."

"Pretty soon you'll know everyone in these parts." He rose and poured two cups of the morning's warmed over coffee. He smoothed his white moustache and settled himself for a long visit with his new associate. "We have a moment here while the clinic is quiet. Why don't you tell me about your life before you came to America?"

For almost an hour Adam made himself homesick as he talked about his homeland.

"I grew up in London, so I'm a city boy and all my schooling was there. With the encouragement of my family I realized my boyhood dream of becoming a doctor. I planned to focus my skills on the upper echelon of London society."

"You don't strike me as the bookworm type. Surely you have other interests?"

"Right you are. We're diehard horsemen in my family. Whenever my studies permitted, I rode to the hounds or played polo. I was a regular substitute for our society's polo team."

"You're in luck, Adam. We don't lack for avid horsemen here in Kentucky. A healthy Thoroughbred business was underway before The War and is coming back strong. We have an excellent local stable where you can hire a mount. Be sure to meet Leon—he's a part Shawnee boy from somewhere up in the hills. He lives over the stables and has a real knack with horses. He'll match you up with a good ride. Of course, you can always borrow Standard."

They laughed and Adam continued describing his life in London.

"I have a new outdoor interest called 'badminton.' I brought my equipment with me."

"Is it anything like our game of horseshoes?"

"No, I've never played that one. My brother learned badminton while serving with the Brits in India. He brought me a souvenir of the required equipment."

"Did he instruct you?"

"Yes, he did. Whenever he trounced me, he reminded me to be thankful because he almost brought me a wastebasket made from an elephant's foot."

Still no one came to the clinic, so the men moved out onto the back porch that overlooked a small pasture. Standard stood grazing in the distance. A few trees still glowed with the colors of fall.

"Adam, you remind me of myself when I was your age—a single, dedicated doctor. I fell in love with a lovely woman who was my wife for over twenty years. Despite my best efforts, she died of pneumonia and I've never found anyone to take her place. But you won't have any difficulty finding someone here to be a wonderful wife for you."

The muscles along Adam's jaw tightened. He cleared his throat.

"Dr. Logan, I think there's something I should tell you." He hesitated, but then plunged in. "You need to know about the dilemma I left behind in London, so you'll understand why I came to Kentucky,"

He described his miserable marriage to Josephine, their separation, her resistance to letting him see Nathan, and her refusal to divorce. He stumbled over explaining Josephine, a layered paradox of beauty, seductive liaisons and rigid social dogmas.

Dr. Logan shook his head. "What a heartbreak to lose your little boy. So, you can never re-marry? Terrible, terrible. Did you come to America to put all that behind you?" He spoke with genuine concern and Adam continued.

"I wanted to keep our family together, but she made that impossible. Even though we had some terrible disagreements, we could've had a decent home together. I'll always grieve for Nathan, a father's delight of a boy. Even though I write to him whenever I can, I'm sure he never sees the letters. I fantasize about having him live here with me, but it'll never happen. He's almost 6 years old now."

"What did you do with yourself when your marriage failed?"

"For a year I did nothing. I struggled to do the simplest things in life. I had my work, but my heart wasn't in it anymore." He paused and looked out into the distance as the pain of old memories flooded over him. "When I heard that my friend, Hugo Perry, was looking for a partner here, I decided to investigate. At least, I'd see some of America—maybe an Indian or some buffalo."

"You're a brave man to start completely over."

"Thank you, sir. Of course, being in Hugo's surgical tents on the battlefields was not in the original plan. I'm extremely fortunate to be in one piece."

"During The War I also put in time treating wounded soldiers. But I was never out with the action." Dr. Logan changed the subject. "I assume that you're Anglican?"

"Our family has a pew in an Anglican church. However, as a boy I had no interest in religion. There are 308 bricks around the stained glass window above the altar, and 28 angels around Baby Jesus in the center of that window. That's the extent of my religious training."

Dr. Logan chuckled. Adam decided not to admit that as an adolescent, he had posed some serious questions about God. Instead of receiving answers, he was punished for asking. A few years later, he immersed himself in the research of Charles Darwin, eliminating the need to believe in a Creator. Now a thoroughgoing atheist, he attended church only on special occasions to please his family.

With a big smile, Adam stretched his hands behind his head and took their discussion down another path.

"When I left England, I certainly never thought I would entertain the possibility of serving a rural clinic in America."

"Don't you rush this decision, young fella. You take your time to investigate my situation here. Now, it's time for my nap. At my age, no one thinks I'm lazy for indulging in a snooze after dinner. You stay here and relax."

Adam leaned back in his chair, propped his long legs on the porch railing and mulled over his decision to leave London. *I had no place to call my own and no one to share my life, so what was I to do? I took a different path.*

Chapter 9

On his odyssey to Kentucky, Adam had enjoyed the Atlantic crossing. He brought little with him—only his journals, his medical instruments, his clothing and a few books. At the last moment, he tossed in his badminton set. The ship passed through a storm or two but arrived in New York on schedule. As he traveled overland across America to Kentucky, the beauty and enormity of the land captivated him. It seemed to go on forever.

To leave his marital problems behind and embark on a new adventure invigorated him. While at sea, he wrote Nathan a letter which he mailed from New York City, and he continued to write whenever he could. Four years later, he still didn't know if Nathan had received his letters or if he would ever see him again.

When Adam arrived in Lexington, he had little time to brood his losses in England. Absorbed at once into a new medical scene, his surgical skills were respected and challenged. Shortly after the Civil War started, Hugo sought him out.

"Norcutt, would you help us over in the wards for the wounded? The CA is sending us more than we planned—terrible wounds. We're desperate for surgeons."

"I suppose I can't refuse."

"I must be sure—do you mind serving with the Confederacy?"

"A wounded soldier is a wounded soldier, Hugo. I'll serve where I'm needed."

Thrust into the military wards where hundreds needed his skills, the pressure on Adam never let up. He stood before an operating table for hours on end. Most evenings he went to his quarters with aching feet and his clothing soaked in the blood of mangled soldiers.

One day Hugo rushed up to him. "Norcutt, we need you in the field hospital if you're willing. Our team out there has fallen apart with malaria and some bad shrapnel wounds. I'm desperate for medics out near the battle lines."

After Adam joined the medical unit that followed the conflict, he was near the fighting and in danger so often he ignored it. This was not his war, but he served the wounded wholeheartedly. In retrospect, he knew he was a far better doctor for his battlefield experiences. He learned to make split-second decisions and to trust his own judgment for diagnosis at an instinctual level. Once in awhile he delivered a baby for a farmer's wife or tended a sick child, but those gentle times were rare.

Adam's experiences as a wartime surgeon, though valuable, had left him deeply scarred and more than a little cynical. When the armistice came, he could not shake the trauma of the battlefields. The horrific memories of operating on soldiers without proper anesthesia or bandages haunted him. He had spent too many days postponing life-saving procedures due to lack of supplies. The sounds and smells of the battlefields stayed with him long after the war ended. Often the faces of soldiers in agony appeared in his dreams. With these difficult memories plaguing him, he recoiled at the prospect of walking into an operating room every day for the rest of his life.

Hugo Perry, recognizing his friend's exhaustion, insisted he take time off. Adam appreciated the rest, but with long, lonesome hours to fill, the ghosts of his life in England surfaced with a vengeance. He grieved afresh for Nathan and longed for him. Perhaps the boy might come to visit or even live with him. But he was sure Josephine would never agree to such a plan.

One evening sitting by the glowing grate in his quarters, he concluded that he'd brought his British struggles with him to America. Rather than spend another sad evening alone, he dressed and went to a reception Hugo and Adele Perry were hosting at their newly refurbished home. The company and the food would be excellent, and he needed a good, stiff drink.

Hugo took Adam on a tour of their new home and tried to encourage him.

"After you've had some time off, you'll be ready for that new operating theater I've promised you."

"I want to stay in the medical field, Hugo, but right now I have little desire to hold a scalpel all day long. To be quite honest, I don't know what I want to do with my skills."

After several more drinks, they were joined on their stroll by Adele, who liked Adam.

"You'll find the right place for your talents, Adam. Meanwhile, you're always welcome here. You don't even need an invitation, does he, Hugo?" Hugo agreed.

"Thank you, both of you. Your boundless hospitality is truly a gift."

Adam lingered with the Perrys long after the other guests left. They enjoyed several more rounds of drinks until Hugo was called out on an emergency. Adam came to the next morning in his quarters with a blistering headache. He looked around and wondered how or when he'd returned home.

He continued to ponder where his original dream of becoming a surgeon had gone. His desire to help people with their physical ailments had never left him. Perhaps a place existed where this part of his calling could be resurrected and put to a useful purpose?

Now, on Doctor Logan's back porch, he recalled meeting him in Lexington.

"I hope I didn't take too much of the good doctor's time," Adam remarked to Hugo.

"Don't worry, we're all fascinated by his clinic out on the fringes of our land."

After several visits with Dr. Logan, when the possibility of serving the clinic in Springdale was offered, Adam jumped at the chance. Here was a complete change of pace and a simpler way of life. He could see patients with milder conditions, deliver babies, or deal with colicky infants. Perhaps this was the place where he could settle down and have a normal life.

Feeling cramped, Adam stood to go inside, but changed his mind. Walking into the pasture, he waited while Standard came toward him. As the old horse's neck was rubbed, he nuzzled Adam with contentment.

"You're quite the special gent around here, aren't you? I wish we'd met when you were younger. No doubt you'd have kept up with the best of my polo ponies." They stood for several minutes together, until Adam leaned into him and said, "I have a proposition for you, old chap. Could you take me out to those shanties someday to see if they need a doctor?"

As a foreigner, Adam had observed how the outcome of The War had affected the freed slaves. As he had disembarked from the steamer the day before, he had seen the dismal conditions of the people standing around in the shanties along the river bank. He suspected that their medical needs were going untreated.

After Dr. Logan's nap, Adam asked him about the deal he had struck with Standard.

Dr. Logan readily agreed. "You two see what can be done for those folks. Stan will be up for the task or get a piece of my mind."

The next morning, Adam tied Standard to a tree limb and set his black bag on a nearby stump. The river rushed by as he looked around the shanty town. Several people peeked at him from behind trees and their flimsy houses.

"Good morning. I'm Dr. Norcutt," he announced. "I'm new in Springdale and I wonder if anyone here needs a doctor. Please step forward. Let me see if I can help you."

He stood for a long time beside Standard before an elderly man spoke up.

"Doctor, we can't pay nothing for no doctor. We 'preciate you, but you'd best go on home now." He saw the man's shadow behind a tree.

"Don't worry about paying me. Maybe you can work for me someday when I need help."

A woman with a seriously ill child came forward first. He urged others to step up and soon several patients waited in line. The former slaves welcomed his solutions for nagging problems like infected sores, ingrown toenails, ringworm, insect bites, poison ivy, and lice infestation. He asked those with more serious problems to come by the backdoor of the clinic.

"Be sure to stop by for that sore on your leg," he instructed one young man. "I need to treat your wound several times to get that infection cleared up." The man's eyes widened when Adam added, "I'd really hate for you to lose that leg. I won't charge you a tuppence." When the man looked puzzled, Adam corrected himself, "I mean a penny."

Appalled by the physical conditions he found on this first trip to the shanties, he decided to make regular visits there when time permitted. . .if he decided to stay. Soon freed folk waited in the shade by the back door of the clinic until he could tend to their needs. One evening after dark he found a chicken tethered to the tree in the back yard. The work satisfied him in a way nothing had since The War ended. He began to experience a welcome set of feelings: He was going to bed happy and waking up with renewed energy.

Chapter 10

Adam settled into Dr. Logan's spare room. Slowly the clinic and adjoining house began to feel like home. He made friends with shopkeepers and citizens as he walked around Springdale. Within a few weeks he approached Dr. Logan.

"If your offer is still open, I'm convinced this is the right place for me."

"Excellent—I'm not surprised. I thought our life in Springdale would appeal to you." They shook hands to seal their agreement.

"So, Dr. Logan, what do we do next?"

"Let's go to the bank and draw up the legal papers, if that's agreeable."

"Absolutely. I look forward to starting this new chapter in my life."

"Tell you what—after we finish at the bank, I'll treat you to a meal at the Excelsior Hotel. It's not much by London standards, but it's tops for our little burg. Their beef is what I order."

Word spread that the new doctor was capable and personable. Around the social circles of the town, the handsome Dr. Norcutt was now on every hostess's most wanted list. Never ill at ease in any social situation, Adam soon felt right at home. He enjoyed meeting the families of Springdale in the large drawing rooms of homes near the town square as much as he enjoyed his work in the shanties. When talk of the War started, Adam could match tales with the best of them. However, he politely turned away inquiries about his life in England. Only Dr. Logan knew why this debonair Brit abandoned London.

Adam found other men who shared his interest in horses. Now they included him on rides that wound through the abandoned plantations. Along the way they stopped to rest their mounts, smoke cigars made of local tobacco and discuss their horses' future breeding lines.

After a round or two of Kentucky spirits from their pocket flasks, they returned to town and turned their horses over to the capable stable hand, Leon.

After one especially pleasant ride into the countryside, Adam reflected on his good fortune to be in Springdale. This small town soothed his shattered nerves and dreams.

How long has it been since I've enjoyed the simple pleasures of life?

Soon Dr. Logan was ready to make his move back East.

"Adam, do you want any of my household trappings?"

"I have no idea what's necessary to set up a household. Tell me what I need."

"What if I set a reasonable tab on the entire contents?"

"I'll be looking at an empty home if I turn you down. Name your price."

"I'll tell the banker to write my offer into our contract. And I'll leave you my books—they aren't for sale. I'll take a satchel of favorites but the rest are yours. I've noticed you love to read, so they'll be in good hands."

"Dr. Logan, I don't know what to say."

"'Thank you,' will do, my friend."

"Then, 'thank you' indeed. I'll think of you whenever I open a new book." He anticipated reading through the elderly doctor's books during the long winter season ahead.

But then he met Nellie Desmond.

Adam had never encountered a female like the beautiful Southern war widow, Nellie Desmond. While her family's ravaged plantation, Murray Manor, remained useless on the outskirts of Springdale, she and her parents struggled to maintain their pre-war lifestyle in a smaller home near the town square. Their wealth, largely held in Confederate currency, had vanished when the South fell. Their cherished southern traditions vanished more each day.

In order to fund the extravagances of his wife and widowed daughter, Giles Murray sold off Murray Manor lands piece by piece to the carpetbaggers. Meanwhile, he and his wife hoped Nellie would marry someone who could support her—and perhaps enhance the family finances as well.

The morning after Nellie met Dr. Adam Norcutt at a party, she talked with her mother.

"Mamma, I met that new doctor from England last night."

"Did you two get acquainted?"

"Not exactly, but I certainly enjoyed making eyes at him." She smiled as she remembered flirting with Adam over her fan.

"Does anyone know about his people? Or what he comes from?"

"He came to America before The War to work with some doctor in Lexington."

"Where does he go to church?"

"Mama, how should I know? I didn't even visit with him."

"You know how I feel about your spending time with someone we know nothing about."

"Mama, don't jump to conclusions. Dr. Norcutt is every inch the gentleman."

"Hmpf, I certainly hope so. Watch yourself with him, young lady. You've hardly finished mourning Roland."

Before The War, Nellie Murray married Roland Desmond, the heir of a tobacco fortune. He died in the first wave Confederate forces up the hill at Gettysburg. To salve her grief, she quickly shed her widow's garb and threw herself headlong into the social whirl of Springdale, Atlanta and Charleston.

"Don't worry, Mama. I've been sad long enough. I want our new doctor on everyone's guest list because I plan to keep him very busy." Any lingering grief over Roland vanished in her determination to attach herself to Dr. Norcutt before another widow caught his eye.

That same morning Adam remembered the gorgeous widow who kept smiling at him over her fan the night before. After being formally introduced to her, he had made a mental note to acquaint himself with her sooner than later. Widow Desmond gave him every indication she would enjoy making his adjustment to Springdale very interesting.

Springdale honored Dr. Logan's departure with a farewell reception at the Town Hall. At the same event, Dr. Norcutt was formally announced as his successor. Nellie never left Adam's side as people came over to promise him a smooth transition. People stared and whispered while the beautiful widow relished every comment.

On a cold, snowy day, a smaller crowd gathered at the clinic to wave farewell as Adam and Standard waited with the buggy to take Dr. Logan to catch the paddle wheeler. Clarissa clung briefly to her elderly friend as they said goodbye.

"You be sure to find someone to clean your spectacles before you operate, Dr. Logan."

"I'll do the best I can, but remember, I'm retiring."

Through her tears she smiled and waved goodbye.

After Adam unloaded the luggage onto the dock beside the waiting boat, the saddest moment came for Angus Logan. He must say goodbye to Standard, who had served him well for so many years. With tears trickling off his white moustache, Dr. Logan boarded the paddle wheeler and left Springdale.

That night Adam went to sleep with a peaceful heart. At thirty-eight years old, he lived in a pleasant community, owned his own clinic and home, and had agreed to escort Widow Nellie Desmond for the coming holiday season—a role which fascinated him.

Adam observed that Nellie's life revolved around card games, late night parties in friends' drawing rooms and the social events of the season. Her family's townhouse was adequate, but not designed for the kind of entertaining Nellie envisioned. Even with Atlanta still in ruins, she told Adam that she wanted to move there to recapture the life she deserved.

Adam fit right into her constant round of activities. Before one event was over, she told him about the next. As long as he escorted Nellie, his social life centered on hers. Her flirtatious ways charmed him and her buttery accent fascinated him no matter what she chattered about. He enjoyed her sophistication and gregarious ways; however, he puzzled that she recoiled whenever he mentioned his medical practice. With few concerns beyond her social life, his profession revolted her.

"Hush, Adam. Don't tell me about all those sick people. Let's be cheerful."

"I only wanted to tell you how many patients I had today. I'd hate to sit in an empty clinic all day."

"Oh, I know that, but I don't want to hear about what goes on over there. It's disgusting."

Still, Adam welcomed her company. What man wouldn't enjoy the whirlwind that was the Widow Desmond? Her lack of interest in his career assured him that her only interest was in having a pleasant companion until she was able to move back to Atlanta. Perhaps he should tell her about his marriage, but he chose to keep his family failures to himself.

What difference does it make? I left all my problems in London... with Josephine.

Chapter 11

The bustle of the Christmas season turned Springdale into a different town. For the first time since before The War, garlands of greenery and shimmers of red ribbon decorated the town hall and the clapboard stores around the square. A light snowfall added a patina of serenity to the town and the countryside. The scent of wood-burning fireplaces permeated the town's atmosphere and brought with it a sense of security welcome in the aftermath of the devastating war. Reconstruction hadn't come easily for the nation or this community, but at last Springdale could celebrate Christmas in peace.

Memories of the tragic conflict hung like ragged webs over Springdale. Painful losses and failures haunted almost every family. Everyone worked with fervor to make this holiday season a time of happiness. The community united to help families who cared for disabled veterans. The joy of the season, missing too long, now seeped up through the tragic past and overtook it.

Clarissa put on a holiday demeanor as she delivered Christmas notes and gifts to her friends. She called out the familiar holiday greetings and received them in return. But because of the secrets she was hiding, she struggled with the goodwill of others. What if people knew the disgusting truth about her baby's conception? Or her marriage? Would they still wish her a Merry Christmas? Nevertheless, pushing her despair beneath her heart, she celebrated God's gift to the world with her friends and church family. She owed them that much. And anyway, the renewed Christmas activities took her mind off her problems.

On an impulse, she gathered her piano students and her church choir into a caroling group. Remembering that Tom Lewis played a small accordion, she asked him to come along to accompany the group. The carolers planned their route through the community and prayed for an evening of clear weather. After their final practice, Clarissa gave some last minute instructions.

"Everyone must wear something red, even if it is just a scarf or mittens. We want to be a festive group." Not to be left out, she tossed caution aside and made a red sash for her black widow's garb.

Early in the evening the carolers met at the town square and made their stops at various homes. Smiling folks came out into the cold to enjoy the carols. One gentleman gave each child a penny in return for their cheer.

Tom and Ida Lewis had invited the group back to their home for cookies, roasted pecans and hot chocolate. When the caroling was finished, the chilled group hurried over for the Lewises' welcome remedies for cold toes and noses. As they passed by the Springdale Clinic, one of the children called to Clarissa.

"Let's sing for our new doctor."

"Does anyone object if we stop and sing for Dr. Norcutt?"

Another child called out, "I like that new doctor, Miss Clarissa."

"Then let's sing for him like he was our first stop tonight. Mr. Tom, please give us a chord for 'Oh, Come All Ye Faithful.'"

The little group sang out loud and clear. Soon the surprised doctor came out on his porch.

"Merry Christmas, and thank you for stopping by. What a jolly memory this will be for my first Christmas in Springdale."

"Doc, we're following orders. These children made us stop," Tom shouted over the carolers' heads.

"Would you like a sweet to help you along?" The children cheered, and in a moment, Adam held out a tin of cookies for the carolers.

"A proper British home would offer you hot wassail, but I guess this will have to do. My neighbor, Miss Olivia, gave me these tea cakes today." No one could deny that he was pleased to be a stop on the carolers' parade through town. When they left he lingered on the porch and shouted out, "Merry Christmas."

Clarissa whispered to Tom, "Dr. Norcutt sounds lonesome, doesn't he? Shall we ask him to join us for refreshments?"

"Fine idea. I'll keep the group headed to our place."

Glory Be!

Clarissa ran back and knocked on Adam's front door. When he answered and before he could speak, she blurted out the invitation.

"Would you like to join the carolers for refreshments at the Lewises? We're going to play games and enjoy Ida's famous hot chocolate. You're most welcome to join us."

"That's an invitation I won't turn down if you are serious."

"Of course we're serious. Just come along as soon as you can." She could tell he was pleased to be included.

"I'll change into my boots and be right behind you. You won't make me sing, will you?

"No, we're done with that. You'll have to wait until next year to sing with us." Clarissa ran off laughing into the light snowfall with her red sash swirling behind her. "I'll tell everyone you're coming," she called back.

Adam watched her run into the cold, dark evening, and remembered his promise to Dr. Logan to watch out for her and her unborn child. Tonight she appeared healthy and energetic. He would just keep an eye on her from a distance and hope she stayed well.

While Adam walked toward the party he wondered how he would fit into a church group's Christmas party. Nellie had invited him to accompany her to Charleston for a week of her glittering parties, but he didn't want to leave his clinic unattended. Tonight he was available for almost any activity that would break the monotony of a chilly holiday evening.

As soon as he arrived at the Lewis home, he was seated at a table where several children played an intense game of "Pick-Up-Sticks." He joined in the game, but lost on his turn. Tom Lewis leaned over his shoulder.

"Doc, I hear you're some sort of fancy surgeon but I hope you find a steadier hand if you ever operate on me."

"I'm never this nervous with a scalpel in my hand."

"What's a scalpel?" asked the little girl who orchestrated their stop at his house.

"It's one of the tools of my trade. Stop by my clinic one day and I'll show you one." He reached over to tug gently on one of her pigtails. The children invited him for another turn at the game.

"This game is testing my mettle!" He twisted his hands in mock despair and continued trying without success to win.

On his way home Adam's footsteps crunched on the snow as he thought about the pleasant diversion of the evening.

"That's the best hot chocolate I've had in America. How many cups did I consume?" He smiled to himself. "I wonder if Nellie ever serves hot chocolate instead of her infamous eggnog stiff with Kentucky bourbon. I'll have to put in a request." He shivered as he hurried along.

Without warning, he was gripped with a wrench of longing for Nathan. Enjoying simple games with the children had brought him face to face with the loss of the son he would never see again. Tears coursed down his face.

Does Nathan ever play Pick Up Sticks? I wonder if his mother will give him the Christmas gifts I sent.

Grief washed over him. He picked up a fist-sized clump of snow and ice and hurled it at a distant fence post. He missed the post, but the misguided snowball hit a different mark. A tiny yowl of pain came from the bushes where his anger landed. Adam swore under his breath and hurried over to see what sort of damage he had caused. He almost gave up the search when he found a shivering orange kitten in the snow. Blood seeped from an open gash on her head.

"Where did you come from?" he asked as he wrapped the injured cat in his scarf and put her under his coat. "I guess I owe you some medical attention and a warm place to sleep."

The pressing needs of the cat diverted his grief over missing Nathan. On Christmas Day, he moved her out into the barn, but she howled so piteously that he brought her back inside and hid her in his jacket pocket. He welcomed a companion of any sort on his first Christmas in Springdale.

Chapter 12

1867

In the early spring, the congregation of the Trinity Church began the Lenten season with a candlelight service on Ash Wednesday. A weary Clarissa thought of refusing to plan the program, but she knew how much the event meant to everyone. After all, she was only fatigued because she was pregnant. Whenever she was tired, she remembered what Dr. Logan often said during The War: "Don't worry about being tired, my dear. We'll rest up when we get to heaven."

Playing the prelude for the Lenten service, Clarissa felt a feathery flicker in her lower body—her baby's first movements. At the end of the prelude, she added a few bars of Brahms' "Lullaby" in honor of her little one. Throughout the program, she smiled with a joy known only to expectant mothers.

"God, thank you for this little soul making itself known this evening. It's the best way I know to begin Lent. After all, Easter is about new life, isn't it? And even Jesus wasn't born into a perfect setting."

Warmer days announced spring's arrival. During the winter Clarissa started some hollyhocks with seeds her mother had sent from Virginia. Now the seedlings flourished in a box on her kitchen windowsill. With difficulty she stooped down to set the plants in their new surroundings. She also planted seeds for foxglove and bachelor buttons. With her spring planting done, she waited for summer—and her baby.

Midwife Betsy Capehart stopped by early in May to see Clarissa and to discuss the baby's delivery.

"Honey, your baby's tiny. That ain't a bad thing, but don't be looking for no big baby."

"It moves around a lot and I've felt well. I honestly don't have any complaints."

"You sure seem healthy. Your baby ain't dropped down yet, so you'll still be waitin' awhile."

Clarissa watched her walk away and whispered, "Betsy, you have no idea why this baby is so tiny, do you? It has five more weeks to go, that's why. Just don't you get too curious."

She had received a lot of attention from the congregation of Trinity Community Church during her pregnancy. Folks, blind to the truth of her pregnancy, often encouraged her.

"Wouldn't Rev. Chambers be pleased?"

Or, "Aren't you happy to have this baby to look forward to? I know it's helping you through your grief, now isn't it?"

Or, "How nice to have a little Ella or Elliot Jr. to carry on the reverend's memory."

She accepted their comments with her usual grace, but worried constantly that the grim story of Pvt. Gary's visit would slip out. She knew her baby would be shunned as a bastard if the truth were known. Honesty was out of the question. She prayed the delivery date wouldn't give away her secret. Elliot died in mid-August and she told everyone her baby was due late in May. Only she knew that her baby was really due in June.

On the last day of May, Clarissa awoke with severe back pain. She made some tea and tried to go about her day, but the pain continued and she noticed a slow rhythm. By her secret calendar, this was a month too soon; nevertheless she wrote a note to Miss Betsy and asked a woman walking into town to deliver it.

Betsy was ready for the note because according to her calculations, Widow Chambers' baby was a bit late. She grabbed her satchel of supplies and hurried out. When she arrived at the cottage, Clarissa greeted her with frantic anxiety.

"Isn't the baby coming too early? I don't feel ready. Can't you stop the contractions?"

"No, Miss Clarissa, you relax. This baby is due, so let your body do the work. Don't be scairt' of them pains. It's gonna hurt, but this be normal. It's the good Lord's way."

Clarissa nodded and promised to follow directions. But she crossed her fingers as she promised and held back on the contractions as much as she could. *My baby and I have a secret to keep.*

If her baby came now, it would fit right in with her trumped up story that Elliot was its father; But if it came later, he or she would have a better chance of surviving. She didn't want to lose another baby born too soon. She labored past noon and finally gave in to the reality of her baby's early arrival. When she stopped struggling against the contractions, the delivery progressed. In the late afternoon, Betsy examined her.

"We can be looking for this baby directly. You don't have much left to do." But the day ended and the evening dragged on. By midnight Clarissa was exhausted.

"What's wrong, Betsy? Can't you do something?"

"Honey, I cain't do nothing more for you. I better send after that new doctor."

"No one is around this late. You'll have to go yourself."

"But I cain't leave you like this."

"Go, Betsy, just go!"

The door slammed shut as Betsy ran out. Clarissa longed for Doctor Logan. He would know what to do. She wept into the darkness through a series of painful, powerful contractions.

Betsy scampered to the clinic and banged on the door until Dr. Norcutt answered.

"Mrs. Capehart? Is something the matter?"

"Miss Clarissa's in trouble. She been laborin' since this morning and she's..."

Dr. Norcutt whirled away from the door as soon as the first words were out of her mouth. "Go back!" he called over his shoulder. "Tell her I'm coming! Try to keep her calm!"

Betsy ran back to Clarissa who calmed down when she heard Dr. Norcutt was coming. When he arrived, he reassured Clarissa, assessed the situation and guided Betsy into the kitchen.

"Mrs. Capehart, I'm not sure this baby will live." He talked while he rolled up his sleeves. "Depending on how things go, we may lose the mother as well. Do you want to leave now so you won't feel responsible if we have a loss? You're free to go if you wish."

"No, Dr. Norcutt. I ain't leaving Miss Clarissa like this. You let me help you now."

"Let's go back and see what we can do." They walked back in and he took Clarissa's hand. "Miss Clarissa, I know you are tired, but you must do exactly as I tell you."

"Of course." Her voice was weak with exhaustion and fear, but the look of determination in her eyes never faded.

"I'm going to see if I can move your baby into a better position. This will take some force and it will be painful, but it won't take long."

She nodded her agreement. With a few deft motions, Adam shifted the baby and continued his instructions.

"I want Mrs. Capehart to sit behind you. Now you lean back on her. She'll push down on your baby during your contractions. Can you work together?" The women agreed to the doctor's plan and began to work in tandem.

A tiny baby girl was born in the early morning hours. Clarissa, exhausted from the agony of the delivery, somehow found the strength to smile and hold her daughter. Adam washed his hands over a basin that Betsy provided.

"Do you have a name for your new baby?" He dried his hands and waited for her answer.

"Yes sir, I do. She's Polly."

"Why that name?"

"Polly was the name of my best friend in childhood. She died in a house fire. I've always wanted to name a daughter after her."

"Excellent—now let me take Polly. I'll bathe her out in the kitchen where I can warm up some water. You and Mrs. Capehart finish up in here and then," he pointed a finger at Clarissa, "I want you to rest."

"How can I thank you, Dr. Norcutt?"

"This baby girl is thanks enough. No one could've prevented what happened here. Let's all be thankful that Polly is here safe and sound. Mrs. Capehart, you can go on home, but I'll stay to keep an eye on our patients. Might I stretch out on that sofa in the parlor?" He looked at Clarissa who agreed.

Clarissa fell into an exhausted slumber while Polly slept beside her in her fluffy yellow blanket. Later in the morning when she awakened to her Polly's cries, Adam helped her sit up.

"When Polly is through with her first breakfast, I'll bring you a cup of tea and whatever I can find in your cupboard. I must leave, but Mrs. Capehart will return to check on you. You must only feed your baby and rest."

"But Betsy isn't supposed to take care of me now. I'll be all right."

"It's all been arranged. You lost a tremendous amount of blood last night. I want you to rest and recover. Polly is a tiny little girl, so Mrs. Capehart will keep an eye on her, too. Be sure she's warm and away from drafts."

"You don't understand. I can't afford to pay Betsy to come out." She began to weep.

"Believe me, Widow Chambers, you and your baby need help. Dry your tears. We'll worry about the money later." He offered her his handkerchief. "I'll stop by off and on." He stooped down and peered at her face. "Did you have those blemishes before you were pregnant?" When she nodded, he added, "I have a salve that will help. I'll bring it when I return."

Clarissa sniffled and fell back onto her pillows, too weak to argue. He left the room and she stroked Polly's sweet head as she nursed. When Adam came back in with her tea, both were sleeping. He pulled the coverlet over them and left for the clinic.

The citizens of Springdale rose to the occasion of Polly's arrival. Everyone wanted to see the miraculous baby girl who had set Clarissa on a new path of joy. The friends who had grieved with her as a widow now rejoiced to see her as a mother. Polly's demands exhausted her, but she learned to pace herself and to sleep when Polly slept. Slowly, she and her daughter forged a routine together.

Chapter 13

On a sultry summer morning Adam received an official letter from an attorney in London. As he opened the letter he reached down to play with the orange cat, now healthy, who batted at his shoe laces.

"I wonder what this is all about, Kitty-Cat."

The news he read shook him to his core. A terse legal document informed him he was now a divorced man.

"But how?" he asked out loud. "How can this happen without my knowledge or consent?"

He read on. The letter explained that Josephine had claimed she had no American address for her estranged husband. Now, she must live all alone with Nathan. Posing as an abandoned spouse, she had fabricated a story of rejection and neglect, and thrown herself on the mercy of the court.

"Of course, she knows where I am," Nathan said with a snort of exasperation. "I've always informed her of my whereabouts. That's the least I could do for Nathan." Kitty Cat yawned in sympathy. "This ruse of hers is ludicrous."

The next day a letter from Adam's parents arrived. When they had heard of Josephine's lies to the judge, Adam's father had gone to the court and told the true story. Now the judge was duty-bound to contact Adam to let him know of Josephine's legal action.

As he thought about Josephine's devious plot to end their marriage, he was consumed with fury. He sent a wire to book passage to England on the earliest possible ship. The departure of the ship meant he must leave immediately to make the sailing date. He sent a scribbled note to Nellie, who had continued to request his presence by her side. He felt no closer to her than he had when they met, but he knew she would expect to be told of his trip. Sparing her the sordid details

Glory Be!

of his marital situation, he wrote that a family emergency called him back to London. He knew she would relish the chance to spread the word of his whereabouts.

He placed a "Closed Indefinitely" sign on the clinic door. His abrupt departure meant that the community would be dependent on a doctor in a neighboring town for some time, but there was no help for it. He couldn't let Josephine get away with something that would have such a profound effect on Nathan without at least trying to remedy the situation. Riding Standard to the stables, he hired Leon to take him and his luggage to meet the steamer. Leon agreed to care for the aging horse until he returned.

As he left town, he felt a growing sense of concern. What if for some unforeseen reason he couldn't return to America? He couldn't put his concerns out of his mind, so when the rig turned onto River Road, he asked Leon to stop at the cottage on the corner.

"I won't be long. I can't miss that afternoon steamer." Adam ran up the path and pounded on Clarissa's door. When she answered, he blurted out the reason for his visit.

"Miss Clarissa, I must speak with you." He pushed his way inside.

"Of course, Dr. Norcutt. Let me excuse my piano student."

Before the little girl could gather up her sheet music, he was telling Clarissa why he was leaving.

"Please slow down, Doctor Norcutt. You aren't making a bit of sense."

"So sorry, but I must be brief. A few days ago I received some unsettling family news and must return to England at once. I decided on my way to the river that I want someone in Springdale to be aware of my circumstances in case something prevents my return."

"Oh, my goodness, what's happened?"

"First of all, I need a pledge of your confidence. I left a note for Miss Desmond, but I didn't divulge what I'm going to tell you."

"Of course, I promise." Alarms sounded in her heart, but he was obviously distressed.

"Only Dr. Logan knows I am a married man, but separated for several years from my wife and son. In a recent post I learned that my wife has divorced me."

Clarissa gasped in disbelief. Her hand covered her mouth as she shook her head.

"Mrs. Norcutt told the court that I abandoned her. This is an outright fabrication, for she locked me out of our home. I've never seen my son again. This happened a year before I left London to come to America. Now I must go to London to settle this."

"You're leaving today? Now?"

"Yes, my carriage is waiting. Forgive me for bursting in like this, but I decided I must tell someone trustworthy about this. I hope I haven't burdened you."

"Don't worry, I won't breathe a word. But I'm floored to be the recipient of your story."

"I didn't think I would tell anyone, but I changed my mind. Now I'm greatly relieved. If I might I borrow a pencil, I'll leave my London address with you." He scribbled his parents' address on his calling card. "Please don't ever doubt your trustworthiness, Widow Chambers, you have it in abundance."

He hurried out, but spun around. "Oh, I almost forgot—I rescued an injured cat the night of your caroling party. She lives in my barn. Could you feed her once in awhile?"

"Certainly, what's her name?" She clasped her hands behind her back.

"She's just my barn cat, but she answers to 'Kitty-Cat.' I hope I haven't forgotten anything else." He hurried out to the waiting coach.

Clarissa shook her head in disbelief. "Forevermore, Polly. He's been married all along."

During the voyage across the Atlantic, Adam had plenty of time to think. He finally resigned himself to Josephine's antics. He could protest the divorce, but after the years of their separation, he decided a legal end to the marriage was best after all.

He determined to leave his rage at sea. On a stormy night at the end of the voyage, he pulled his gold wedding band from his watch pocket, threw it as far as he could and watched it vanish in the white foam of the turbulent sea. What remained of his heart followed the ring.

His tears of regret and sorrow blended with the rain dashing against his face. He had long ago lost hope of reuniting with Josephine, but he didn't realize how deeply he had buried the hope that he might somehow reconnect with his son until now, when it seemed the last opportunity had been snatched from him. Despite the storm, he stayed huddled in a deckchair until a thin rim of light on the horizon announced the dawn.

When the ship docked, Adam welcomed the sights and sounds of England. Even the familiar scents of London had not been forgotten. He visited relatives and colleagues, watched his polo team win an important match, and played badminton with his brother. After seeing some of his medical colleagues, he knew he couldn't put off the reason for his visit any longer. He made an appointment with the family attorney and traveled by hired coach across London. He couldn't shake his dread of the negotiations ahead.

The lawyer made the legal process as painless as possible, but he delivered more distasteful news. "A few days after the divorce was granted, your former wife married a wealthy nobleman, Sir Lloyd Chokeberry. She's added the title 'Lady' before her name."

"I know the man. As I remember, he brags constantly about his family's wealth."

"What an abominable way to be abused by our legal system and a wife. Frankly, I expected the judge to fine her when he heard she lied in court. I suspect her family paid him off."

"Or perhaps her new husband?"

Adam stared at the papers placed in front of him, reached for the pen on the lawyer's silver inkstand and signed his name to the documents of divorce. He blotted his signature and his marriage was over.

"Now I'm free of this marriage, but being divorced is going to take some getting used to." His voice choked.

"You'll have time to make adjustments to your new status on that long voyage back to America." He looked sympathetically over his glasses at Adam's slumping posture. "Remember, Norcutt, now she has to live with what she has done."

"I doubt Lady Chokeberry harbors any remorse about the infernal mess she's created. If anything was predictable, her actions are. Eventually, she would have wanted her freedom for some reason or another." He folded his copies of the documents, slipped them into his waistcoat pocket and left the attorney's office with a profound sense of sadness.

After Adam told his parents about the morning's ordeal, his father cleared his throat and addressed another distressing topic. "Son, we've been told that Nathan is poorly cared for. We've heard that he is unkempt and running about at all hours. It's high time you step in, don't you think?"

That afternoon, Adam took a walk past his former home. He strolled on the green nearby and saw some children playing. He recognized one—his son, Nathan. His father was correct; the boy, dressed in dirty, rumpled knickers, badly needed a haircut. He was taller, but otherwise little changed since Adam last saw him as a two-year-old. He would have known him anywhere and knew he must speak to him.

"Hello, young man, are you Nathan Norcutt?"

"Yes, sir, I am." The boy brushed his hair out of his eyes.

"Do you know who I am?"

"No, sir. Don't think so."

"Nathan, I'm your father. I've just arrived from America." The boy stood stock still with widening eyes. Adam reached out his hand which Nathan accepted.

"I knew you were coming, sir!" His grimy face broke into a grin.

"Who told you I was coming?"

"No one, but I knew you were coming." He shouted to his friends, "Come meet my father!"

Adam shook hands with the boys who had the last names of some of his closest friends.

"Nathan, might I call on you before I go back to America?"

"Yes, sir, I'd like that."

Adam kicked a rock all the way back to his parents' home as he fumed over Josephine's obvious neglect. She was not taking care of their son. He must do something, but what?

That evening he wrote a note to Josephine's parents. He was sure their daughter would reject any request from him to see Nathan. He asked them to arrange a visit for him with their grandson. By return mail he was invited for tea the next day. They assured him that Nathan would be present.

When Adam was ushered into his former in-laws' drawing room, both Nathan and Josephine's parents were present. Used to being at ease in any social situation, Adam was surprised to find himself ill-at-ease. He longed to visit with his son, but he was tongue-tied. Nathan was also uncomfortable.

"I've brought out some of my best lead soldiers for you to see."

"Thank you, Nathan. I used to have some just like yours and I set up many fierce battles. Let me show you how I planned my attacks." For a few moments the father and son set up a makeshift battlefield. But Nathan was still curious.

"Do you have any pets, sir?"

"Yes, I have an orange cat that I found last Christmas. She was hurt and I took her in to help her recover." He recalled the sadness that was responsible for the poor cat's injury.

"What's her name, sir?"

"She doesn't have one. Would you like to name her? I'll tell her her new name when I return home."

"Really? I'll think of a name before you leave."

Because Adam wanted to know everything about his son, he kept making small talk.

"My, Nathan, you've grown a lot since you were two."

"Yes, sir."

"Are you learning what your governess is teaching you?"

"Yes, sir."

"Would you like to hear about America sometime?"

"Yes, sir. I should like that. I want to know all about Indians and buffalo."

Adam smiled at this echo of his own early ideas about America. As they continued to talk, Nathan gradually warmed to his father's attention. When a servant came in with a silver tray loaded with pastries and small sandwiches, his grandmother asked Nathan to pass the refreshments. Josephine may have neglected the boy's clothing and hair, but his manners were perfect.

"Please, help yourself, Father." Adam's chest expanded with a warm glow to hear himself called "Father" for the first time.

When his son left the room to get more soldiers, Adam lowered his voice and blurted out his dream. He knew he was taking a huge risk, but decided it was worth it.

"I'd like to take Nathan back to Kentucky with me."

"What? Take him to America?"

"Yes. I'll provide a good home for him. You can see he is comfortable with me. Every young boy needs his father."

Nathan's grandparents agreed to convey his request to Josephine. Their ready assent made Adam suspect that they were as concerned about the boy as he was. As his father was leaving, Nathan whispered in his ear, "Might I name your cat 'Bonnie?'"

"She'll like that. You've picked an excellent name. I'll tell Bonnie that my son in England named her."

Adam didn't dare hope for too much and kept himself busy with his preparations to return to America. When a letter arrived two days later from Josephine herself, he ripped it open. He was stunned to learn that she had agreed to his plans. Nathan would be ready to leave with Dr. Norcutt the next morning at her parent's estate.

Adam shouted with relief. "This is too good to be true!" He rushed to tell his family who congratulated him. His brother was a bit skeptical.

"You bloody well better be ready for a monstrous change of pace, Old Chap." He clapped him on the shoulder and wished him well. "I promise to do my best as Nathan's uncle."

Along with his joy, Adam felt a twinge of sadness over Josephine's indifference toward their son. Her decision was yet another example of how their opinions had never meshed. Now that he'd had time to think about it, he realized her decision to send Nathan to America with him was as predictable as the divorce. She'd never wanted to be encumbered by a child, and now she was free of both of them.

He made hurried arrangements for Nathan to join him in America. To raise a child on his own was overwhelming, but he was determined to take advantage of the unexpected privilege of being a father.

When he called for Nathan, to his surprise, Lady Chokeberry was present. After their formal greetings, there was a brief, awkward pause.

"I see you finally have the title you always wanted," Adam finally said. "You wear it well."

Whoa, where did that come from? I'm sounding like a brash American.

He saw a brief flicker of surprise in her eyes that he would comment on her new status in society.

"I believe I've packed everything he'll need," she said and ignored Adam's comment.

"Thank you," he replied, just as cool. "I'm sure I'll be able to supply anything else that he needs. Kentucky isn't as uncivilized as you might think."

"The boy has been asking questions about you for a long time." She patted Nathan's hair, but she never quite looked Adam in the eye.

"I can't wait to go to America, sir."

Nathan and his mother shared a stiff farewell embrace. Though no tears were evident, she dabbed her eyes with the lace handkerchief in her hand—the site of an enormous diamond ring. Josephine directed a footman to carry Nathan's trunk to Adam's waiting carriage. When the door closed behind them, Adam knew he was headed home a different man.

Now I'm a father with a son.

Chapter 14

The next few days were busy with preparations for the Norcutt men's trip to America. Adam made sure that all the official documents were ready for Nathan. He shopped for current books of interest for himself and made several choices for a six-year-old, including an elaborate set of wooden blocks and more lead soldiers. He bought a set of Pick-Up-Sticks, two new badminton racquets and a croquet set. When everything was packed, he marveled at how much luggage a son required.

On the morning of their departure, Nathan peeked in on his sleeping father. "Papa, shouldn't we leave? We mustn't miss our ship." He jumped onto the bed where Adam feigned deep slumber. "Papa?" Nathan shook his father's shoulder.

"Growrrrrr!" Adam growled and gathered his son up with a massive hug. "Yes, we can leave, but first let's get dressed and have some breakfast."

When both were ready for travel, Adam carried their luggage downstairs. After sharing a hurried breakfast with his parents, he pulled his napkin through the sterling napkin ring bearing his initials. His glance rested for an instant on the polished ring, a symbol of the British way life he was leaving again.

"The time has come, Nathan. Let's not put this off any longer." Laughter mixed with tears as they said their goodbyes at the door.

"What an adventure you two will have," said Grandfather Norcutt.

When his mother embraced him for the last time, she slipped his silver napkin ring into his hand. "Don't forget us, son."

"Not possible, Mother." He tossed the ring in the air, caught it deftly then slipped it into his valise. "Thank you."

Nathan stood with a little bow. "You're welcome to visit us in America any time."

Their adventure began when they entered the shipyard full of vessels coming and going.

"Wow, Papa! Look at the size of our ship!" Their ship seemed enormous to him. After all, he'd only seen miniature ships sailing on the pond in the neighborhood green. When the passengers behind them complained, Adam urged him to keep moving along. After they found their stateroom, Nathan looked in every cabinet and drawer.

"Where's our food? Aren't they going to feed us?"

"Of course they are. Every ship has a kitchen called a 'galley.' Tonight you may choose whatever you want to eat."

"Really? I can do that?"

"Of course. You may even have dessert twice a day if you want. But when we're home, you'll eat what you are served."

"All right, Papa."

On their first night at sea, Adam stood close by to tuck his son into his berth. Nathan's next request puzzled him, but he did not object.

"Wait, Papa." He knelt to say his prayers. "Dear God, thank you that I'm going to America with my father. Help me be good. Amen."

Life on board the ship and the magnificence of the sea took away all other distractions. From time to time Adam saw Nathan staring out at nothing in particular.

"What are you thinking about, son? Something serious—am I right?"

"When I grow up shall I be an Englishman or an American?"

"Good question, son, but you won't need to decide for a long time."

Once when Adam found Nathan crying, he took his son by the hand.

"Let's go for a walk and watch the sunset from the front deck."

Once outside, the grandeur of the sunset filled the sky. Nathan sniffled several times and wiped his eyes on his cuff.

"Why are you crying, son? Are you sad about leaving London? About leaving your mother?" He offered his son his handkerchief.

"A little bit." He wiped his nose. "I'm sorry, Papa, I guess I'm not very brave."

"Do you know that I felt the same way the first time I made this trip?"

"Honest? You were afraid?"

"Yes, I was a bit fearful. But this time, it's different. I'm happy to be returning to Kentucky and I'm glad that we will be there together." Adam put his arm around Nathan and looked him in the eye. "This is what I've always wanted."

Nathan's tears turned into smiles. "Me, too." He snuggled closer to Adam to stay warm.

Several dolphins shot out of the water which still glowed blue and orange in the setting sun. Nathan applauded the show and Adam enjoyed it with him. The captain rang the dinner bell and the moment was over.

Adam marveled at the boy's curiosity and endless questions:

"Shall I be allowed to see Indians?"

"Do you have horses we can ride out to see your buffalo?"

"How many nannies are at our house?"

"May I ride Standard?"

"Where do Indians get their war paint?"

Adam raised his hands in mock despair. "Whoa! Where do these questions come from?"

"I heard all about buffalo and Indians from our butler, Henri. He went to America, but came back because Indians covered with war paint attacked his wagon train."

"I doubt that really happened, Nathan."

"Oh, yes it did. Henri told me all about it."

Adam knew old Standard was far from his son's dream of having a mighty steed, but perhaps someday soon he could teach his son how to ride. The thought thrilled him in an unusual way—he'd never known that parenting a six-year-old could be so rewarding.

When their Atlantic voyage ended, Adam found them passage on a small ship that delivered them to the dock at the end of River Road in Springdale. On the dock surrounded by their luggage, Adam waved to a freed man he recognized.

"Willy, please run into town and ask Leon to bring out a carriage for my son and me. We are ready to go home."

Willy's eyes lit up with surprise and he took off at a run. Adam wondered if the news of his new role as a father would be all over town before they reached home.

Chapter 15

Adam hurried out the next day to introduce Nathan to Springdale. Now the details of his marital disaster could be unveiled in a joyful context. Their first stop was the Murray home to meet Nellie Desmond. He told Nathan that she would be upset if she were not the first to meet him.

Dressed in a blue organdy gown over wide hoops, which she still wore despite shortages of whale bone, Nellie breezed into the room. "Halloo, my world traveler—I thought you'd never return." She threw herself into his arms. "You'll never know how much I've missed you."

Once Adam extracted himself from her embrace, he cleared his throat.

"Nellie, I'm glad to see you, too. And I've brought along someone who wants to meet you." He reached back for Nathan's hand. "Allow me to present my son, Nathan Norcutt. Nathan, please say hello to Widow Nellie Desmond."

"Widow Desmond. I'm pleased to meet you." Nathan offered his hand which she took in total silence. Her mouth opened and closed a few times until Adam broke the silence.

"Nellie, I never dreamed I'd have the joy of bringing my son back to Springdale with me. This is a surprise to a lot of people, most of all to Nathan and me."

"So I see." She called for the serving maid hovering nearby. "Sally May, take Master Nathan out into the backyard and serve him some lemonade and cookies."

Nathan balked, but Adam reassured him. "It's all right, son. We'll join you in a moment."

As soon as they were alone, Nellie launched herself into a flurry of questions. Adam skimmed over them as he told her there had been a marriage, a son and a divorce.

"What on earth, Adam?" Her voice was at a pitch he'd not heard before. "Do you mean that this—this boy is your child?"

He began to explain the recent divorce proceedings, but was interrupted.

"What divorce? When were you . . .?"

He stopped her mid-sentence. "Wait, Nellie. I don't intend to keep any secrets from you. Nathan is my son from a marriage that is finally over. I went to London to tend to the legal details of my divorce."

"You mean you were married?" She took a seat. "And now you're divorced?" Her voice was high pitched and raspy.

"Yes, my divorce was final when I signed the documents in London, but the marriage was over a year before I came to Kentucky before your Civil War. This is the family matter I mentioned in my note to you." He leaned forward in his excitement. "Nellie, I thought I had lost my son forever. You can't imagine how pleased I am to have him living here with me."

Nellie stood, turned her back on him for moment, and then spun around.

"How could you do such a thing? I had no idea you were a married man with a son. You should've told me immediately."

"I am sorry, but. . ."

Her tirade gained momentum. "Why did you keep this from me?" She stomped her foot. "How could you have a wife and a son and never mention this to me or anyone else in this town?"

"For the record, I informed Dr. Logan of my circumstances before I bought his clinic. I wasn't trying to deceive anyone. I simply chose not to discuss my former life in England. I've been living here as a single man for several years."

"Well, I certainly feel taken advantage of." She pouted and wanted him to be well aware of her misery. "You should've let everyone know you were married."

"Hindsight may make it seem so, but let me explain. Because my former wife said she would never allow a divorce, I assumed I would live as a single man for the rest of my life. I was most certainly single. What was there to discuss?"

"Don't you see? You've been acting like the most eligible bachelor in Kentucky and no one was the wiser."

"Eligible, my dear? Don't worry. I'm not out in search of a wife. No one in Springdale has any serious designs on me. I certainly have none on any of them."

Nellie was suddenly embarrassed and speechless.

"You didn't think . . ." Adam stammered. "Aren't you still mourning your dead husband, Nellie? You aren't exactly eligible either, are you?"

"That's beside the point. I think you should be humiliated to be caught up short with a son and a divorce—of all things."

He hesitated. "I'm not proud of this divorce, Nellie, but at least it ends a most unpleasant chapter in my life." She continued to glare at him as he straightened and turned to look directly into her eyes. "But make no mistake. I'll never be humiliated by Nathan. He's all that I could wish for in a child. Now shall we join him so you two can get acquainted? Or shall we leave?"

She stood in silence for a long moment, then nodded. "I suppose you can stay, but it will take some time to adjust to your new situation. And your old one, I might add." A chilly tone in her voice remained for several days.

Adam's excitement about introducing Nathan to Springdale faltered somewhat after Nellie's tantrum, but later that day they found a gift by the door of the clinic. A basket addressed to 'Dr. Norcutt's Son' waited for them on the front porch. Nathan peeked under the napkin and found several gingerbread men with raisins for their eyes and buttons. He reached for a cookie, but Adam stopped him.

"You must read the note before eating your cookies." He was curious to see if Nathan could read the note.

"I'll try. 'Dear New—comer,'" he stopped. "Does that mean me?" Adam nodded and he continued. "'Welcome to America. Ask your father to bring you soon for tea at my house.'"

"Who signed the note?"

"I can't read the names."

"Let me see." He took the note and smiled. "Your cookies are from Miss Clarissa and her daughter, Polly. She's a nice widow I met the day I arrived here, and Polly is the first baby I delivered here in Springdale."

Nathan helped himself to a cookie. After biting off the head of the gingerbread man, he offered one to his father.

That evening, Adam wrote in his journal: Why is Nellie so unreasonable about past events which are none of her concern? Why can't she join me in my pleasure over having Nathan with me? Why all the questions? Thank goodness for Widow Chamber's basket of cookies.

The truth about Adam's failed marriage and his new role as a father spread quickly throughout Springdale. To his relief, most folk praised him for his commitment to his son rather than criticizing him for not disclosing his marriage. As the father and son became familiar around town, shopkeepers made it their business to know Nathan's favorite treats. Everyone showered attention on the youngster with the impeccable manners and British accent.

Tom and Ida Lewis took a liking to Nathan. One day Ida told Nathan to pick out a straw hat for himself from the display along the wall of The Lewis Mercantile.

"You mean a hat like those stagecoach drivers wear?"

"That's right."

Nathan took a long time choosing a straw hat with a red headband.

"Do I look like an American now, Papa?"

"Yes, you do. Now say 'thank you' and let's allow Mrs. Lewis to take care of her customers."

Nathan left with a smile on his face. For days he only removed his new hat when he slept.

Adam did his best to meet the challenge of raising his son. At first the simplest solution was to keep Nathan by his side. But he still had a clinic to run. Feeding the two of them loomed as a huge hurdle.

"Come on, son. Let's see what we'll eat tonight." A simple meal would appear as they worked together on hot oatmeal or scrambled eggs. But they were not always successful. "Son, you'll have to be patient with me while I learn to cook," he told Nathan as he scraped a gray mound of mashed potatoes into the garbage pail and took them to eat at the Excelsior Hotel. He couldn't seem to stop himself from throwing the word *son* into almost every sentence.

"Let me tend to this last patient, son, and then we'll saddle up Standard and have a ride together," was a frequent promise Adam made, but sometimes broke when patients' needs interfered. On those evenings Nathan went to bed with a sad face.

Adam soon realized he needed some assistance with Nathan. After a few inquiries, he found a gracious helper in his elderly neighbor, Miss Olivia. She agreed to come over and stay with Nathan for a few hours each day.

Nellie continued to resist Adam's new role. She demanded answers to endless questions about his past and showed no interest in becoming acquainted with Nathan. One fall afternoon as they sat on the Murrays' veranda, Adam lost his patience.

"Nellie, please. I don't want Nathan overhearing your constant questions behind your pretty little fan. I was married, I'm divorced and I have a son. It's a closed book."

Perhaps he should've disclosed his failed marriage before, but he couldn't go back and change that now. He refused to explain himself further, so he looked away and said no more. She snapped her fan shut and stalked inside to refill their mint juleps.

Nathan ran onto the veranda. "Papa, may I look for pecans in the front yard?"

"Good idea. How many do you need?"

"Miss Olivia told me to fill my pockets twice."

Their elderly neighbor, shocked that the Nathan had never heard of pecans, promised to make them a pecan pie if Nathan collected enough nuts—and cracked them. Adam sent Nathan off hunting for the mysterious American nuts. He didn't want him privy to another unpleasant conversation between him and Nellie.

Adam's divorce caused Nellie only a brief pause in her determined flirtations. She planned her wardrobe and her days to win the handsome doctor's heart. She decided that Nathan didn't concern her, so she rarely spoke to him. In her opinion, Nathan was "that little boy from England." When she did pay attention to him, she told Adam to clean him up, dress him better or make him behave. Her own children would be clean, well-disciplined and well-bred. And they would never have a runny nose.

Still, even with her faults, Nellie made Adam's social life a bright interval in his adjustment to Springdale and he was reluctant to lose her company. In his mind, the relationship suited both of them. He enjoyed squiring a beautiful, vivacious woman, and she enjoyed being accompanied by a handsome man who was prominent in the community. He either didn't know or blinded himself to the idea that she was planning their future together.

If he suggested an outing, Nellie would trump it with her plans. "Adam, dear, you've forgotten our schedule for that evening."

He learned to inquire, "What's on the docket this weekend?" He thought of proposing to her, but Nathan's face was a thundercloud whenever she was with them. He was focused on his new medical venture and the care of his son. Marriage seemed irrelevant.

Nellie was puzzled that he kept his distance around her. Perhaps refined British gentlemen weren't as amorous around their sweethearts as southern men. She had no idea how determined Adam was to remain romantically aloof. Still, she relished her role with the desirable doctor. She felt sure she would someday have her way with Dr. Adam Norcutt.

Chapter 16

Springdale sizzled with terrible news and Prudence Philips hurried to spread it. She rushed around to each place of business on the square.

"Typhoid is in the shanties! Stay away from the river! Don't let them freed folk near your property!"

Typhoid hadn't surfaced inside the city limits, but the citizens were uneasy. The sheriff took a wagon load of staples to the shanties to keep the freed folk from coming into town. Adam went out to beg everyone to boil their water, clean up their outhouses and limit their travels. Everyone hoped Springdale was far enough away to avoid the epidemic.

Not so for Nathan, who fell seriously ill. Adam suspected his son was exposed to the disease when they were fishing on a pond near River Road. The shanty folks often fished there, but the Norcutts had the place to themselves that afternoon. Nathan played in the water more than he fished. Neither of them caught any fish, but Nathan caught typhoid fever.

To complicate matters, Adam had never had the disease himself. It was imperative that he find some way to isolate Nathan away from their home. When Miss Olivia refused to help with a case of typhoid, he was at a loss. Clarissa was mentioned as a possible caretaker but he hesitated to impose on her. However, when she heard about the doctor's dilemma, she sought him out.

"Dr. Norcutt?" She rang the bell and waited in the clinic with Polly balanced on her hip.

"Hello, what can I do for you ladies today?"

"I hear you need a place to quarantine Nathan. Perhaps I can help."

"Thank you, but I can't expose you two to this terrible disease."

"But that's why I'm offering. I survived typhoid as a child, so I'm immune. Correct?"

"Yes, but there's a slight chance you can be re-infected. . ."

"And since Polly isn't weaned, she's protected as well?"

"Yes, Dr. Clarissa, you're correct. But can you care for a sick youngster? He's quite ill."

"Don't you worry about that. I'll go home right now and get ready for him. We must move him out of your house immediately."

Desperate, Adam accepted her offer. By that afternoon Nathan was settled in his new surroundings. The town clerk tacked a bright yellow quarantine sign on Clarissa's door.

Adam stopped by often to see Nathan, but he could only venture onto the front porch. From behind the screen door Clarissa described his son's progress. When she told him Nathan was teaching her to play checkers, he warned her that the boy was a determined competitor.

"Don't expect any favors from him."

"I'm learning to hold my own. He's very intense, no doubt about that."

"I can only wave to him, but I'll keep calling. I really miss him. I regret adding him to your busy life."

"Honestly, Nathan's a good patient and seems content with his books and those lead soldiers. But I don't think I can keep him in bed much longer."

"I'm sorry that I haven't inquired about you lately. Dr. Logan may descend upon me for neglecting you. How are you doing with Polly?"

"Quite well, thank you. At almost five months, she's tiny but healthy. She eats well and is sleeping through most nights."

"Good! She's a beautiful little girl. With those white curls of hers she's going to break plenty of hearts."

She looked down at her daughter with her fair complexion and blonde ringlets. The resemblance to George Gary was uncanny, but Dr. Norcutt didn't need to know that, did he?

"Her ringlets aren't from my family. She must've inherited them from her father's side." She enjoyed telling that much truth about her daughter, however veiled.

"Or perhaps you had a great-great-grandmother with blonde curls. Anyway, she's a lovely baby and Nathan is fortunate to have such a good caretaker. I can't imagine a better place for anyone to be quarantined with typhoid."

Dr. Norcutt would not have long to imagine.

Later that week Willy found Standard hitched to Dr. Norcutt's carriage and meandering with it along River Road. He stopped the carriage and discovered the doctor slumped over on the front seat. Since Clarissa's cottage was close by, he tied the horse and buggy to her hitching post and rushed up the path. When Clarissa saw Willy, she could tell some sort of trouble was brewing.

"Oh, Willy, what's wrong?"

"Something terrible bad is wrong with that doctor. He's passed clean out in his buggy." He pointed to the doctor's rig. "Could you have a look so's I'll know what to do for him?"

Clarissa hurried down the path and leaned into the carriage. When she felt Adam's hot, moist forehead, she knew at once what the problem was: typhoid had struck Dr. Adam Norcutt.

"Willy, the doctor probably has the typhoid. Don't take him into town. I'm keeping his son here with the fever. I guess he'll have to stay here, too."

Fear rose along her spine, but not about the disease. Her old fear of men rose to confront her good heart. *How can I have a man stay here? Who'll take him in if I don't? I have to do this.*

"Ma'am, you sure 'bout this?"

"It's not up for discussion, Willy. Now let's move him inside."

Willy feared the disease as much as the next man, but he didn't hesitate to help. "The doctor's helped my people. I'll jes' trust the good Lord to keep that bad fever off me."

"I have a bucket of coal oil in my shed. I want you to scrub down with it after we get the doctor inside."

Together they managed Adam up the front steps. Nathan heard the commotion and came to the door. "Papa! What's the matter?"

"Don't worry, your papa will get well just like you have. You can help me take care of him. Now, hold that door wide while we bring him inside."

Nathan's face crumpled with tears, but he followed Clarissa's instructions. Adam remained unconscious while they settled him on the horsehair sofa in the living room.

"Willy, please bring in the doctor's black bag and take Standard home. You'll need to brush him down. Give him some oats and water, and then let him out into the pasture. Wait, I'll give you some scraps for that cat out in the barn. Let's see what else. . . ."

Willy's face broke into his gap-toothed grin. "Don't you trouble yourself none, Widow Chambers. I knows what to do." After he wiped himself down with the coal oil, Clarissa paid him for his help and gave him a note to put on the clinic door:

"Due to Dr. Norcutt's illness, the clinic is closed indefinitely."

Chapter 17

Adam was seriously ill with raging fever and violent chills. In desperation, Clarissa tried to bring his fever down by applying towels soaked in cold spring water to his head and neck. She poured out the medicine he had sent out for Nathan.

"Dr. Norcutt," she said, shaking his shoulder gently, "You have come down with typhoid. I need you to take this medicine. Open your mouth and take it. It's Nathan's medicine."

"Madam, I'll take nothing from you." He growled at her with unseeing eyes and knocked the spoon out of her hand. She cleaned up the spilled medicine and loosened his collar, but knew of nothing else to do. So she prayed.

"Dear God, I beg You, come down and touch Dr. Norcutt with Your healing power. Show me what to do for him. And help me not to be so afraid of him. He's sick and needs to be cared for somewhere."

She worried that he would roll off the sofa, but she couldn't move him into the study by herself. As a last resort, she sat on the floor by the sofa with her back to him and fell asleep. When Polly cried out in the dead of night, the commotion awakened Nathan. Clarissa covered the ailing doctor with a quilt and went on tiptoe to the children. After nursing Polly and singing to Nathan, she found the doctor shivering with chills. Still fearing to leave him alone, she made a pallet on the floor beside the sofa and tried to sleep.

Adam had no idea where he was. He drifted through nightmares where he was back in the field hospital during The War. He amputated the leg of a soldier named Johnny again and again. He agonized aloud over lack of pain killing drugs. "I need more chloroform over here— send for more!" His foul language blistered her ears until she covered her head with a pillow. When he argued on and on with someone named Josephine, she reached up and rocked his shoulder back and forth. She tried singing the same lullabies to him that soothed the children, and somehow they helped.

As morning came on, Adam rested with a delightful sense of peace. He dreamed of walking in a fragrant meadow full of wild flowers and lush grass. He drifted in and out of awareness. He came fully awake with his arm off the couch and his fingers tangled in Clarissa's long auburn hair.

"Ouch! Stop it, sir. You're pulling my hair."

"Dear lady, I'm so sorry. Where am. . .?" He grabbed his temples as the room spun around him. His voice drifted off as he sat up.

"Dr. Norcutt, please lie down. It's me, Widow Chambers. You're at my cottage. I'm taking care of you."

"What day is it? I have patients waiting. I must go." He stood up and fainted onto her. She leaned him back onto the couch and scurried to find her smelling salts which she held under his nose until he raised a hand.

"What's happened?"

"I'll explain when you're feeling better. For now, you must be still. Later I'll help you over to my study where I've made a bed for you." He drifted off into a feverish slumber once again. Before dark, he was coherent enough to ask some questions.

"Why am I in your parlor? So sick—bad headache—dizzy." He tried to lift his head.

"You've come down with the typhoid and Willy brought you here."

"You must get the small. . .vial out of. . .my black ba. . ."

"Dr. Norcutt, hush. Don't talk. Remember, you've already told me what to do for Nathan. Please, save your strength."

Adam managed to nod. When Clarissa offered him the medicine again, this time he took it. She persuaded him to take a few sips of warm tea from a china cup she held to his lips. She helped him move to the bed in her study, which she had transformed into a sickroom for him.

The Norcutts slowly improved. Nathan played with his soldiers by the spring and one day marched them to the creek at the back of Clarissa's property. Adam, trying to be a decent patient, convalesced in the tiny study. When he was up for short intervals he played with

Polly and tried to distract her when she cried. Nathan often joined in with funny antics.

Having the Norcutt men in her home reminded Clarissa that she and her daughter had a broken family. But she stopped her thoughts and prayed that maybe someday God would send her a husband and Polly a father. She was surprised when her fear of the doctor subsided a bit. After all, he was a sick man with no family on this side of the Atlantic to care for him.

She found she enjoyed the evenings when they debated the doctor's atheism and affection for the scientific mind. His education and training included all the new theories of evolution. He regaled her with quotes from Charles Darwin and told her about attending meetings where the scholars and thinkers of London debated crucial issues. In return, she asked questions, prompted him to explain his opinions and often clarified an issue. This fascinated Adam.

"Widow Chambers, you surprise me. If I bring up Darwin's theories with my new friends in this town, they look at me like I've bumped my head. Miss Desmond, whose company I often share, hasn't even heard of him. Where did you learn about all this?"

"My late husband was a brilliant student," she said. *I have to grant Elliot that much.* "Before his illness, we held lively discussion groups at the parsonage. Many people here know about these current issues. You must be spending too much time in the wrong drawing rooms." Adam looked out the window which framed a full moon before replying. He chose his words carefully.

"Might I assume your church doesn't agree with my philosophies?"

"You're right about that—and, for the record, neither do I. You aren't surprised, are you?"

"So you still hold to an antiquated Christian view, which means that I'm a poor, helpless invalid trapped with no escape in this hostile space called 'Widow Chamber's Cottage.'" He smiled as he teased her.

"That's correct, and you'd best behave or the proprietress may turn you and your son out onto River Road. But honestly, you don't know if my views are antiquated or not. If I'm not mistaken, we've only discussed yours."

"Right you are." He nodded in her direction. "Please divulge, Widow Chambers. You have my word, I'll listen with an open mind

Glory Be!

and not be too critical." He held up his right hand as his pledge and stifled a yawn with his left.

"No, not tonight, Doctor. I can see you're weary. I'll do you a disservice if you stay up a minute longer. Off to bed with you. My opinions can wait."

As he left the room, she realized that taking care of the Norcutts hadn't been the chore she'd expected. Despite her fears, she enjoyed having them around. Even though the doctor was still weak, he now insisted on doing whatever chores he could. He even carried out their bath water and emptied their chamber pots.

Clarissa did not take care of the doctor's small family alone. Sympathetic church members rallied around the cause with food, firewood, notes of encouragement and supplies. However, they always made a quick departure after leaving things on the front porch. No one dared come near the oddly matched foursome in quarantine. Several church members questioned the propriety of the doctor staying with the widow, but no one had a better solution.

Aunt Mag spoke up. "Miss Clarissa is an angel to nurse them Norcutts. No one else'll do it. I hear a candle is burning for the doctor in her study every night. So don't no one be finding fault."

Miss Nellie came to call on her sick sweetheart, but Clarissa and Polly met her on the porch to remind her of the quarantine. She handed Clarissa a large box of expensive chocolates wrapped in gold paper.

"Widow Chambers, see that my Adam receives these chocolates as soon as possible." With no other word, she turned and left.

"Who in their right mind would bring a man as sick as 'my Adam' a huge box of chocolates?" Clarissa whispered to Polly. Nevertheless, she gave Nellie's gift to the doctor. Whether or not they were good for his health, he devoured several candies on the spot. When his back was turned, she tried to put the delicacies out of sight.

"Madam, I see you hiding my candy. You'd best not get between me and my chocolates."

"I most certainly will. Tell me, Doctor, would you allow one of your patients to eat almost a half a box of chocolates?"

"I'm begging for a little mercy."

"I'm fresh out of that commodity." She took the chocolates into the kitchen. That evening, when he excused himself and went to bed early with a stomach ache and a raging headache, she resisted the urge to say, "See. . .?"

One night Adam heard screams coming from the back of the house. He bolted out of bed and hurried to investigate. The screams led him to Clarissa's bedroom. He knocked on the door several times, then cautiously went in and found her thrashing around in the bed and crying out. Debating what to do, he stood at the end of her bed.

"Miss Clarissa, it's Dr. Norcutt. Wake up, you're having a bad dream." He kept repeating himself and shook the bed frame. When as a last resort he touched her foot, she bolted upright in terror.

"Don't be afraid, Miss Clarissa. It's only Dr. Norcutt. You were crying out in your sleep and I came to see what all the commotion was about. You must've had a bad dream."

"Oh, was I dreaming? I'm so sorry I disturbed you." Clutching the bed linens around her, she pushed her disheveled hair out of her face. Old fears and the lingering remnants of her nightmare consumed her. She huddled behind her quilt and stared at Adam with huge amber eyes filled with fear.

"It's all right—nothing to be afraid of now. I thought perhaps someone was harming you or the children. I'll bring you some water and perhaps you can go back to sleep." She drank the water he brought and drifted back to sleep.

But Adam did not go back to sleep, for he had noticed that the widow was not only afraid tonight, but she was often ill-at-ease around him. Whenever he was near her, she would shift away. Her evasion was subtle but predictable. Once, when he reached to help her lift a heavy tray, she dropped it when their hands touched. Tonight her terror brought these concerns into sharp focus.

Why is she so fearful? Is this about men in general or only me? He wished Dr. Logan were around to give him some wisdom about the puzzling little widow—who was surprisingly pretty with her long hair mussed and her hazel eyes huge with fear.

After long days of songs at Clarissa's piano, endless games of checkers and pick-up-sticks at her kitchen table, not to mention deep conversations about religion and politics during the long evenings, Adam and his son improved. They no longer suffered from fever

Glory Be!

and the annoying skin rash had healed. The doctor declared them fit enough to return home.

Nathan disagreed. "But I'm still sick, Papa. I think we should stay a bit longer, don't you?"

"You want to stay near that creek where you can set up battles with your soldiers. And close to Widow Chamber's cookie jar."

Nathan grinned and ducked his head. "I like it here."

"We can't take advantage of this kind lady's hospitality forever. We are well enough to be back at home now." He glanced at Clarissa with a plea for agreement. "I'll take care of us."

"Nathan," Clarissa whispered, "I often need the help of a strong young man around here. Would you come out to help me sometimes?"

"Yes, ma'am, I'll do that. Right, Papa?"

"I'm no match for you two. We'll come any time we're needed." He bowed to Clarissa.

He sent word for Willy to bring out their buggy, and by late morning the Norcutts were back home at the Springdale Clinic. The helpful former slave unloaded everything and sent Standard into the back pasture.

"Now, Mr. Doctor, you send for me any time you needs help."

"We'll manage things now, but I'll remember your offer. Thank you for taking care of the place." He handed Willy some folded bills.

"Master Nathan, you know what's happened while you's been gone?"

"What, Willy?" begged Nathan. "Tell me, tell me."

"Your Bonnie had a bunch of babies. I put her and them kitties in a big basket out in the barn. I think their eyes 'bout open." Nathan took off at a run.

When Clarissa and Polly finally had the house to themselves again, she was reminded of how alone they were. Despite her fears of housing a man, she had felt much safer with the Norcutts under her roof; even a sick doctor and a little boy felt like safety. When she changed their beds for the last time, she found an envelope under the doctor's pillow with several bills, a small jar of salve and a note.

"Thank you for your care during our recovery from typhus. Try this ointment for your skin. I promised it to you when Polly was born. *Mea culpa*."

She was thankful for the salve, but embarrassed that the doctor had noticed her blemishes again. Somehow, despite her best efforts, her complexion problems never completely went away. She folded the money and spun around in front of the hall mirror.

"Hooray! I'll order Polly's baby carriage."

Adam was glad to be home. They were fortunate to be survivors, but he was still quite weak. Now he owned a fresh compassion for patients who suffered similar illnesses. However, he knew that most of them lacked the excellent care Clarissa had provided.

Miss Olivia came over and talked to him through the screen door.

"Dr. Norcutt, you need help so you can rest and get well."

"Thank you, Miss Olivia, I'll take things easy. We'll get through this."

"Now, you listen to me. I know the right person to help you. I've already asked her to come work for you."

"Thank you, I'll think about it."

"She'll be here tomorrow morning and don't you send her away."

"What's her name?" He rubbed his throbbing forehead.

"Magnolia. She ran the house on a plantation on River Road before The War. Be glad she's available."

"Fine, I'll be expecting her. Now, I'm afraid I must go." He shut the front door in Miss Olivia's face and almost collapsed with weakness. As he fell onto his bed, he realized that he didn't know what to pay this Magnolia.

No price is too high. I hope Nathan is entertained with those kittens for awhile. Perhaps we should've stayed at Widow Chamber's house.

Weakness took over and he fell asleep with the day only half done.

Chapter 18

After Polly finished her nap, the spectacular late fall afternoon beckoned to Clarissa. She bundled them both against the chilly wind before going outside to enjoy the sunshine and the last colors of fall. Polly watched her mother piling up mounds of fallen leaves and smiled at someone coming up the path.

"Well, if this don't beat all. If I can count right, we got us a baby girl, don't we?"

Clarissa froze. Horrified to hear a male voice behind her, she feared even more when she turned and saw Pvt. George Gary greeting her and wearing a spotless uniform. She reached for Polly as old fears rolled over her.

"How—how long have you been there watching us?"

"Long enough to figure out this baby girl looks like her daddy and his family. Now, don't you be alarmed, Miss What's-Your-Name."

"I have no business with you, sir."

"I'm here for a friendly visit." Clarissa's eyes filled with fear, but she said nothing. Gary continued. "I thought I'd look around for a place to settle in this area."

"There's nothing for you here. You'd best move along."

"That's what you said last time. But now, I have a right to get acquainted with my daughter. She's about six months old, ain't she?"

Clarissa backed away. "Go away! I want you to leave. Now!"

"You know I don't take 'no' for an answer." George Gary came closer.

Clarissa turned and ran toward the front steps of the house. He caught her arm and tore the sleeve of her dress. She screamed but he didn't relent.

"Why don't you hush your pretty mouth?"

Clarissa begged him to stay away, but her fear only encouraged him.

"Wouldn't you like to have us a little boy, pretty lady?" He grabbed for Polly, but Clarissa gripped her so tightly she began to cry.

"Leave us alone! Get off my property!" She tried to climb up the front steps.

He planted his heavy boot on the lowest step, "You gonna to make me?" When he reached for Polly again, Clarissa lost any remaining composure.

"Let go of my baby! Get away from us!" Her hair was in disarray, her dress torn and now her hem dragged on the steps.

Without warning, Pvt. Gary was tackled from behind and pinned to the ground. Jacob and Luke Featherson were delivering a wagonload of pumpkins into town when they heard Clarissa and Polly screaming and rushed to their aid. Face down in the dirt and leaves, Gary tried to excuse his behavior.

"Boys, I was only asking for directions."

Jacob reached into Gary's holster for his pistol. "Then why's this nice lady so upset? Why's her dress all tore up? We saw what went on here, so don't deny nothing. You're going in to the sheriff. You can't treat one of our women like this and get away with it."

"Let me go. I won't cause any more trouble, I promise."

Jacob cocked the pistol and pointed it at the soldier's temple. "Luke, fetch me a rope yonder in the wagon. I don't want this Yankee running off on us. Widow Chambers, why don't you and your baby girl g'won inside? We got this situation under control."

"Please don't let him go," Clarissa whispered.

"He'll be behind bars as soon as Sheriff Olsen hears what he done. I reckon he'll ride out later to talk at you about what happened here."

When Clarissa was inside, a shock went through her—Polly had just seen her father. She changed her torn clothes and made herself a cup of strong tea but her hands still trembled. *What if the Feathersons heard George Gary's remarks? What if they heard what he said about Polly?*

In an hour Sheriff Olsen knocked on her door and Clarissa hurried to let him in. "Come in. I'm mighty glad to see you."

"Widow Chambers, are you all right? Are you hurt?"

"Nothing serious, but I have a bruise or two on my arm and a torn dress."

He examined the bruises and dress, then made some notes along with a rough sketch on a pad of paper. "With your permission, I'd like to take your tore up dress as evidence."

When she handed it to him, he began his questions. "This Pvt. Gary claims he knows you and visited you when his unit stopped here last fall. Is this true?"

Is my secret out? What did he tell the sheriff? How much should I say? Did he tell what happened in my shed? She chose her words with caution.

"He stopped by and took some food. He was a Union straggler and told me that he had missed muster. He was filthy and still drunk." Her voice trembled as she tiptoed around the truth of Pvt. Gary's former visit. "I'd never met him before."

"I'll keep him in my jail until the army comes for him. I'm sure the military will discipline him, but we'll also bring him before our circuit judge so his behavior goes on county records. We can't have this sort of thing going on."

"Thank you, Sheriff. Sorry to be so much trouble." At last someone was defending her against Gary. Nothing ever felt so good. But what if her horrible story came out?

"You know you'll have to testify under oath against him, don't you?"

"I understand."

"I'll get this taken care of. I'll let you know the court date."

Clarissa saw him out and collapsed at her kitchen table. She thanked God for sending the Featherson brothers along as she rubbed her sore muscles and the bruises on her arm.

The farmers stopped by on their way home. "This'll get taken care of by the judge, Widow Chambers," Jacob said. "Don't you worry no more."

They had no idea what a huge request that was. *How can I not worry?* She sent them home with her profuse thanks and their hands full of cookies.

That night her nightmares about Elliot returned with a vengeance.

Chapter 19

The news of Private George Gary's rough treatment of Widow Chambers circulated like wildfire throughout Springdale. The guilty, obnoxious soldier fretted and paced in a jail cell until the judge of the circuit court arrived. Because of the size of the crowd expected, the trial was moved to the town hall. By the time Gary was ushered in, most of the town had gathered for the event.

"All rise," the bailiff called out when the judge entered. The witnesses and the prisoner were sworn in and the hearing began. When the judge called on the Feathersons, they gave identical accounts. Jacob ended his comments with a flourish.

"Your honor, thank the good Lord we come along because things was heating up, not cooling down."

When Clarissa rose to testify she noticed Dr. Norcutt seated with Nellie Desmond at the back of the room. He gave her a small salute and she felt a tiny surge of confidence. She handed Polly over to Ida and took her seat before the courtroom.

"Widow Chambers, is this Private George Gary before you the man who came uninvited onto your property and mistreated you and your daughter, Polly Chambers?"

"Yes, your honor, that's the man."

"I see here in the sheriff's documents that the defendant claims to have met you before. Is this true?"

"Yes."

"When?"

She hesitated. She glanced toward the doctor who nodded. "He came to my back yard sometime last fall. He took some breakfast with him and left."

"You've never seen him before or since?"

Glory Be!

"No."

"Do you agree with the accounts given by Jacob and Luke Featherson?"

"Yes, sir, I do."

"Has the sheriff presented his evidence correctly?"

"Yes."

"Thank you, Mrs. Chambers, you may take your seat."

Awaiting his turn to testify, George Gary smirked and stared down at his boots. Clarissa feared he might divulge the truth about his first visit. But if he did, the charges against him would escalate, wouldn't they? She shivered, nearly sick with the knowledge that they shared such a diabolical secret.

"Dear God, seal his lips for Polly's sake—and mine." She prayed silently and wiped her damp palms.

Gary took the stand. "Your honor, all I wanted from Widow Chambers, whom I met when my regiment was in town last year, was some information and directions."

After a few more question, the judge ruled.

"Private George Gary, I accept your testimony about needing directions and meeting Widow Chambers before, but in no way does this permit you to mistreat her and her child. I have read Sheriff Olsen's description of the bruises you inflicted and have seen her torn dress on exhibit. I have heard the Feathersons' and Widow Chamber's testimonies which match up completely. Your actions caused damage and harm. You are to be kept under arrest here until the army can take you into military custody. Our court records will go with you. I find you an embarrassment to the troops that serve this mighty nation and I am sure that a military tribunal will find you guilty of assault, as I do."

He brought his gavel down with a loud crack. Clarissa jumped at the sound and started shaking. She wept with relief as Ida leaned over to comfort her.

Private Gary resisted when the guards came to escort him back to the jail. They seized both arms and forcefully ushered him toward the exit. As the bailiff held the doors open, Gary turned toward the courtroom. In a hoarse voice, loud enough for everyone in the courtroom to hear, he shouted,

"Clarissa, darlin,' you take good care of our baby girl. You hear me now? I'm counting on you 'til I get back."

The swish of heads turning toward Clarissa and Polly was the only sound in the room. Clarissa felt all the blood drain out of her head. She slumped over as stars swam before her eyes, but she managed not to faint. The audience began to leave, but instead of a celebration of justice accomplished, there were only whispers, stares and silence. Tentacles of human tension slithered into the makeshift hall of justice. Like a protective gladiator Tom hovered nearby and allowed no one to come near.

Ida gripped Clarissa's hand. "Clary? What on earth?"

"Wait until everyone leaves." Clarissa still felt lightheaded and dizzy. In an instant, with one sentence, her reputation had collapsed along with Polly's only hope for a decent life.

George Gary has taken so much. How dare he destroy more of my life?

The bailiff walked back into the hall and gave the huddled group a curious stare. Tom held up his hand. "May we have a moment or two here?"

The outside doors flew open and Steven Jackson rushed back inside.

"Miss Clarissa, why on earth would that soldier say an awful thing like that?"

In a flash of clarity, she knew she couldn't live with her deception any longer. The time to speak her truth was now, right here in a court of law, before God, her close friends and her pastor. She noticed the doctor was still standing in the back. She stared at him as she whispered.

"Because it's true."

"What on earth?" Ida's eyes glistened with shock.

"It's true." Clarissa rocked Polly back and forth. "He's her father."

"Elliot isn't Polly's father?" Tom asked.

Clarissa slumped lower in her seat. "No, he isn't."

A moment of bleak silence surrounded the huddled friends. Rev. Steven spoke up.

"This is a horrible shock, Widow Chambers. Why, the reverend couldn't have been cold in his grave...."

"He. . ." she began, but stopped, too ashamed to say the words that would prove her innocence. "I'll move away tomorrow." She stood to leave. "I'm sorry, so sorry."

"Wait. Everyone wait a moment." Dr. Norcutt hurried over to the group around Clarissa. "Private Gary assaulted you against your will. Isn't this what happened, Widow Chambers?"

Clarissa nodded as tears streamed down her cheeks.

"Why don't you tell your friends the truth? They'll understand."

Her friends in the small circle murmured their support and leaned in to listen. She began her story in a whisper.

"After I moved into Ida's cottage, I went out one morning to clean up that old shed in the back. I didn't know this Yankee soldier had slept in there overnight. When I opened the door, he pulled me into the shed and. . . ."

". . .there was a rape." The doctor lowered his voice and finished her sentence. Her fragile reserve abandoned her and she shook with sobs while Ida held her.

"Clary, how horrible. Why didn't you tell us?"

"I couldn't talk about it. It was too vile. I was going to tell you when you came to visit, but you assumed the baby was Elliot's. I took the easy way out and let all of you believe a lie. Please, please forgive me."

Ida whispered words of encouragement and stroked Clarissa's hair as if she were a child. But she still sobbed. "Pastor Steven," she managed at last, "will God ever forgive me?"

Adam interrupted before the pastor could speak. "Widow Chambers, you are an innocent victim and we commend you for all you've endured under these trying circumstances." He took off his hat and bowed, "My hat is off to you." The others agreed and the pastor chimed in.

"Miss Clarissa, today God's abundant grace frees you from the web of deception into which you placed yourself. You were trying to protect yourself and your baby. You caused no harm to anyone. We all know that God forgives every child of His who repents." Everyone in the circle said, "Amen."

Tom brought his buggy around to the front of the town hall. Clarissa walked out into the sunshine with Ida, Polly and the Lewis twins. A few curious onlookers still gawked. Adam went to Tom and spoke in a low voice.

"Tom, the widow needs a great deal of support right now and I know you and Ida will take good care of her. Please send for me if she needs any medical attention."

"Thanks, Doc, we'll do that." He guided his mare into the flow of traffic around the square. Adam walked over to where Nellie Desmond drummed her fingers and waited for him.

Chapter 20

After the Lewises ushered Clarissa and Polly into the security of their home, everyone stood around in awkward silence until Tom spoke up.

"Ida, why don't you put that tea kettle of yours on the stove? The Jacksons will be here when they find someone to mind their children. Lester and Lydia, you have chores to do."

Ida nodded and went out to the kitchen. The twins followed her and kept whispering questions and glancing back into the living room. Clarissa tried to help Polly out of her sweater and cap, but her hands wouldn't stop shaking.

Tom made a welcome suggestion. "Would you like a few minutes alone?"

When she agreed, he took Polly from her and left the room. She walked over to the tall mirror on one side of the parlor and stared at her reflection. Straightening a stray hair or two, she smoothed her navy blue bodice of serviceable linen and took several deep breaths.

"All right, Clarissa Francine, calm yourself down." She closed her eyes and prayed in a whisper. "God, You've stood by me through all of this. I didn't know what to do today except to tell the truth. All I can do now is cast this bread of mine on my troubled waters and let You take it to where You want it to be . . .somehow."

After Steven and Sophie arrived, the friends spent the afternoon adjusting to the truth surrounding Polly's birth. They agreed that Springdale would understand and that in a few days, things would get back to normal. But this did not happen.

Clarissa's friends were alarmed when ten days passed and twisted rumors were rampant. Never had anyone doubted her good character, but now many believed exaggerated rumors about a romance between her and the Yankee soldier. Some decided that Widow Chambers had always been of questionable morals. A rumor started that she was seen with the soldier down by the river on a Sunday afternoon. Two of her sewing customers wrote notes to inform her that they no longer needed her services.

Upon hearing that Clarissa claimed to be an innocent victim, Prudence Phillips harrumphed, "A likely story. Of all things—and with a Yankee."

Even Aunt Mag spoke up with feigned authority. "Maybe this is why there weren't no tears from the little widow at the parson's funeral."

Steven Jackson decided that something must be done.

"Sophie, we can't sit idly by while these terrible lies keep going around, can we?"

"The gossip just keeps getting worse and worse, doesn't it?"

"I'd like to help, but I don't know what to do."

"Let's pray on it overnight," Sophie yawned. "Maybe we can come up with a solution tomorrow."

By morning, Steven had a plan, one that Sophie agreed might work. He confirmed his idea with the Elders, and then called on Clarissa. After she invited him in, they discussed pleasantries for a few moments, but he had more on his mind.

"Miss Clarissa, I know you're upset by all the rumors going around about you and that Pvt. Gary. Would you be willing to you tell your story at an open gathering over at the church? If you do this and people can ask you questions, perhaps we can put these rumors to rest."

"No, Pastor," she recoiled at the idea. "I'm too ashamed."

"It will be difficult, but I'll be right beside you. People need to hear your version of what happened. You won't have to give details, but I think hearing your truth will stop the rumors."

"Then I'm ready."

"Do you know of anyone else who could speak on your behalf?"

"I can't think of anyone. There were no witnesses," she answered with sarcasm in her voice.

"How about Mrs. Capehart or Doctor Norcutt?"

"What can they add to this story?"

"Mostly credibility. We need to hear from someone besides you and your best friends."

"Pastor, please ask anyone who might help."

With Clarissa's agreement to his solution, Rev. Steven posted a notice announcing the open meeting on the front of the church.

Near dawn the next morning, Clarissa was terrified by a nightmare in which she was listening to Elliot preach as she stared at her clenched fists. When she looked at the pulpit, the preacher was no longer Elliot, but Private Gary who leered at her over the pulpit. "Come on up here with me, pretty lady."

Barely awake, she stumbled into the kitchen and lurched against the kitchen sink. *Will they never leave me alone?* When she splashed a ladle of spring water on her face she calmed down enough to return to her bedroom. She tossed and turned until Polly awoke—a welcome reality.

On the day before the meeting at the church, Dr. Norcutt called on Clarissa.

"Welcome, Dr. Norcutt. Come in before this wind blows you away. You haven't been out our way in too long."

"Your place seems like my home away from home. I certainly have not forgotten your excellent care when we were so sick. I'll always be grateful."

"And I want to thank you for your support in the courtroom. Tom told me you offered to come over later."

"What a difficult day that must have been for you. I'm sorry so much gossip has resulted." He hesitated, then continued. "I've been asked to comment at the meeting tomorrow, but I must discuss something with you beforehand."

"Of course—please, come in and I'll bring you a cup of tea."

Once they settled in the parlor, he went straight to the issue.

"I've been asked to shed some light on the situation surrounding Polly's birth, but I can decline if you wish."

"I think I'm ready for this. I hope I can cope with the backwash I'm sure it'll stir up."

"May I speak candidly with you?" He gulped his tea without his usual English grace.

"Yes, of course. Go on."

"As you know, I'm a surgeon, but I delivered many babies in England and Lexington before coming to Springdale. Healthy newborns have a certain look at birth. I suspected your tiny Polly was premature when I delivered her."

Clarissa gasped as fear clutched at her throat. He held up his hand to reassure her.

"At the time, I did some calculating. If Rev. Chambers died in mid-August, your baby would've been a full term infant. To me she appeared to be at least a month early. When you said nothing and Mrs. Capehart acted as though Polly's birth was right on schedule, I kept silent."

"So you knew?" The color drained from her face.

"Yes, but I didn't know what to do with my conclusion." Clarissa's eyes were riveted on his as he continued. "Because premature babies often have problems, I've kept an eye on Polly. Frankly, it's a wonder she lived. She was so tiny. But so far, I see no complications."

"But why didn't you say something?" She fought back hot tears.

"Because I was still a newcomer at the time, I kept quiet. I thought an experienced midwife like Mrs. Capehart might say something, but all she said was, 'Too bad this ain't a son to bear the reverend's name.' Who was I to trouble the waters, Miss Clarissa? You never offered any explanation."

She could only whisper, "What on earth did you think of me? Something terrible, I'm sure." She turned away from him.

"On the contrary, I failed you. As your doctor, I should've spoken with you about my concerns."

"No one questioned the timing of my Polly's arrival or her size, so I let it be. When I look back on it, I marvel at how everything fell into place."

"Everything came together in your favor, didn't it?"

"Yes. I want Polly to have a normal life. Claiming that Elliot was her father seemed the best way to insure that."

"If your doctor wasn't asking questions, why put yourself through a lot of explanations."

"Exactly," Clarissa said. "Thank you for understanding."

"Now about this meeting tomorrow. Do you want me to validate the fact that you became pregnant after your husband's death? As your doctor, I can do this but only if you agree."

"What I want is to stop the rumor that I was involved with that soldier. People are going to have to take my word for it, or not." She grimaced and smoothed the hem of her apron across her knees.

"All right. But if you want me to stop my remarks, look at me and shake your head."

"Agreed."

As he was leaving, Polly was waving toward Standard and squealing. Clarissa wrapped both of them in her warm shawl and walked out to the hitching post so Polly could see the horse. She held Standard's bridle while Polly patted the horse's velvet nose. Adam mounted up and smiled at them.

"Little Girl, will you go for a bit of a ride with me?"

He sat Polly on the saddle in front of him and pulled his topcoat around her. He whistled to Standard who trotted along River Road and back again. He handed Polly down to Clarissa, who shivered in the brisk wind. He tipped the brim of his hat and nudged Standard into a canter toward town.

"I'll see you at the church house tomorrow afternoon."

Chapter 21

Steven Jackson stood at the front of the church as the pews filled. The afternoon sun sent dusty beams of light through the tall, clear windows. Not only were elders and church members arriving, but Clarissa's sewing customers and the parents of her piano students filed in. The town leadership was well represented by the likes of Giles Murray and his wife. Willy and a few folk from the shanties huddled along the back of the balcony.

The large turnout both impressed and frightened Clarissa. "I didn't know people would be so curious," she said to Ida as they found their places on the front row. Shafts of sunlight glinted off her auburn braids and warmed her simple brown frock.

"Most folks are here to support you, honey," Ida reassured her.

"Maybe, maybe not," replied Clarissa.

Dr. Norcutt and Betsy Capehart were ushered in and stopped to greet her. Rev. Jackson opened the meeting with a prayer and explained the purpose of the meeting.

"George Gary made a comment as he left the courtroom a few weeks ago. Many of you were present. In the aftermath, a flood of derogatory rumors about Widow Chambers have been going around. We've come today to hear the true story from this dear lady, whom we all know and respect. I've invited Dr. Norcutt and Mrs. Capehart, both of whom assisted in Polly's birth, to add their observations and comments. Miss Clarissa, please join me and go ahead with your remarks."

She rose, wiped the palms of her hands with her wrinkled handkerchief and began in a strained, but clear voice.

"My story is difficult to tell, but I want you to hear the true story from me." Stopping off and on to regain her composure, she gave a guarded summary of both assaults by George Gary. Her closing remarks explained why she chose to remain silent.

"God's gift to me is my daughter, Polly. Hoping to give her a better future, I allowed all of you to believe Rev. Chambers was her father. You have my sincere apology for not exposing George Gary and his cruelty to me from the beginning. I have come to regret that decision."

When she paused, Prudence Phillips stood. "This is all very easy for you to say now, Mrs. Chambers...."

Clarissa cut her short. "No, Miss Prudence, this is not easy. Telling the details of the most devastating shame a woman can endure, easy? I don't think so." She wiped away her tears and continued. "But I'll no longer hide the truth when it is being twisted to make false assumptions about Polly and me."

The preacher stepped in front of Clarissa and spoke to the group.

"Please, hold your comments until the midwife and the doctor have made their remarks. Mrs. Capehart, why don't you go first?"

Betsy came forward. "Miss Clarissa told me 'bout some problems early in her confinement, but by the time I came on, things was routine. I didn't know her pains was premature so I warn't alarmed when she sent for me. When things got bad for the widow, I ran for Dr. Norcutt. There was never no mention of that Private Gary."

When Betsy finished, Adam rose to give his comments.

"I've been asked to comment and I do so with some reservation. Part of what I have to say is of a private and sensitive nature. However, Widow Chambers tells me I may continue. Is this correct?" He glanced over at her and she nodded.

"First of all, from a medical perspective, it is not impossible but rather improbable that a man dying of brain cancer could father a child so close to his death. The location of his tumors would've caused the intimacies of married life to cease some time before his death." The men in the room shuffled in their seats and the ladies stared at their tightly folded hands.

"My next comments are about Polly. She was born nine months after Elliot Chambers' death and assumed to be his child. However, at the time of her birth, I recognized signs of prematurity and knew she was not an infant of nine months development. Therefore, I knew she was conceived after the reverend's death. I remained silent about my observations because no one questioned the paternity of this baby girl and it did not seem appropriate for me, still a newcomer, to do so. My role was to see that the mother and child were in good health.

"As many of us observed, the resemblance between Polly and George Gary is striking. Remember, even Gary recognized this baby as his own. So, based on these factors, and confirmed by Widow Chambers' own statement that Gary is indeed the father of this child conceived against her wishes, I do not hesitate to believe that her story of an assault is accurate."

Reverend Jackson interrupted. "Dr. Norcutt, please comment on the time when you were quarantined with typhoid at Widow Chamber's home? Did you ever see Gary on the premises or was there any evidence that he and Mrs. Chambers were involved in any way?"

"When my son and I lived at Widow Chamber's, there was no evidence that she was involved with Private Gary or any other man. She is a woman of impeccable decorum. She used great discretion as she nursed me and my son. However, during the time we were in the confines of her cottage, it appeared to me that she must have suffered some sort of past trauma. She put on a cheerful countenance, but she went through times of profound sadness. I regret now that I, along with every other person in this community, failed to provide the support she needed during this trial. It is true that she did not disclose her circumstances, but we all witnessed their aftereffects.

"I feel strongly that Polly's parentage should not condemn mother or daughter. Rather, this should be a time when understanding is extended to a woman who has been through a dreadful experience. We should all support and accept Clarissa and Polly Chambers."

Steven Jackson stepped to the front again. He opened the floor for questions, but received only silence until Rosalie Featherson spoke.

"Miss Clarissa, you're such a dear. I am so sorry for all this talk that's been going 'round. Shame on us!"

Another woman called out. "Please let us know what we can do to help you now that we know the truth."

Elder Ira Philips spoke from the front of the room, "Don't you worry about that Yankee. If I have anything to do with it, he'll get his comeuppance."

Glory Be!

Encouraging comments continued as tears streamed down Clarissa's face. Rev. Jackson closed the meeting with prayer. "Dear God in heaven, heal the aftermath of the regrettable experience that brings us together. We humbly ask You to bless Mistress Polly and Widow Chambers. Grant that we may all go forth in peace from this gathering. In our Savior's dear name we pray, Amen."

He added a spontaneous announcement. "A love offering basket for Widow Chambers and her baby will be at the back of the church. Thank you and be careful going home." The meeting had accomplished exactly what Steven Jackson had intended. He and Sophie smiled at one another as the crowd left.

Clarissa waved to Max and Betsy Capehart. "Thank you, Betsy. You didn't have to be here today. I appreciate your support."

She also stopped to thank the doctor. "Thank you, Dr. Norcutt. Your remarks helped turn the tide. I honestly didn't think people were going to believe me. Some still wanted to believe the worst. If only Private Gary had kept silent, no one would've been the wiser. I guess it wasn't meant to be that easy."

"I'm glad he spoke out."

She mouthed a horrified, silent, "Why?"

"It's time you let people help you. and above all, now Gary will get the punishment he deserves."

"I hope my confession won't make Polly's life too difficult."

"Don't torture yourself with thoughts like that. You can't control what people want to believe. This way, you and Polly can live your lives with nothing to hide." Clarissa nodded and sighed. *But I still have another secret, one hidden in the parsonage that no one will ever believe.*

"Might I offer you and Polly a ride home? I took delivery of a new buggy and mare this morning and we need a destination." His new rig glistened in the sunshine and the mare tossed her mane, ready to be on her way.

Several men stood nearby admiring the doctor's excellent taste in horseflesh. The arrival of a fine horse was always of great interest in this horse-loving Kentucky town.

"How kind, Dr. Norcutt. Your new rig is beautiful."

"Miss Desmond talked me into making a change. For a long time she has complained about Dr. Logan's antiquated buggy."

"Have you taken her for a spin yet?"

"No, I offered to bring her to this meeting, but she had some invitations to post today." He shifted the conversation back to his new horse. "I'm not sure if Standard will tolerate this intruder in his kingdom, but I think he'll appreciate the time off."

"Don't worry. Old Standard will have a new lease on life with this beauty in his pasture. What's her name?"

"It's shortened from 'Fancy Petticoats' to 'Fancy.' She was a brood mare in a racing stable and, if I let her, she runs like the wind. I don't think she ever expected to be hitched to a country doctor's rig." They laughed as he helped them into the buggy.

"We are honored to be your first passengers, aren't we, Polly?" Waving her arms, Polly bounced up and down on Clarissa's lap.

"Ready, Little Girl?" He smiled at Polly and flicked the reins over Fancy's hindquarters. They moved along until Adam stopped the rig at Miss Olivia's.

"We're stopping for Nathan. He's frantic to go somewhere, anywhere, in our new rig. I promised him a ride as soon as this meeting ended. He'll be happy to have you along with us."

Chapter 22

On arriving at Clarissa's cottage, Nathan jumped from the new buggy and begged to run to the creek. "I think I left some of my soldiers down by the willow trees. Please, please! I'll come right back."

"It's all right, Dr. Norcutt. Let him go and why don't we join him? We could all use some fresh air after today's inquisition."

"All right, Nathan, run ahead. We'll follow along with Polly." He was reluctant to admit any weakness left over from his illness. Blaming his slower pace on Polly saved his pride.

The chilly breeze off the clear water was invigorating. A great blue heron croaked and rose from the sand bar on his huge wingspan. He landed a short distance away but kept his eye on them as he searched for fish. Adam sat down on a log to catch his breath.

"I hate this weakness. Maybe I shouldn't be walking so far yet. How can Nathan bounce back so fast? Look at him!" They watched Nathan splashing in the shallow water. The solitude and beauty of the scene stole their voices until Clarissa broke the silence.

"Strange, I'm relieved to be honest about Polly's birth. I'll always grieve over how her little life began, but at least I'm not deceiving people anymore."

"I'm surprised you've kept your secret this long. These things have a way of coming out eventually."

"At least I have Polly. She's such a comfort. She is God's gift to me since. . ." she paused and turned aside, "my marriage ended prematurely."

Nathan, enjoying being back at the creek beside the willows, scurried about looking for his lost soldiers. They all watched as the regal heron caught a large fish and struggled to swallow it down his slender throat.

"Look, Papa, you can still see the fish in that big bird's neck." Nathan was enthralled by the heron's eating habits. When the lump in his neck disappeared, the bird went back to stalking along on his long legs. Nathan ran after him, but Adam stopped him.

"Stop, son. Don't harass him, just watch. His kind has lived here longer than we have. This is his kingdom." Nathan ran closer to the creek.

"Miss Clarissa," Adam paused, weighing his words. "You and I became friends when you provided a hospital for Nathan and me. We'll always be in your debt."

"I was just returning the favor. After all, you also saved my life and Polly's."

"Might I ask you something not only as your doctor, but as a concerned friend? Remember, I promised Dr. Logan I'd watch after you."

"Of course, I suppose so. What's your question?" Her expression turned quizzical.

"Earlier today when I said that I didn't see any evidence in your home of a relationship with any man, I was saying more than you thought. While staying at your home, I saw no evidence that you were ever married to this Reverend Chambers. Other than his books, it's like he never existed." He waited for her response. When there was only a chilly silence, he went on. "You never mention your late husband. You don't wear a wedding band or a locket with a strand of his hair. Your home has no memento of him, not even a portrait. You never visit his grave."

"Hmmm, I hadn't thought of all that."

Adam risked one more comment. "For a grieving young widow this is puzzling, isn't it?" More silence. "Forgive me, perhaps I'm reading too much into these small things. But is this all coincidental or can you give me a reason?"

"Is it still open season on my personal life, Dr. Norcutt? I thought we were done with that over at the church."

"I don't mean to intrude, but I think I know the answer. If I'm correct, this is another regrettable secret you're keeping." He looked beyond the sand bar and shook his head.

Propelled by a surge of fury, she stalked away from him. *How dare he presume to know so much about me? He has no right to pry into my privacy.* She wandered over to a willow tree and began stripping the remaining yellow leaves off a slim branch. Her difficult history started bubbling up out of its dark recesses near her heart and demanded to be acknowledged. Suddenly, she needed to talk. After staring at the gurgling creek a few moments, she motioned to him to come within earshot.

"All right, Mr. Fancy British Doctor, since you think you know so much, I'll tell you." But she choked on her words. Embarrassment and rage wrapped around her throat. She twisted the long willow branch around her fingers until they turned white. Adam took the branch away from her and rubbed her throbbing fingers. He dropped her hands and waited for her to continue.

"I never dreamed I would thank the good Lord that someone was dead and buried—certainly not my own husband."

"I've felt for some time that you must have endured something traumatic at the hand of one or more men. I came to this conclusion while we were staying with you. You seemed afraid of me when there was nothing to fear."

She nodded and held up her hand to request a pause, then continued in halting phrases.

"Elliot was a difficult man. I didn't know this until after we were married. I could never please him. I came to believe that he enjoyed making me miserable."

"I'm terribly sorry to hear this. I truly am."

"We looked like a perfect match, but when we married we didn't know each other very well. Since he was away in seminary we had only brief visits together. Instead, we wrote daily love letters—mine were on lavender stationery written in purple ink. I was younger than he by five years and very naïve. To this day, he's my only serious sweetheart."

"You never saw this other side of him?"

"No, I thought he was a wonderful young man of the cloth. In some ways he was—when he was on his good behavior and away from the parsonage."

"The ministry can be a dark place for a duplicitous man to hide. Some professions, including my own, can give you a stalwart reputation whether or not you've earned it."

She was relieved that he believed her. "I was so pleased to be married to a minister, but I soon found out that he was downright mean."

"He mistreated you?"

She resisted another intrusive question, but found herself thankful for his brand of curiosity. Her voice came in a whisper.

"Yes. When he was angry, if he was not shouting and cursing, he was throwing things around. Once he locked me for hours in our privy on a snowy night. Fortunately, I had a shawl around me. He thought it very funny."

Adam braced his arms on a tree limb over his head and leaned toward her.

"No one should be treated like this. You understand this, don't you?"

"He was brutal, Dr. Norcutt. One of the saddest things for me now is that I kept loving him and expected him to love me back. I'll never understand why I thought I could change him."

"He expressed no love for you?"

"Never, but he expected constant affection from me."

"This must have been terribly difficult."

"I was pleased to be pregnant once. I thought having a baby would help us, but I lost the baby—a boy born too soon." Her voice disappeared as she wept. When she could speak again, she begged, "Please, no one must know about this."

"Don't concern yourself. Your secrets are safe with me."

"You're the only one who knows all this, so I'll know who told if talk gets around." She sniffled and tried to smile. By now, her handkerchief, fresh when she went to the church meeting, was a sodden wad in her fist.

"People may know more than you think."

"That's the irony of it. As far as I know, Elliot deceived everyone. Once I had a bruise on my face and told folks that our cow knocked me against the shed while I was milking her. He even said to me in private, 'Lovely story about the cow, Clary.'"

"You had a cow at a parsonage?" He tried to lighten their conversation.

"Yes, she was donated to the church and I became very attached to her. She'd listen to anything I told her while I was milking." *Things I probably shouldn't have told you, Dr. Norcutt.*

"Why didn't you tell anyone besides your cow about this? Perhaps they could've helped you. I know Angus Logan would've."

"You don't know how much I wanted to, but Elliot would have made my life a living hell if I told on him."

"But they would have defended you."

"He would've told them I was crazy and stupid. That's what he always told me."

"So you let eight years go by and did the best you could?"

She was silent while a few more tears slid down her cheeks.

"Thank you for trusting me with your story. You've been hiding inside your soul with these horrible secrets. I hope talking about it helps a bit."

"Yes, I do feel relieved." On an impulse she asked him a question. "Now I have a question for you."

"What's that?"

"How did a skilled British surgeon end up in this little Kentucky town with a little son?"

"Yes, we'll talk about that someday, but right now we'd best leave while I still have some breath left."

Clarissa splashed cold creek water on her tear-stained face as Adam called to Nathan. They walked through the trees into the sunset toward the house. Nathan clutched his misplaced soldiers and Polly rode at Clarissa's waist in a shawl tied across her mother's shoulders.

"Have you picked out a Christmas tree yet, Miss Clarissa?" asked Nathan.

"No, I haven't, Nathan. If you pick one for me, I'll have Willy cut it down."

He carefully chose a small spruce for her parlor window.

"Why not pick a tree for your home, too? The Lewises won't object."

"Say 'yes,' Papa, say 'yes!'" The Norcutts chose a larger tree for their parlor.

"Nathan, come out someday soon and I'll show you how to make paper chains to decorate your tree. And speaking of Christmas, I hope you both will join our caroling group this year. Last year I told you we'd expect you. Remember?"

"The last person you want in your caroling group is someone like me who is tone deaf, but I'll come if Nathan can join in."

"Of course, you're both welcome and I'll find something useful for you to do. Perhaps you can accompany us with some harness bells? I hope we won't need a doctor."

Their stressful day ended with amazing peace.

As Christmas came closer, Nathan was often busy making paper chains at Clarissa's kitchen table. When he had more than enough for their tree, Miss Olivia's tree, and the tree at The Lewis Mercantile, he wanted to make more.

"Miss Clarissa, would you like a chain for your tree? I'll make one for you if you want."

"How thoughtful, Nathan. I think my tree needs more decorations, don't you?"

Nathan went to work and soon a paper chain graced the small tree by her front window.

"We have a lot to celebrate this holiday, don't we, Nathan?"

"Yes, ma'am, we do. It'll be my first Christmas in America."

During Clarissa's second annual caroling event, Adam proved to be proficient with the harness bells. He noted that Ida Lewis's hot chocolate was still the best. On their walk home from the caroling party, he showed Nathan where he found Bonnie, hurt and shivering in the snow, exactly a year ago. The memories of the tears he shed that night over his loss of Nathan brought him to tears again. But now the tears were for his joy as a father, a role he'd never expected to be his.

Nathan reached up to take his hand as they walked the rest of the way home.

Chapter 23

1868

One snowy Sunday afternoon in January, Adam finished a visit to the shanties and traveled toward Springdale along River Road. His bout with typhoid was over and done with and he had resumed his normal routine. Guiding Fancy over to the hitching post in front of Clarissa's fence, he opened the gate to walk up the path. The bell on the gate alerted Clarissa and she walked out onto the porch to greet him.

"Beautiful snowy afternoon, isn't it, Widow Chambers?" He removed his wide-brimmed hat and stamped the snow from his boots.

"I agree. Come in and let me serve us a cup of tea." She walked ahead of him into her parlor. "I've been sitting with my sewing by the front window to watch the snowflakes come down. You sit down and warm up a bit."

"Thank you, it's always colder down by the river." He eased himself into the creaky chair. His long legs barely fit under the table that held Clarissa's mending. At times like this he longed for the sturdy English furnishings of his homeland. She returned with cups of steaming tea for both of them.

"Just what I needed, thank you. Now I have a question for you." He fiddled with the teacup's dainty loop, one much too small for his forefinger.

"It's not another one of those awful, prying questions of yours, is it? I don't have any more secrets." They both laughed as they recalled their conversation down among the willows before Christmas.

"No, it's of a different sort."

"What's that?"

"How would you like to work for Nathan and me?"

She looked up at him, startled and momentarily speechless.

"It's no secret I need someone to look after Nathan while I work. I can't take care of patients properly with him underfoot. He tries to stay out of the way, but a clinic is no place for a child and house calls also present a problem. Miss Olivia has been helping us, but she is moving away next month."

"You do have a problem, don't you?"

"You aren't the only one who's made that observation." He paused to see her reaction. "So," he slapped his palms on his knees, "I'd like for you to help me with Nathan on a permanent basis."

"What made you think of me? I'm not sure how it would work when I live so far out."

"First of all, Nathan is fond of you. During our quarantine here, he became attached to you and Polly. We could work out some sort of schedule. You and Polly can walk to our house or I can bring Nathan out here and come for him later. I'm sure we can devise a plan. Of course I'll pay you fair wages. What do you think?"

The night before she had struggled and prayed over her finances. Even with free housing and her widow's stipend, money was scarce. She resisted the urge to say "Yes" on the spot.

"More income would be a help. Let me think about it. I'll give you my answer in a few days."

"I'm really desperate for a governess." He hastened to add one more advantage. "In bad weather, I'll call for you and Polly in the buggy."

"I must pray about this, Dr. Norcutt. Thank you for thinking of me. I'm really quite flattered."

"I hope those prayers of yours give you a resounding 'yes.'"

He was teasing her for praying, as he often did. She resisted the urge to argue with him for she was pleased that he had considered her for Nathan's care.

"I'll stop by in a couple of days for your answer. I think I'm warm enough to make it home now."

Clarissa stopped herself from calling after him with a hasty decision. She didn't want to seem too eager. She pulled back and forth on the measuring tape tossed around her shoulders and thanked God for this possibility.

As she prayed about the doctor's request, she felt less and less confident about being Nathan's governess. How could she care for him with a child of her own and a home to care for? How could she contain Polly, now constantly in motion? The more she thought and prayed about it, the less sure she was that it was a good idea. A day or two later, she came up with a solution that might work, if Dr. Norcutt agreed.

True to his word, the doctor stopped by two days later. Nathan, impatient to find out Clarissa's answer, ran up the front steps where she waited for them.

"Welcome, gentlemen, come in and let me take your coats."

"We can't stay, but you know why we're here. What's your decision?"

"I wish you'd stay a moment so I can explain my answer."

"Does that mean 'no'?"

"I'm afraid it does, but I have another idea for you."

"If you are turning us down, I need some suggestions."

"I'd like to become Nathan's piano teacher. He's the perfect age to begin and he can practice on Dr. Logan's piano. I have all day Mondays without a student. He can come out here for his lesson and stay all day. Or, I'll come to your house for his lesson. That takes care of one day for you. Also, I want Nathan to come here if you're ever in a pinch. Don't forget, Nathan, you promised to help me around here."

"Your plan has a lot of merit and I don't have any options. Nathan is probably ready to learn piano, aren't you, son?" He looked over at Nathan who looked the other way. "We're sorry for your decision, but I like your idea of piano lessons. He'll get used to the idea."

"Won't Widow Desmond help you care for Nathan?" She had heard the recent rumor that Nellie Desmond and the doctor were marrying in the spring.

"I doubt Miss Desmond will ever supervise a child on a daily basis."

"Well, surely the right governess will come along. Meanwhile, Nathan, you're always welcome here." She knelt down to hug Nathan and reminded him to come Monday for his first lesson. "Bring your soldiers and plan to spend the day."

She looked up at Adam, and they grinned at each other over Nathan's clear disdain for piano lessons. She noticed the man's striking blue eyes. Had she ever looked directly into them before? She felt herself beginning to fall into the warmth of his gaze and quickly looked away. "I'm sorry but. . ." she glanced up at him. He was still regarding her with sympathetic blue eyes. She took a quick breath to calm the strange flutter in her heart and started again. "I'm sorry but this isn't a good time for me to take on a new job. After I prayed about it, I knew I wasn't the one to help you. I'll try to think of someone else."

"Please do. As you can tell, I'm at a loss for a solution. Right now I must rush back to the clinic."

As she watched them leave, Clarissa wondered if she had made a mistake by turning them down. Throughout the rest of her day, she tried to think of someone to help the doctor with his son. When she was ironing in the late afternoon, the perfect solution came to her:

Rosalie, Luke Featherson's daughter.

PART TWO

"One's progress through difficult
terrain is heading somewhere."
—Kathleen Norris

Chapter 24

Adam acted on Clarissa's suggestion about hiring Rosalie Featherson, and the young girl soon became an enthusiastic caretaker for Nathan. Lively and energetic, she enjoyed spending her days with Nathan and away from endless chores on the Featherson farm.

Once Clarissa was asked to help when Rosalie was sick. She and Polly came and stayed with Nathan for the day. That afternoon as she and Adam chatted on the clinic porch, he expressed a concern.

"Do you know Nathan now insists we say a prayer before we eat? I guess you and Rosalie tell him his food will be poisoned if he doesn't pray—or something equally frightening."

"My stars, Dr. Norcutt! Neither Rosalie nor I would force our personal beliefs on Nathan, but we do say a prayer of thanks before meals. It's an expression of gratitude, not a superstition meant to frighten him. Being thankful is the farthest thing from frightening, don't you agree?"

"I suppose I won't forbid a mealtime prayer. It's a social grace he should understand. He's always said bedtime prayers which seem to give him some sense of security. Between you and Rosalie, I don't stand a chance of keeping religion out of that boy's head, do I?"

"Knowing how you feel, I'm surprised he knows about God. Actually, your son often teaches me about God." She glanced uneasily at him, for she had never challenged one of his caustic remarks about her faith.

"That's absurd. He doesn't know anything about God." His derision rankled the air between them.

"But he does, Dr. Norcutt. Surely you've noticed he has quite a repertoire of children's Bible stories and choruses. He believes in God in a lovely, childlike way."

"Where on earth has he learned this?" He snorted and answered his own question. "Probably in London from another saint of a nanny."

"Just resign yourself to having some happy Christians in your new circle of friends. We go with the territory here in Springdale." Clarissa laughed and the tension between them eased.

"I don't suppose you could at least agree that there are other reasonable possibilities?"

"I know what you are asking. Honestly, you and I have chosen to believe in different possibilities, as you call them. Don't you see that your atheism is as much a choice of belief as my faith in God? This isn't about arguing things out until one of us delivers the winning point of view—this debate is ageless and endless."

Adam wrote in his journal about his conversation with Clarissa that night: "Even though I disagree with the ladies' beliefs, I appreciate their strength of character and humanitarian fervor."

On another day, Clarissa spoke to Adam about his careless use of God's name around her and the children.

"Miss Clarissa, it's only an expression."

"You're missing the point. You're not supposed to use God's name as a term of profanity or call upon Him unless you are speaking to Him. That's what the Bible means when it says, 'Thou shalt not take the name of the Lord thy God in vain.'"

"That's preposterous. People use these expressions when something needs an—uh—an, you know, an emphasis. Don't make so much of this. I feel like you are preaching at me."

"I don't mean to offend you, sir, but I do expect you'll curtail your profanity around these children and me."

"Yes, madam." He stomped off.

Another time, after a competitive game of checkers with Nathan and Clarissa playing against Adam, he started down this same critical path.

"Please, Dr. Norcutt, you cannot dictate what I believe about God."

"No," he lowered his voice rather than be overheard by Nathan who was in the kitchen looking for cookies, "but I can and will restrict what you teach Nathan." His eyes flashed steel blue as he reinforced his demands.

"That's your prerogative as a father and I will always respect that. But children often have a faith that's important to them. If you're curious about Nathan's faith, ask him how he arrived here with you in Springdale. It's quite a story."

"How he arrived here? Surely, you haven't taught him some sort of bizarre fable about being delivered by a monstrous stork across the Atlantic?" His voice had a touch of acid in it. He was annoyed and felt she had overstepped the boundaries between them. He decided it was best to refrain from saying, *"What I teach Nathan about God is none of your bloody concern."*

Clarissa didn't hesitate, "No, his account is much better than that, although that stork theory is fascinating. If you ask him, I'm sure he'll tell you all about it."

Adam took Clarissa's challenge as he sat on Nathan's bed that evening.

"Nathan, would you would tell me something?"

"What, Papa?"

"Something about how you arrived Springdale. Miss Clarissa says you told her and I wonder if you'll tell me too?" He held out his hand for a man-to-man agreement. Nathan slipped his small hand from under the comforter to shake Adam's.

"I guess I know what she's talking about, but it happened in England."

"Many things happened there that I don't know about. Would you like to start telling me about them?"

"Mum was gone a lot. I had nannies, but they just sat around when Mum was gone."

Adam nodded. "That is precisely why I brought you to America with me. Is there something else I don't know?"

"How you were sent to England for me."

"What do you mean, son? I came to England to sign some papers. I wanted to see you, but I wasn't sent by anyone to England." He spoke with authority.

"Yes, you were, Papa. God brought you back for me."

Adam stared at him. "You think God sent me to London?"

"I missed you so much. Didn't you miss me?" Adam nodded. "So, I prayed every morning and every night that God would send you back for me."

"You what?"

"I asked God to send you back so I could be your boy again."

Adam's eyes welled with tears as he pulled Nathan into his arms.

"Nathan, you've always been my boy. Nothing can ever change that. Some days you were on my mind all the time, but I thought I'd never see you again."

"I couldn't remember your face, but I thought a lot about you when I was lonely."

"So, you prayed that I'd come back to London for you? Who taught you how to pray?"

"I don't know. I talk to God. That's all."

"Is this what you were talking about when I saw you in the park in London? Something about how you knew I was coming?"

Nathan yawned. "Yes, Papa. Is that what Miss Clarissa wanted me to tell you?"

"I suppose so. Now, why don't you say your prayers?"

Nathan was almost too sleepy to pray, but he asked God to bless his father, then Standard, then Fancy. He paused to add, "And take care of Mum."

Adam sat beside the candle in his parlor that night. Were things beginning to make a bit of sense or were they coincidental? Josephine, never one to back down, made it clear that she would never divorce him. If a child's prayers could be heard by God—if one existed—then could Nathan's prayers have been a factor in Josephine's changed attitude about divorce? He kept reasoning with himself.

He knew he would never have returned to London without the legal nightmare of the divorce. By then he had resigned himself to never seeing Nathan again. His ties to England were cut. He had assumed that since Nathan never really knew his father, he wouldn't miss having one. But the simple story Nathan had related tonight made Adam realize how deeply Nathan had felt his father's absence. Adam found himself heartsick that Nathan had suffered because he couldn't find a way to deal with Josephine.

Adam's past decisions and their implications swirled in his head. When he went to bed, he jerked the quilts up under his chin, and continued his conversation with himself.

I wanted to do what was best for Nathan when I invited him to come live with me here. Some sort of hovering deity did not orchestrate that decision. I'm not about to believe that the prayers of a little boy manipulated me all the way over to England to take him away from his mother.

"This is insanity," he muttered into the darkness. "This confounded childhood God of Nathan's better get out of my head and leave me alone."

With his well-ordered mind a bit shaken, Adam hoped that Clarissa would forget to ask him if Nathan had told him his story yet. He didn't want to talk about it. But before he fell asleep, he realized he had spoken to himself as though Nathan's God were real.

"Sometimes that boy sounds just like Widow Chambers."

Chapter 25

Farmer Jacob Featherson was a confirmed bachelor when he and Luke rescued Clarissa from Private Gary. His wife and their unborn child died in childbirth before The War. He rarely thought about finding a new wife because his days were consumed with his farm chores and raising his lazy sons, Claude and Bubba.

On the evening after he and Luke took George Gary to jail, they talked on their way home about how pretty Clarissa was. With a quick jab to his brother's ribs, Luke challenged him.

"Now there's a possibility for you, Jake."

"Huh?" He stared at Luke.

"Don't be acting all big eyed. I'm talking about you and Widow Chambers."

"Me and the preacher's widow?"

"Why not? If you and them boys cleaned up a tad, that lady and her pretty little girl might fit right in." He gave his brother another poke in his rib cage.

"Think so, do you?"

One day while plowing, Jacob mulled over his brother's suggestion again. Maybe he should find a wife, and no doubt about it, Widow Chambers was pretty. Not only was her waist almost small enough for him to reach around with his big hands, but he liked the way her thick auburn braids nestled against her neck. One of his mules stumbled, crossed over a row and canceled his day dreams about Clarissa. *Quit your dreaming about some silly woman and pay attention to your plowing.*

Luke brought up the subject again. "Jake, what you got to lose? You won't know 'til you go over and spend some time with the little widow. I see how you been looking at her in church."

Jacob decided to take charge of the possibilities with Widow Chambers. He made a point of greeting her when they crossed paths in town. He cleaned his fingernails, trimmed his beard and put on a clean shirt for church. Maybe she'd talk to him after church was over.

One Sunday afternoon he mustered up enough courage to call on her. Another time, when he brought her an armload of clothing to mend, she wouldn't let him pay.

"Jacob, I'll always be in your debt for taking care of Pvt. Gary. Your mending won't ever cost you a penny." Now he was more smitten than ever.

Jacob's Sunday afternoon visits went on until Clarissa suspected he was interested in more than friendship. Knowing him to be a decent man, she was polite to him, but in a distant way. She decided to see what Ida thought about her suspicions.

"Ida, Jacob Featherson is showing me a lot more attention than he should. Almost every Sunday afternoon he plants himself on my front porch."

"Really? I don't know him very well, but he seems nice."

"He's a decent man, but I don't have the slightest interest in him. All he talks about is how his hens are laying or which cow is about to freshen."

"I know Jacob isn't the most sophisticated man in Springdale, but he's a good provider. Don't forget he's in church every Sunday with that entire Featherson clan in tow."

"But I don't have one lick of affection for him. He and Luke rescued me from that soldier, so I don't want to be rude to them. But I don't want to spend every Sunday afternoon with Jacob."

"Then just be polite, but don't encourage him. He'll catch on. Or maybe you'll change your mind?"

"Don't plan on it, Ida. I want my Sunday afternoons back."

Whenever Jacob visited, Claude and Bubba would go down to the creek to skip rocks and fish. They would come back to the cottage soaked to the skin, beg Clarissa for more lemonade and loll around on the porch steps.

On one Sunday afternoon Clarissa heard them brag about throwing rocks at the heron.

"Jacob, you tell Claude and Bubba not to torment that bird down on the sandbar. Let them know that this won't be tolerated."

"It won't happen no more. I'll warm their britches when we get home."

"Don't whip them, Jacob! Just speak to them about it."

"Yes, ma'am, whatever you say." She wondered later if she had saved the boys' backsides.

One time when Jacob came calling without Claude and Bubba, Clarissa served him lemonade out on the front porch. When she took their empty glasses inside, hoping his visit was over, she bumped into him as she left the kitchen.

"I'm sorry, Jacob. I didn't hear you come inside."

"I've been thinking you and me should have an inside visit."

"An inside visit?"

"Yes, ma'am, I think you and me might enjoy a kiss or two, don't you?"

The look on Clarissa's face warned Jacob, but he persisted.

"Us is both lonesome. It'll be just fine. You'll see." He reached his big hands around her waist, but she pushed him away.

"Is this why Claude and Bubba aren't with you this afternoon? If you planned this, you can change your tune right now."

"Aw, Miss Clarissa, come on now."

"No, Jacob. I don't want to kiss you."

Clarissa retreated backwards into the kitchen, but Jacob followed her. When she bumped into the pie safe, her hand came to rest on her iron skillet. She grabbed the skillet and raised it over her head.

"Jacob Featherson, leave me alone! You get out of my house this minute and don't come calling again!"

"Aw' right, Miss Clarissa. Now put down your skillet." The menace of a fierce little lady brandishing an iron skillet at him sent a clear message. "I was only hoping to romance you. If you don't want it, you just say so."

"You need to leave, Jacob."

"Yes, ma'am, I believe I do."

Later that evening when she was still angry and upset, Clarissa realized Jacob's intentions had resurrected her bad memories of Elliot and Private Gary. Why on earth would I threaten Jacob like that?

With my iron skillet? I didn't want to kiss him, but he's not like those others. Or is he?

"Lord, forgive me for being so belligerent. Most of all, thank You for giving me back my Sunday afternoons."

The next day, a beautiful Monday morning, Clarissa grew impatient with Nathan as he finished up his piano lesson. His dawdling had worn her to a frazzle. Adam waited on the front porch of her cottage and listened to Clarissa struggle to teach his son. He needed to hurry home to open the clinic, but the lesson dragged on and Nathan was not cooperating.

"Let's do that scale once more. Now pay attention to what you are doing with your right hand. Nathan, where is your mind today?"

"I guess it's outside." He made another mistake.

"Play it again and do it correctly this time. You know how to do this." The lesson slowed to a close and Nathan scampered out the door.

"I'm going outside with my mind!" He gave her his most brilliant smile. She followed him onto the porch where an amused Adam waited.

"You all right today?" he asked.

"I'm fine, thank you. And you?"

"I've never seen you struggle so with Nathan. I'm afraid he's like his father. We enjoy music, but not the making of it." She rolled her eyes and looked away. "Come on, it's not worth another war between the Brits and the Yanks, is it? We've already had two of those."

"I'll try to replenish my patience by his next lesson. Meanwhile, may I serve you a quick cup of tea before you leave?"

"Why, thank you. I'll linger for that tea of yours, but then I must hurry into town." He followed her in and sat at her kitchen table while she fumbled around with the tea kettle.

"You're not yourself today, Widow Chambers. Don't rush too much on my account. You'll break something." She clattered their teacups. "Are you quite sure you are all right?"

"I'm fine. It's a new week and I haven't collected myself yet."

"Really? Did you hit a wrong chord at church yesterday? If that what's gotten you rattled, it must've been a horrendous mistake." He tried to cheer her up a bit.

"No, it was nothing like that." She set two cups of tea on the table.

"Well? What was it?"

"I lost my temper and to make it worse, it was on a Sunday." She hesitated before adding, "I almost hit a man yesterday. I honestly intended to hurt him."

"You what?" He sputtered, slid his cup back onto its saucer and pointed at her. "You intended to hit a man?"

"Yes, I did. I've never, ever done anything like that—not even with Elliot. I can't quit fretting about it." She shook her head in disbelief and felt of her face which must be turning red.

"Can you tell me what this was all about?"

She hesitated to say what happened in her kitchen the day before, but felt he most likely would be sympathetic.

"I've had a gentleman visitor lately and the only way to convince him to stay away from me yesterday was to shake my iron skillet at him. He was very persistent. I don't know why I'm telling you this," she muttered. She pressed her hands again to her burning cheeks. "I'm so mortified that I lost my temper."

Adam lost all ability to be solicitous. The vision of her diminutive form combating an amorous suitor with her iron skillet was too delightful.

"Oh, my," he clapped his hands on his knees and roared with laughter. "You must've been a sight to behold!"

Clarissa recoiled, then joined in his laughter. Tears rolled down their faces and neither could stop. Soon Polly joined in the laughter. Nathan came inside to see what was so funny.

"It's all right, Nathan. We're laughing about something that happened to Miss Clarissa."

When Adam could catch his breath, he ventured a guess. "Was it Farmer Featherson? On my way to the shanties, I've seen his wagon tied to your hitching post most Sunday afternoons."

She nodded and he began laughing again. He finished his tea and stood to leave.

"Farmer Featherson is no match for you, Miss Clarissa." He gave a little bow as he clicked his heels together. She stood and curtsied in return. She wanted to change the subject, but was puzzled by his comment. He noticed her quizzical look.

"I predict that someday a fine young man, a man without two scrawny sons and a broken down farm, will win your heart."

Clarissa shook her head. "I'm not ready for that yet. I seem to attract only difficult men. First there was Elliot, then Private Gary, and now Jacob. Although he isn't awful like the others. At least I don't think so."

"Whoa, hold up. Don't lump us all together. Most of us try to behave around women."

"But how do I sort men out? You're the doctor. Tell me how to do this."

"As if I'm one to give anyone advice on relationships."

"But you and Widow Desmond seem to do well."

"Hmmm, some days that's debatable." He looked away for a moment. "Here's what you must do. Look for the warning signs and disconnect from someone before you have difficulties. Perhaps Jacob misinterpreted your hospitality. You can prevent most men's advances if you speak up before you have to use an iron skillet in self-defense. George Gary, of course, is an unfortunate exception to this rule."

"I'm trying to learn this skill, but it still frightens me. Elliot was the picture of a mannerly gentleman until we married. Sometimes it's hard to tell."

"I think you've already learned what to look out for. After all, you sent Jacob packing yesterday, didn't you? Someday, when the right young man comes along, someone with integrity, intelligence and the right sort of heart, you'll recognize him. Someday you'll know."

"I hope so, but right now no man in the state of Kentucky better darken my door." She smoothed her apron. "Of course, the fathers of my piano students are always welcome."

"Thank you, but might I make a suggestion?" Clarissa nodded for him to continue. "Please send any of your future beaux to me so I can forewarn them. I don't want to sew up some bloke's scalp because he couldn't dodge your skillet."

Clarissa laughed. "Yes, sir. Now promise me you won't tell anyone what happened yesterday."

"You have my word, but it will cost you something." He left his challenge hanging in the air and opened the front door to leave.

"What's that?"

"A batch of chicken fried in that iron skillet. We need to put it to proper use."

Clarissa laughed. "I'll do that, but only if your promise is official."

"It's ironclad, but don't wait too long or I'll weaken. I'll have Magnolia pluck the chickens and bring them when Nathan comes for his next lesson."

"That'll be fine."

Nathan persuaded Clarissa to let him stay with her for the rest of the day. As Adam hurried in to the clinic, he chuckled as he thought about Jacob Featherson's dilemma.

"Poor chap, I doubt it occurred to him that he'd be rejected. But then, he doesn't know what Widow Chambers has been through with men, does he?"

Later that day, when he told Magnolia about the promised chicken dinner, she looked up from scrubbing clothes in her laundry tub.

"Don't she want me to cook them chickens for her?"

When Adam told her why Clarissa was duty bound to fry the chickens in her own skillet, Magnolia began to chuckle. "Whew-wee, waving a skillet at that big, strapping farmer? S'wanee, wish I'd seen that...mmmmh-HHMMM."

Later, when Adam realized he had inadvertently broken his promise of secrecy to Clarissa, he called to Magnolia. "That's a big secret between you and me. Don't tell anyone. Just get the chickens ready next week for Miss Clarissa."

"Yessuh." She covered her laughter by scrubbing harder on her washboard.

Chapter 26

Late in the day Clarissa and Polly waited on their front porch with Nathan. Rosalie had brought him out to the cottage when she was needed at home for the afternoon. When Adam arrived and Clarissa walked Nathan to the buggy, she saw Nellie Desmond seated in the front.

"Nathan, don't forget to play your recital piece for your father and Miss Desmond. I know you'll be proud of how well your son is doing, Dr. Norcutt."

As Adam started to turn the rig around, she overheard Miss Nellie say,

"Adam, dearest, weren't we going to give Widow Chambers some medicine?"

"Right, I almost forgot. Son, look there in my black bag and find that small white jar." Adam reached down with the jar for Clarissa. "Nellie reminded me to give you more of this ointment. Sorry it has taken me so long."

Clarissa was thankful for the ointment which always helped her skin, but she was mortified that Nellie, whose complexion was flawless, brought it to Adam's attention—apparently more than once. Nellie never looked her way.

"Nothing if not perfect," she whispered to Polly as the buggy headed toward town.

That evening she sat in front of the mirror on her dressing table and glared at her reflection. Dr. Norcutt's ointment was improving her complexion, but her hair was a mess, she was thin as a rail and her well-worn clothes were frumpy and out of style. Giving in to waves of self-criticism, she broke down in tears. But she could only blame herself. In struggling to get by from day to day, she was sadly neglecting herself. After a good cry, she spoke to her image in the mirror.

"Clarissa Francine, you must make better care of yourself. No more excuses."

The next day Clarissa honored the promise she made to herself the night before and bought a length of flowered cotton sateen at the Lewis Mercantile. Before bedtime she cut out the pieces of her new dress from a stylish customer's pattern.

The next morning she put Polly in her carriage and walked to Ida's to tell her about her plans to take better care of herself. "I started on the dress last night, but it's time to change my hair. I've worn these braids too long. The only change I've ever made is to move them from the top of my head to the back of my neck. What should I do?"

"We could experiment if you aren't in a hurry."

Before Ida finished her comment, Clarissa started to unravel her long braids. Ida assembled her combs and brushes and the two tried out various hair styles.

"It's high time you quit wearing those tight braids like your mother always braided. It's all right for a curl or two to show, Sweetie."

Ida brushed out the long tresses and trimmed off some of the excessive length. After trying several styles, they settled on one that enhanced Clarissa's features.

"I think you look beautiful. Now your hair is stylish and your skin isn't pulled back by those school girl braids."

They consulted with the twins and Polly for their approval, and the new style passed inspection. The soft waves around Clarissa's face brought a noticeable difference in her looks. Rosalie noticed the change right away.

"You look so pretty, Miss Clarissa. Isn't something different about your hair?"

"Why, thank you. I wanted a change and Miss Ida helped me find a new style."

"You're glowing like someone in love. Do you have a new boyfriend?"

"No, no, no, a thousand times no. There's no one here for me."

"I don't know about that. You'd make a wonderful wife for someone."

"Well—maybe someday."

In the late spring, Clarissa's parents, the Sinclairs, sent word they were coming to visit. She cleaned her cottage, raked the front yard and made a dress for Polly out of remnants of her own new dress. When the Sinclairs arrived, Clarissa and Polly greeted them wearing their matching dresses. Her efforts to improve her looks were not wasted. Her mother wept to see how well their daughter was doing. Her father strutted around the cottage and noted repairs he could make. Both were thrilled with Polly, and Clarissa was delighted with their gift of local perfume made near their home.

Clarissa dreaded the day she must tell her parents the truth about Polly's birth. Because they lived so far away, she had kept the sordid tale from them. She didn't want to spoil their visit, so the bad news could wait. She and her mother cooked family favorites and worked together on bound buttonholes for a demanding socialite's spring outfit. Her father stayed busy with his repairs and turned over a patch of soil for a garden. They played with Polly and bought gifts and essentials for her at the Lewis Mercantile.

One day as they sat on Clarissa's porch enjoying the morning, Willy, with Nathan beside him, stopped the Norcutt wagon and called out to them.

"Widow Chambers, there's been a bad accident at that sawmill. Mr. Doctor says he be tied up the rest of the day with the foreman. He 'bout cut off his hand."

"You don't mean Max Capehart, do you?" When Willy nodded, Clarissa turned to her parents. "Max and Betsy go to our church and he helped move me from the parsonage. Betsy was my midwife with Polly. I do hope Dr. Norcutt can help him."

"Mr. Doctor wants to know, could you see to the boy 'cause Miss Rosalie ain't there today. He can't sew up that hand with Master Nathan running in and out."

"Of course, Willy, he'll be fine here with us."

"He's got them soldiers with him and wants to play out by your creek."

Nathan ran to Clarissa who welcomed him with a hug. They waved goodbye to Willy as he headed back to Springdale.

"Nathan, can you and your soldiers wait for me to pack up a picnic? If you can, we'll all go out to the creek. It's a lovely day for a picnic. Come meet my parents."

When Dr. Norcutt arrived to pick up Nathan that afternoon, Clarissa invited them to stay for supper. He didn't hesitate to accept her invitation when she told him left over chicken and dumplings was on the menu.

"Mother and Father, meet Dr. Adam Norcutt, Nathan's father. Dr. Norcutt, my parents, Mr. and Mrs. Sinclair." Her parents stood to greet him.

"So how is Max's hand?" She blurted out her question before any other conversation could start. *What if he mentions my horror story?*

"Unfortunately, I don't have good news. Max's hand was lost. I don't know what he'll do. His livelihood depends on the strength of his arms and hands."

Everyone absorbed the tragic news and discussed Max's dilemma for a few moments until there was nothing else to say.

"Well," Clarissa spoke up, "Let's sit down and I'll put our food on the table."

After supper, when the doctor still seemed unsettled, she suggested a game of checkers. Nathan teamed up with Mr. Sinclair against Adam. They played until Nathan fell asleep on Mr. Sinclair's lap. As he left, Adam shook hands with the Sinclairs and expressed his appreciation for Clarissa's help with Nathan.

"My son's not much of a piano student, but he certainly enjoys your daughter's company."

When Adam mounted Fancy, Mr. Sinclair gave a drowsy Nathan a lift up onto the saddle in front of his father. Adam smiled down at Clarissa, then stared.

"Wait a moment. Something's different about your hair, isn't it?"

"Yes, Ida and I trimmed my school girl braids the other day."

"I've wondered if those tight braids ever gave you a headache. Well, thank you for a quiet evening with good company. This would've been a difficult evening to be alone."

Hmm--pity she cut that hair.

She breathed a huge sigh of relief when they left. All during the evening she had feared Adam might mention the George Gary incident.

"Clary, I think that doctor has taken a shine to you, don't you?" her mother asked as they sat around the table with their breakfast the next morning.

"Heavens to Betsy, no! He's much too old for me. Before Dr. Logan left, he asked Dr. Norcutt to look after me because I was expecting Polly. He's my doctor and has become a friend, that's all."

"Wouldn't he be a good match for you?"

"Probably not. He knows way too much about me."

"Why would you say something like that?"

She could put off the inevitable no longer.

"Because it's true." She set down her cup of tea and looked up at them. "It's time you know that after Elliot died, I was assaulted by a Union straggler who is Polly's father."

There was a long, tense silence as Clarissa stared down at her lap. She forced herself to look up and make a feeble attempt at humor.

"Now don't you agree that I could never be the next Mrs. Norcutt?"

More silence until Father Sinclair stood to his full height.

"Do you mean your departed husband is not the father of your child?"

"Yes, Father. I hadn't planned to tell anyone, but the terrible story came out recently. You'd surely hear about it someday."

Mother Sinclair left her breakfast unfinished and hurried to the guest room for the rest of the day. Clarissa tried to discuss the difficult truth with her father, but he refused to listen. Finally her mother re-appeared.

"Clarissa Francine, please do not bring that illegitimate child with you when you come to Virginia. We will not tolerate this sort of humiliation in our family."

"Mother, no one in Virginia will ever know what happened. Don't reject your only grandchild. She's so sweet and beautiful. None of this is her fault or mine. How can you be so cold hearted? Aren't you concerned for what I've been through?"

"Someday you'll understand," added her father.

She wanted to lash out but held her tongue. *How old do I have to be to understand I was raped and bore the villain's child?*

Her parents never relented. For the rest of their visit, they showed no compassion for what she had endured. This new wound opened a bruised compartment in her heart, one that hid her parents' distant affection. Throughout Clarissa's childhood, they were attentive and controlling, but never cared to share deep emotional issues. They would only go so far in their relationship with her.

She wanted to scream at them, "Where's compassion? You take care of surface necessities so well that everyone feels beholden to you." But she knew they were a closed book when it came to her tragic situation. *I should never have told them.*

She whispered to Polly under her breath as the steamer carried her parents away from Springdale. "They didn't sympathize one bit about the bad things that have hurt us, did they? I guess this means we'll never move to Virginia. I won't take either of us anywhere near that rejection of theirs again."

Polly kept waving to the departing ship.

Chapter 27

In the days following her parents' departure, Clarissa's emotions spiraled downward into a lingering, foggy depression. Apart from Polly, she was alone in this world and she agonized afresh over her past. The wounds of an abusive marriage, the violent assault, and this unexpected rejection from her parents went deep into her heart and churned there. She battled persistent bad dreams and prayed that God would take them away. She often awoke in hysterics and walked around the dark cottage to calm down.

"God, I'm so alone in this world. Thank goodness You delight to find lost sheep and keep us safe. I know You won't desert me in this wilderness."

Friends noticed her moodiness and Ida tried to talk to her.

"Why are you so blue these days? You look so sad. Is there something I can do?"

"No, I'm trying to be cheerful, but I can't seem to find that place inside myself right now. I'm determined to let God carry my burden, but it's hard."

"That's the best thing you can do. You know God's loving kindness will carry you through anything, don't you?"

"I'm trying to see it that way."

Adam also puzzled over her profound sadness. Once, when he passed her in town, tears flooded her cheeks. She tried to dry her eyes before he could speak to her.

"Don't hide your tears from me, Miss Clarissa. Is there anything I might help you with? I hope this isn't about Nathan?"

"Your Nathan is never a problem," she sniffed. "I'm just a bit sad today."

"You have a lot of these sad days, don't you?"

"You needn't trouble yourself about my personal problems." She still tried to hide behind her handkerchief.

Her downcast eyes missed the warm concern in his gaze. "Please cheer up. After all, everyone in America struggles nowadays with some sort of past or present difficulty. Everyone has lost relationships. Entire parts of folk's hearts and lives vanished in The War and won't return. Except for Nathan, I lost my life in England. We're all in the same boat." Their conversation paused as others passed by.

"So," she whispered through her tears, "we should all grab an oar on this boat of yours and start paddling?"

"That's the way I see it."

"What if I can't even find an oar?"

"Then you must keep trying!" He punctuated his words with a clenched fist.

"Dr. Norcutt, I'm beyond trying. I'm tired. If it weren't for Polly, I don't know what I'd do. Some nights all I can do is to hold my Bible and pray." Her sobs now came in gulps she couldn't control.

"You're still upset about what happened to you."

"Please don't bring all that up. I'll be all right. I know God is holding my hand."

"You aren't just going pray and hold your Bible about this, are you? You're much too strong for that. Can't you see that God is an arcane excuse for people who won't solve their own problems? When they believe in God they feel better because they can shift their struggles to some sort of ethereal 'other place' and not face them head on. You aren't that sort of person."

His words cut through her heart. He insisted she be strong—the very thing she could not be. At the same time, he attacked her faith, the only piece of fragile strength she could still claim.

"Yes, Doctor Norcutt, I'm afraid I am. Holding onto the Bible and praying is exactly what I'm going to do. This isn't about being strong or weak. Many of the strongest people in history have had the habit of praying." Before Adam could speak, Clarissa spun around and hurried away.

"I don't want to be at cross purposes with him, but sometimes he can be downright insensitive and intrusive," she lectured herself. She tried to calm down, but she felt a glut of emotions like hot, angry lava coming from the core of her being. Her flash of temper at the doctor opened an emotional wound that had festered for a long time.

At the cottage, she pushed the carriage into the shade and walked behind the spring. Overcome with sobs, she fell face down. In angry frustration, she dug her fingers into the dirt and grass. The distant willow trees stood like silent witnesses as she wept and gave back to the earth the losses and tragedies that continued to ravage her life. When her tears subsided, she prayed out loud.

"Dear God, help me accept this path in life. I don't want to stay caught in the past. It's too terrible. Help me give my burden to You and don't let me keep looking back. I don't care what that high-falutin' doctor says, I need You and Your comfort—and I need it right now."

With renewed faith in God's constant care, she brushed the dirt and grass off her dress, and stopped by the spring to wash her muddy hands and tear-stained face. Polly's carriage moved slightly and she went to rock her daughter back to sleep. Standing beside the carriage she hummed a hymn and felt more calm.

At the clinic, Adam thought back over his visit with Clarissa. He found himself smiling at her eloquent defense. He found it admirable, even though he disagreed. He hoped he hadn't offended her by contradicting what she said about prayer. Above all, he didn't want to cause Clarissa Chambers any more grief. Or lose her help with Nathan.

Chapter 28

Excitement hovered over Springdale as the townspeople anticipated their first Fourth of July celebration since The War. The community hummed with preparations as everyone prepared for the displays by local artisans, racks of handmade quilts, cake walks, and canning contests. Farmers groomed their best livestock and poultry. Sheaves of tobacco from re-opened plantations hung on long display racks. A spanking new grandstand stood ready for the animal judging and the horse races. To win a blue ribbon motivated every participant. And they anticipated endless tables of food, plenty of music and a bonfire after sundown.

Before The War, the horse races had always caused the most excitement. Now everyone welcomed the beautiful horses back to the festival. A win at the racetrack meant not only bragging rights in Springdale, but also clout in the Thoroughbred business that was making a strong comeback in post-war Kentucky. Behind the grandstand, money exchanged hands as gentlemen bet on their favorite mounts and enjoyed a sip of Kentucky bourbon from their pocket flasks. Fancy Petticoats became the talk of the gamblers. Maybe the doctor would enter her in the races. When he announced that she wasn't ready to race this year, the owners of the other mounts were relieved that Fancy was not in contention.

Yards of red, white and blue bunting were brought out of storage. A new event was added to celebrate the re-opening of the fair: The Watermelon Seed Distance Contest. Those using the term "spitting" were shushed. Men of all ages were to compete and the winner would take home a blue ribbon and the largest watermelon.

Local seamstresses stitched on their quilts for months to compete for the 'best in show' ribbon. To raise money for the Trinity Church's

Benevolence Fund, a quilt made by the Ladies' Christian Guild would be raffled off. Before The War, Clarissa always helped with the quilters' booth. This year, though she was no longer the preacher's wife, she agreed to manage the quilt show.

The festivities began at noon and soon the fair was a beehive of activity. Cheers went up as prizes were awarded and competition was fierce at the Distance Contest booth. Later in the day, Nathan bought the last raffle ticket for the Ladies Christian Guild quilt as Adam stood with Nellie at a distance and waved. Now Clarissa was free to enjoy the fair.

While fiddlers tuned up for the evening's dancing, local children twirled around on the makeshift dance floor. Clarissa was dancing around with Polly when Nathan ran over to join them. The three spun round and round until Adam approached them with a big smile on his face.

"Miss Clarissa, you are outnumbered. Might I join your little circle and even things up a bit?"

"Of course, but where is Miss Nellie?"

"She and Mrs. Murray went off to look at jams and jellies." The four joined hands and danced in a circle. When the fiddlers started the familiar dance tunes, the doctor put Nathan on his shoulders, picked Polly up in one arm, and extended his other hand to Clarissa.

"Let's see if we can make this work. Nathan and Polly, you two hold on. I don't want to lose anyone." He began to dance with them in time with the music. Elliot forbade dancing, so she hadn't danced in years, but tonight Clarissa was determined to follow the doctor's lead. With her other hand on Nathan's knee, she tried to follow Adam's lead but stumbled against him.

"Oh, dear, I can't remember how to dance." Her cheeks flamed with embarrassment.

"Don't fret over a misstep or two. After all, we can't really call this dancing, can we? Nathan, hold on to Miss Clarissa's hand and let's try again."

Nathan and Polly squealed with delight until Nellie cut in.

"Adam, dear, our supper is served. You and your son come along."

Adam shifted Polly into Clarissa's arms. "That's the dinner bell for the Norcutts."

Nathan scowled as he jumped down from his father's shoulders. Without speaking to Clarissa, Nellie reached for Adam's hand, and they walked off together with Nathan lagging behind. True to form, the Murray family had brought along their own elaborate meal complete with table, chairs and starched table linens. Two uniformed servants hovered nearby.

Clarissa thought it odd that Doctor Norcutt and Miss Nellie never danced together. And she was pleasantly surprised when several men from the county asked her for a reel. Aunt Mag asked to hold Polly for the evening. The little girl, worn out with all the excitement of the day, was soon asleep on the older woman's lap.

Clarissa's hair slipped out of its combs and flowed behind her as she circled around the dance floor. Reverend Chambers died almost two years ago and his pretty young widow was not ignored.

Preparing for bed, she brushed the tangles out of her hair and thought back over the evening. The faces of the men who had danced with her still danced in her head. She enjoyed their attention, but no one caught her eye, much less her heart. Even though she congratulated him on winning the Watermelon Seed Distance Contest, Jacob Featherson never requested a dance. She noticed he had forgotten to clean his fingernails.

With a little smile she remembered Adam's attention to her and the children. To watch him playing and dancing with children at a festival was something new. She could not stop thinking about how their foursome laughed and danced together. And she lectured herself:

"Clarissa Francine, it is improper for you to dwell on how the doctor enjoyed dancing with us. He probably sheds all his British manners and turns into a monster at home."

But why doesn't he relax like this more often? Why does he only work at his clinic and socialize with the likes of Miss Nellie? Why doesn't he find a loving wife and have more children?

In spite of her own stern lecture, she fell asleep remembering the delighted squeals of their happy children and Adam's smiles for her as they all danced together. She snuggled into her pillow and murmured, "Mmm, he has nice blue eyes when he's happy."

Chapter 29

When Nellie invited Adam to a formal concert at the town hall, he arranged for Clarissa to stay with Nathan for the evening. She and the children ate the supper she prepared, and Adam's plate waited for him. To pass the time, she sat on the back porch while the children played. As the shadows lengthened, she knew his food was getting cold. Finally, she knocked at the clinic door.

"Something amiss?" He opened the door with a brusque tone in his voice.

"No, nothing, but we've eaten and your supper is getting cold. Is there anything I might do to help you?"

Adam thought a moment. "As a matter of fact, there is. Have a look at that grey formal suit you'll find in my wardrobe. I'm not sure it's presentable. I'll also need the dress shirt on the top shelf. Honestly, that would be a big help." As she left, he remembered, "Also, I'll need a silk cravat to match. Just choose one from my top bureau drawer."

"I used to keep a preacher presentable, so maybe I can remember what's necessary. I'll see what I can do."

She hurried back to tend to his requests. Nathan showed her where she could find everything, but she still felt awkward in the doctor's bedroom. When she opened his pine wardrobe she admired several exquisitely tailored suits made of fine fabrics. As a seamstress she marveled at the workmanship before her. What kind of life would demand such fine clothing? Was this attire normal for his life in England—and now with Miss Nellie and her gaggle of friends?

She found the gray suit he described and selected a silk cravat to go with it. His shirt was clean, but she ironed the cravat and touched up the crease in his trousers. She spread the formal wear on his four poster bed and went back to tending the children.

When Adam came in from the clinic, he ate his supper and rushed back to his room to dress. Nathan sat in the middle of the bed to watch him change into his formal attire.

"Papa, why do you have to wear such fancy clothes?"

"I'm escorting Widow Desmond tonight for a special occasion. You've never seen this suit, have you?" Nathan shook his head. "I brought it with me when we returned to America. So? How do I look?"

"Just fine, I guess." He ran to find Clarissa.

Clarissa was settling down in the parlor to read to Nathan when Adam walked in ready for the evening. She saw him almost daily in the rumpled clothing of a busy doctor, but tonight he looked the part of a well-to-do, sophisticated gentleman. He kept pulling at his collar and softly cursing as he stood in front of the hall tree mirror.

"Is something the matter, Dr. Norcutt?"

"I've made a mess of this cravat you ironed. I can't tie it right and Nellie will be unhappy if I don't pass her inspection. I was told to look my best for her parents' big event. They've outfitted the town hall as a theater for the evening." He turned to face her. "What do you think?"

"You're right, something's crooked."

"Perhaps Mrs. Murray won't notice in the dark." He pulled on gray kidskin gloves as he watched for the carriage.

"Would you like for me to tie it for you?" Her own boldness surprised her. "I helped Elliot every Sunday morning. He was never good at tying his cravat straight either. If it was crooked, without fail some little lady would fuss at him after church."

"Yes, I could use some assistance, little Widow-of-the-Rector. I don't see the carriage yet, so why don't you give it a try? Maybe you can save me from a lecture from Mrs. Murray or her daughter."

Nathan set aside his storybook and stood on the couch to supervise. Clarissa struggled to straighten the doctor's cravat, but with his height, it was impossible. Frustrated, she put her hands on her hips.

"Perhaps if you sat down, I could reach around?"

"Nathan, is she doing a good job?" Adam smiled at his son as he took a seat.

"Yes, Papa, I believe she is."

As she reached from behind him to re-tie the cravat, she complimented him on its fine quality. With his head turned away from Nathan, he whispered.

"... the last gift from my former wife."

"Uh-oh, should I choose another one?"

"No, you picked the one she bought to go with this suit. It's only a cravat and England's a long way off tonight."

"All right, stand up and let's see how you look." The three looked at the reflection of the well-dressed man in the mirror. All agreed that he would now pass Nellie's muster. On an impulse, Clarissa moved closer to make a minor adjustment to the back of his collar. He looked down at her as she put the finishing touches on his attire.

"You didn't know you'd be dressing me as well as Nathan, did you?"

"No, sir, I didn't." She smiled and patted his lapel. "But I'm glad we've made you presentable. We can't have the Murrays' big event ruined because of the botched cravat of their daughter's escort."

"My thanks for serving as my emergency valet, Miss Clarissa." He clicked his heels, chuckled and kissed her lightly on the forehead before backing away. Clarissa also laughed, but inwardly she cringed. Adam continued to check his appearance in the mirror as he pulled on his topcoat.

"By the way, Widow Chambers, what's the name of that perfume you wear?" He looked out the window for the carriage. "It's like a part of your personality."

Shy about going into his wardrobe, flustered about assisting with his cravat, caught off guard by his playful kiss, she could only whisper, "'Fresh Meadows.'"

"Ah, 'Fresh Meadows,' is it? That explains why springtime always comes into the room with you."

"Back home in Virginia our local apothecary makes it. My father stocks it at his store and sends it to me. The flowers for the perfume are gathered by some local ladies."

"Interesting," he said and waved out the front window. "Here's the Murray carriage. I'll be late tonight."

"Don't you worry. Have a lovely evening and enjoy the concert."

Adam gave Nathan a goodnight hug, tipped his hat toward Clarissa and was gone. As the carriage clattered away, she checked her appearance in the hall tree mirror and tucked in a strand of auburn hair. Thankfully, her striped lavender dress showed no signs she had cooked dinner. Trying to bring her thoughts and emotions under control, she whispered to herself.

"Honestly, do you have to get all flustered by a little peck on the forehead? Clarissa Francine, don't be such a ninny."

"Did you say something to me?" asked Nathan.

"No, just talking to myself. Now, back to our story—where were we?"

Nathan knew every word on the page, but insisted she read the familiar tale to him. Next they sang his favorite songs until he fell asleep against her. She helped him stumble back to his bed, straightened up the parlor a bit and went back to her mending. But as she passed the mirror, she checked her appearance one more time.

Chapter 30

"I'm hosting a dinner party." Adam announced with a flourish. "When I returned from England, my mother sent along enough old family silverware and china to serve twelve. I will invite ten guests plus Widow Desmond, who will be my hostess."

Rosalie and Magnolia tried to absorb the magnitude of these plans. A concerned glance flashed between them, but Adam never saw it. He went on to tell the women what must be done.

"Rosalie, please unpack everything in those wicker chests in the cellar." She had no idea what his request entailed, but nodded her agreement. He continued his instructions.

"Magnolia, I'd like to serve beef roast with Yorkshire pudding, scalloped potatoes, creamed spinach and baked squash. Rosalie can help you prepare the dinner."

"Mr. Doctor, I ain't never cooked that pudding."

"It's my favorite with roast beef but we'll get by without it. Do you have any ideas for dessert?"

"Nobody turns 'way from my chocolate cake."

"Ah, perfect. I'll want several slices left over, so bake two cakes with lots of frosting." He gave the women a wicked grin. "Ladies, I want this place to look its best—everything polished and ready. My guests will be my new friends who have entertained me from my first day in Springdale."

"Yessir, Mister Doctor." Magnolia already looked forward to the challenge. She and Rosalie had two weeks to prepare and they would need every minute.

Full of the news about the dinner party, Rosalie took Nathan on a brisk afternoon walk to Clarissa's house.

Glory Be!

"I shouldn't talk out of turn, Miss Clarissa, but the doctor's house is in a mess. He cain't have dinner guests there, can he? And there's only two of us to do all that work."

"Maybe Dr. Norcutt will let me lend a hand."

"Would you really? Maybe you can help us serve the night of the party?"

"I'll do it if Nathan will entertain Polly."

Rosalie looked at Nathan. "Will you help with Polly...especially the night of your father's party?" He nodded." That's mighty nice of you. I'll go tell Magnolia right now." She grabbed Nathan's hand and they ran home with the good news.

The women worked day and night preparing for the party at the doctor's modest home. They washed, starched, and ironed table linens. They rinsed vases for flowers. They struggled to place extensions in the dinner table. They scoured the house from top to bottom. Willy helped with the heavier chores. Whenever Clarissa found a few moments between her piano students and her sewing customers, she and Polly joined in the preparations.

One evening, Nathan looked over Adam's shoulder as he worked on his seating chart for the big event. "Papa, where is my place? Where will Miss Clarissa sit?"

"Son, at a party like this, children aren't seated at the dinner table, only adults. You'll be with Rosalie and Magnolia out in the kitchen."

"But what about Miss Clarissa?"

Adam said the first thing he could think of. "We don't have enough china to set a place for you and Miss Clarissa. Don't forget that Polly will also be with you at the kitchen table."

"Oh." His face mirrored his disappointment, but Adam was looking down at the seating chart again.

Now preparations for the meal began. The kitchen was rarely silent; Magnolia worked all the time. Every shelf creaked with food and delicious scents filled the house. Clarissa took some items to the cold storage box by her spring. Except for Adam, everyone was exhausted.

The day before the party, Miss Nellie arrived to inspect the premises. She ran her white-gloved finger over all the furniture. Clarissa, helping Magnolia in the kitchen, found something urgent to do in the pantry. However, Nellie searched until she found her.

"I need you in the dining room to receive my instructions, Widow Chambers."

Clarissa straightened her hair, retied her apron and went out to where Rosalie and Magnolia stood side by side—terrified. In her haughty voice, Nellie announced to the three what they needed to do and some things they were not to do.

"Widow Chambers, the front windows are still streaked and must be washed again. Will you see to that?" She noticed the cakes waiting to be frosted. "Magnolia, those chocolate cakes won't do. I want you to serve fruit compote with whipped cream. You have plenty of time to make the change. I'll speak with Dr. Norcutt about this. I'm expecting him momentarily."

Clarissa went out the side door as Adam came into the front hallway. Nellie assailed him with of her list of changes. He kept nodding until she came to her dessert suggestion.

"No, Nellie, now you've gone too far. I want to serve that chocolate cake of Magnolia's I've heard so much about."

"But following a dinner of roast beef, fruit compote will be more refreshing."

"Nellie dear, the chocolate cake stays. Perhaps you can serve this favorite of yours at one of your parties, but not at this one."

Nellie pouted and acquiesced on the dessert, but as she left she made one last announcement. "I'll bring proper white aprons and caps for your three maids."

Rosalie started to protest, "But Miss Clarissa. . ."

Adam put his finger to his lips and whispered, "Don't worry, Rosalie, I'll take care of it."

When Rosalie reported what had happened, Clarissa was relieved. She would help, but wearing a maid's uniform she would not do.

On the day of the dinner party Adam went outside before the clinic opened. He was pleased that the weather promised a fine evening. He set up the croquet set for the ladies and his badminton equipment for the men. He wanted his guests to relax on the lawn before dinner was served.

"Nathan," he said over breakfast, "I have everything set up on the lawn for tonight. I want you to leave the equipment alone, understood?" Nathan replied with a disgruntled nod.

Chapter 31

At the appointed time Clarissa, Magnolia and Rosalie stood ready for Adam's guests. Clarissa wore her new dress and a matching apron created for the event. Miss Nellie arrived with heavily starched white caps and aprons. She gave instructions on how to wear them and went to find the man of the house. Clarissa wondered if she had been relegated to the role of a maid after all.

Magnolia assessed the situation. "Miss Clarissa, I can wear them things. I done it befo'."

"Well, I plan to wear my own apron. I won't kowtow to Nellie Desmond."

Magnolia nodded as she put on her white cap and apron. Rosalie sighed and did the same.

Soon the elegant guests arrived and the party was underway. As everyone enjoyed the cool of the evening on the lawn, drinks were served. Adam's games were a big hit. Nellie made a show of playing croquet, but quickly gave her mallet to another lady.

"Here, you take a turn." She made a hasty exit to freshen up inside. It wouldn't do for her to perspire.

Nathan begged to join the party until Clarissa dressed him in his best and sent him out to greet the guests. Even though this was not in Adam's plan, when he saw Nathan, he was surprised and pleased. He stopped the conversation around him as he took Nathan's hand.

"Ladies and gentlemen, look who's joined us. Allow me to introduce my son, Nathan. He always makes his father proud. I'm glad he's here to meet each one of you." He waved to Clarissa in appreciation.

When the guests gathered around the dinner table Adam, on an impulse, asked his son if he would say a prayer before the meal.

Glory Be!

Although Nathan had not expected this request, he bowed his head and prayed in his high-pitched British accent.

"Dear God, thank You for our food and for our guests tonight. Amen." The dinner guests applauded Nathan's short prayer. Adam leaned over and whispered in his ear.

"Well done, son. Now your supper is waiting in the kitchen. Time to run along." Nathan obeyed, but his disappointment was obvious as he left the room.

Rosalie and Magnolia served the guests from steaming platters of food. Clarissa passed a silver tray mounded with buttery rolls kept warm under an embroidered napkin. When a guest dropped her dinner knife, Clarissa retrieved it.

"Don't worry. I'll bring you a clean one."

As she left, Nellie rose and followed her into the kitchen. Clarissa looked up with the soiled knife in her hand, but said nothing.

"Widow Chambers, why aren't you wearing your apron and cap? You were told yesterday that I would bring them. What do you have to say for yourself?" She pointed to the unused cap and apron on a table nearby. Clarissa began washing the soiled knife.

"Why aren't you wearing these?" The more silent Clarissa was, the more Nellie fumed. Clarissa dried the knife as the one-sided conversation continued.

"I demand an explanation for your insubordination."

"Insubordination? Is that what you think, Miss Desmond? I don't agree." She handed the clean knife to Magnolia. "Magnolia, I believe I hear the doctor's son calling me. I'll be with him if you need me." Resisting the urge to slam the door behind her, Clarissa spun around and left.

Magnolia returned the knife to the dinner guest and hurried to find Clarissa, who was slumped against the wall of the hallway sobbing and shaking with anger.

"I knowed you was fibbin' 'bout Master Nathan needin' you." She was as angry as Clarissa. "Don't you mind what that lady say. No, ma'am! You go back in there and hol' your head up high."

"I can't stay, Magnolia." She choked on hot tears.

"Yes'm, you can. Don't you let her run you off." She muttered under her breath what sounded like "that no-count woman."

Clarissa shook her head. "Please, tell Dr. Norcutt how sorry I am." She gathered Polly up and spent the walk home in tears. *I'll never help that doctor again as long as Nellie Desmond is his hostess.*

When his guests were gone, Adam wondered what had become of Clarissa. He walked toward the kitchen to find her and thank her for her help.

"Oh, Adam," Nellie reached for his arm. "That widow woman left. She simply did not understand her place. But never mind, she's gone now. Your party was a wonderful success. Did you notice that I enjoyed your chocolate cake after all?"

"Wait—that widow woman? You mean Miss Clarissa? She left?"

"Yes, and I'm glad she did. She was very rude to me."

"Rude? How so?"

"Honestly, the way she talked back to me. She needs to be spoken to."

"What the blazes are you talking about?"

"She was downright insubordinate. When I went back to the kitchen to inquire why she wasn't wearing her white cap and apron, she was quite snippy. You really must do something about her defiance."

Adam stalked back to the kitchen.

"Magnolia, where is Miss Clarissa?"

"She left out a spell ago. She say to tell you she be sorry."

"Is it true what Miss Desmond says? Something about those things?" He pointed to the unused items.

"Yessuh."

Adam swore under his breath.

"Yessuh."

"Excuse me, Magnolia." He returned to his hostess with the cap and apron in his hand.

"Nellie, I told you not to bring these confounded things over here."

"We southerners expect servants to be properly attired when serving." Her voice rose to a sharp pitch. "I won't have that woman with her scandalous baby. . . ."

"Nellie, Mrs. Chambers is neither a maid nor a servant. She is a genteel young widow who helped me with this party out of the goodness of her heart. I never expected her to dress like a maid. And Polly is not scandalous. Babies can't be scandalous."

"Adam, I find your excuses inappropriate. You'll have to understand that this is how things are done in Springdale."

"No, you must understand this, my dear. This is my house and Widow Chambers is not my servant. She was not being insubordinate. What's gotten into you tonight?"

Nellie rose to gather her things for the ride home. Adam walked out to the waiting carriage with her, but other than a perfunctory goodnight kiss, nothing more was said.

That night Clarissa tossed and turned before falling asleep. She had never cared much for Nellie Desmond, but after being demeaned by her, she thoroughly disliked the woman. She talked aloud to God in the darkness.

"Dear Lord, best I can tell that woman's not cut on the straight of the goods. When those two marry, I hope and pray she'll treat Nathan right, but I don't plan to be around to find out. I'm sure she'll have plenty of servants to take care of him. Please, forgive me for losing my temper."

The next Monday after Nathan's weekly piano lesson at her house, Clarissa, Rosalie and Polly walked back into town with him. Adam stood with his hands behind his back as Clarissa opened the door to let everyone in ahead of her. He sent Nathan over to the piano to put his music away.

"Dr. Norcutt, I am terribly sorry for leaving in the middle of your dinner party." Clarissa looked down to avoid his eyes, but her voice was firm. "But I'm not a servant. I won't take orders from Widow Desmond."

"I understand. It is I who should apologize to you."

"So, you've heard what happened?" She looked up, straight into his smile.

"Yes, I've spoken with Widow Desmond and Magnolia." He brought a pale pink rose from behind his back for her. "I am sorry you were upset enough to leave. Worst of all, you missed Magnolia's chocolate cake and I fear the rest of it has vanished." He handed her the rose. "Please accept this and my apology."

She hesitated. "I do regret leaving Rosalie and Magnolia to deal with everything."

"I think we should put the entire incident behind us. We can't have you deserting us again, so I'll make sure Widow Desmond understands. Is all forgiven?"

What can I do? The man is genuinely sorry. She held the cool velvet of the rose petals to her nose. "Most certainly. But our disagreement did bring something to mind."

"Yes?"

"Widow Desmond did have a point."

"What's that?"

"I'm not sure if a gentleman notices these things, but have you noticed Magnolia's tattered clothes? I know she's wearing her best."

"Since you call it to my attention, I have to agree."

"Are you aware that it's customary to provide some sort of suitable clothing for your servants? Maybe this is just in America?"

"We Brits do the same thing but it was never my responsibility to see to it. Tell me, what should I do for her?"

"I will make a dress or two for her if you will let me buy the fabric. Tom Lewis can put it on your account at The Mercantile."

"Please, do that. Choose something suitable and let me know your charges for the sewing. Ask me about medicine and perhaps I can give you an answer. Ask me about my household and I'm lost. You should have spoken up sooner."

"Consider it done, Dr. Norcutt."

"Someday I'll know all these American customs. I'll be sure to tell Magnolia that you straightened me out." *Once again.*

She went back to the kitchen to tell Magnolia the good news.

"Awww, I'se wearing the only dress I got." Her embarrassment was painful.

"Don't you worry. You always come to work clean and ready to serve this family. You know that's what matters most. Just consider these new dresses a blessing."

"Yessm, I can do that." She smiled from ear to ear. "I sure can."

"Good! I'll buy some fabric on my way home. Now let me take some measurements."

Within a week Magnolia was wearing one of her new dresses with its matching scarf. When Adam noticed and complimented her, she beamed and thanked him profusely.

"'Preciate you, Mr. Doctor."

Chapter 32

Late in the fall, Ida and Clarissa planned a picnic by the creek with their children. Ida stopped by the clinic for Nathan so he could join them for the day. While the children ran around on the sand bar, the friends sat in the sunshine and wrapped themselves in blankets to keep warm.

"It's so beautiful here. If I weren't so busy I could enjoy it more." Clarissa said.

"Why are you so busy? No one is in charge of your time but you."

"The problem is working for that doctor. I started out as a piano teacher, began helping Rosalie and now I'm the one who does whatever is left over."

"What's the matter with Adam Norcutt? Doesn't he see what he's doing to you?"

"Maybe I've been too available." Clarissa went on to tell her about colliding with Nellie Desmond over the starched caps and aprons. "Ida, do you think the whole town sees me as a maid? When Widow Desmond ordered me around she acted so hoity-toity. Honestly, I'm not that doctor's extra servant."

"Can't Magnolia manage his chores? Should he hire more help?"

"Magnolia's not the problem. She sees to it that all the work gets done. Dr. Norcutt needs to hang on to her, she'd be hard to replace."

"Sounds to me our Dr. Norcutt has a blind spot when it comes to you. After all, you have no outside help, and you must keep up with Polly, your music students and sewing customers. He's asking more and more of you and doesn't reckon with the toll it's taking on you."

"You're right. Absolutely right."

"Clary, he's being downright inconsiderate and you're too nice to complain."

The more Clarissa listened, the more her sense of injustice rose.

Ida continued. "Our fancy British doctor should tie on an apron and do some chores himself."

"That's not likely to happen. He's too busy at the clinic to help around the house. Any extra time he has is spent with Nathan or Nellie Desmond—or playing badminton or riding that new mare."

"There's a simple solution. Why doesn't he marry her?"

"Honestly, I don't know why. I can assure you if he doesn't marry Miss Nellie, he won't have any trouble finding another social butterfly. He's Springdale's most eligible gentleman."

"What's keeping him from proposing when he needs a mother for his son and a wife to run his household?"

"They're quite attached to one another. They'll probably marry someday, and I can promise you something—when that day comes, Nellie Desmond won't be a housekeeper. She'll need a wagonload of servants to run her household, and every blessed one of them will wear a starched white cap and apron."

Dissolving in hysterical giggles, they fell back onto the quilts. When Ida could catch her breath, she pleaded with Clarissa.

"Be reasonable! Why should the doctor marry anyone if you're doing everything for him?" Then she added with not a little sarcasm, "Have you thought of proposing?" While she laughed at her own preposterous idea, Clarissa felt a rush of emotion.

"I certainly don't want to marry the likes of Dr. Norcutt. For one thing, he's too old."

"You might reconsider. He'd be quite the handsome catch."

"He's handsome all right, but remember how handsome Elliot was? That didn't make him worth a bent pin as a husband. Besides, the doctor wouldn't take a second look at the likes of me. All Dr. Norcutt does is play doctor or socialize with Springdale's upper crust."

"Where do he and Nathan go to church?"

"They tag along with Nellie to the Catholic Church. But he's a sworn atheist and you can be sure I don't want that in a husband. I must admit he's a good doctor and father, and he has a gentle streak a mile wide, but I shouldn't do all his extra housework, no matter who he is."

"Thank goodness you're getting some gumption."

Glory Be!

"You're right. I was hired to be Nathan's piano teacher and agreed to help when Rosalie can't be there, but I'm not his spare servant. What's the matter with me?"

"Right," Ida said, nodding her head decisively. "Now let's back up. What's this about Elliot not being worth a bent pin?"

Clarissa dropped her eyes. The words had slipped out while she was thinking about Adam. Now she was trapped; she did not want to lie to her friend. She stared at her quilt and traced the pattern with her finger.

"Clary? What—what is it?"

"All right, let me check on the children, then I'll tell you about the Elliot you never knew." When she returned, the story of her horrendous marriage to Elliot poured out. She stopped, but not before both were in tears.

"Clary, you poor thing, I had no idea our preacher treated you like that. No one in this town suspected a thing about what you were living with over in our parsonage."

"Now please don't spread this around. Only you and Dr. Norcutt know about Elliot."

"Dr. Norcutt?" She stared, wide-eyed at her friend.

"Yes, Dr. Logan told him to watch out for me when I was pregnant. Since he delivered Polly, he feels beholden to inquire about us. Honestly, he can be so nosey sometimes. Somehow after he and Nathan were quarantined with me, he put two and two together about Elliot and me. When he pushed me about it one time, my troubles came out. He promised not to tell." She looked up at Ida, "He's very good about confidences."

"Honey, Elliot's behavior was not your fault. You were the sweetest wife to him. If this ever does come out, people will be shocked, but all their sympathy will be for you. You never did a thing to deserve being treated like that. I'm so sorry."

Even though Clarissa promised Ida that she would talk to the doctor about her schedule, she put it off for several days. Down deep inside she knew she tolerated being overworked because it gave her something to do with her days—if only she weren't so tired. For several days she procrastinated before finding enough courage to speak to Adam. During a lull in Nathan's piano lesson at her house, she took a deep breath and spoke up.

"Doctor Norcutt, may I talk with you about something while Nathan plays his scales?"

"Of course, what is it?" She motioned for him to follow her into her study.

"I would like to go back to just being Nathan's piano teacher."

"Isn't that what you are doing?" He pointed to Nathan playing his scales.

"Yes, but the job has expanded. I don't mind helping Rosalie in a pinch, but I'm doing more and more around your home these days."

"Really? Explain what you mean."

"I'm doing a lot more extra work for you, but it's become too much. I'm really exhausted all the time." Her voice trembled as she explained her concerns.

"I certainly regret taxing you, Miss Clarissa. I thought you wanted the additional work. Haven't I paid you for your extra time?"

"My salary is fine, you're always fair. But you need more help than you realize. Excuse me, but you need a wife and a mother for your son." *I can't believe I said that!*

"I see."

She quickly changed the subject. "Anyway, I know Magnolia would gladly work more."

Adam was taken off guard. He had accepted her willingness to help without thinking of her situation.

"Although I agree that Nathan and I need a lot of help, I'm not so sure about your nuptial suggestions." His blue eyes teased her. "Don't worry about this, Miss Clarissa. I'll work something else out."

"I know you will. You always do." Nathan was almost finished with the drudgery of his scales. "Oh, by the way, there's one more thing and then I need to go back to Nathan."

"Yes, what's that?" *Does she have another problem? I thought she was satisfied.*

"I'm waiting for you to keep our other agreement."

"Excuse me?" He tried to remember any sort of agreement he'd made with her.

"The promise you made that day I told you my secrets about Elliot."

"I'm still in the dark here."

"You agreed to tell me how you ended up in Springdale. All I know is whatever gossip is going around."

"Gossip? What gossip?" Now he was fully attentive.

"If people don't know the facts, they tend to make things up."

"What's being said about me, Miss Clarissa?" He scowled as he leaned toward her.

"Usually something about you and Miss Nellie, but sometimes it's speculation about your life in England." She held up her hand and called out to Nathan, "Nathan, that scale has F # in it. Now try it again."

"Why on earth are people so blasted curious? My past isn't noteworthy, Widow Chambers. I left England, came to Kentucky to work with a surgeon and ended up a medic on some battlefields. After The War, I settled here, went back to England concerning my divorce and returned with Nathan. That's it—spit spot."

"You still don't understand life around here, do you? Springdale isn't London or Lexington. You can't expect the anonymity you find in larger cities. You are beginning to be well-loved and folks are asking the same question I asked: 'Why did you pack up and leave England?'"

"All right, I do have a vague recollection of this agreement. Someday I'll be glad to answer your questions." He hoped this conversation was over but she smiled and waited. The little bead of perspiration on her upper lip made him know she was quite determined to have her question answered. He was out of options and cleared his throat. "Perhaps a walk on the sand bar before supper will do. We'll talk while Nathan and Polly play."

"Very well, I'll expect you back later this afternoon."

As Adam walked back to town with Nathan, he thought about his marital situation. A wife would simplify some things, but complicate others. Despite their row after his dinner party, he felt sure Nellie would accept if he proposed. But was marriage to her wise? They often argued over the simplest decisions and even though he enjoyed her affection and attention, he was not in love with her.

He muttered to himself as he neared the clinic.

"Why the devil are women always so curious? First Nellie and now Widow Chambers. But perhaps it's time someone around here knows what happened."

Nathan ran back toward him and they tussled a few moments.

"Want to walk down by the willows with the Chambers this afternoon? The creek is still warm enough for you to wade in the shallows. I'll close the clinic a bit early and we'll go over there this afternoon."

Chapter 33

Nathan skipped ahead of Clarissa and Adam as they headed down the path toward the creek. Polly held her arms up to be carried by the doctor. Oblivious to the cool afternoon, Nathan took off his shoes and waded up to his knickers in the cold, clear water. On an impulse, Clarissa joined him with her skirts held a respectable distance above the stream. Adam looked at Polly.

"Well, Little Girl, let's not be left out." Soon all four were wading in the shallow pools that reflected the colorful, late afternoon sky. Clarissa walked up on the creek bank to sit on an old fallen tree while she dried her feet on the grass. Adam began circling the moss covered log.

"So," she began, "I'll get you started. How did you end up in Springdale with a six-year-old?" She turned aside to pull on her stockings.

"Could we start with an earlier question?"

"Why did you come to America?"

"My marriage to a woman named Josephine ended in a complete disaster."

"So that's the 'Josephine' you were arguing with when you were delirious at my house."

"Great Scott—that's frightening! What did I say?" Memories of long, ugly shouting matches surfaced.

"Nothing I could understand, only that you were angry with Josephine. And your language was appalling. So go on."

He paced back and forth in front of her. "My marital problems became a huge embarrassment for me. After all, I had an impeccable upbringing and expected a brilliant career. I struggled because I didn't want our marriage to fail. After she locked me out and refused to allow me to see Nathan, I lived alone for months. I soon realized I could no longer live anywhere near Josephine or London. Even the air there seemed foul—I could hardly breathe. When I discovered a professional opportunity in America, you could say I escaped to Kentucky. I sailed for America one year after Josephine ordered me out."

"How did you first meet her?"

"Our families—people of substance on both sides—ran into one another frequently. We even socialized with the royal family during the social season." He snorted at her shocked expression and went on. "During my medical studies Josephine began appearing by my side at parties and receptions. Even though I squired my share of sweethearts, some rather serious, I was quite naive about her kind of seduction." This part of his story was difficult to divulge. He paused and took a deep breath. Still barefooted, he sat down on a log across from Clarissa.

"Yes, go on."

"Josie had a legendary way with men, but I didn't know this at the time. No one told me about her reputation. My friends, who should have warned me about her, took great delight in my infatuation. In hindsight, I think I knew but chose to ignore the obvious. I guess you could say she was a high society coquette and I was her willing victim."

"You're avoiding calling her a derogatory name?"

"That Bible of yours would call her behavior 'fornication.'" He grimaced and said nothing for a moment. "But to be quite honest, I have to own my part in this. I'm not proud of it now, but I didn't resist her advances." He hesitated to offend Clarissa with the rest of his history.

"But you married her?"

He stared down at his toes curled into the grass. With a nod he continued but didn't look up.

"When she told me she was pregnant, she threw a terrible tantrum when I wouldn't perform a surgery to dispose of our unborn child—to think I might have destroyed Nathan." He shivered—lost in dark memories. "Anyway, I proposed, she accepted and we eloped."

"So, are you sure you're Nathan's father?"

"You get right to the point, don't you?" He was resistant and looked off into the distance.

Glory Be!

"Shall I retract my question?" After a long silence he sighed and continued.

"As far as I know, Nathan is my son. With Josephine's penchant for illicit liaisons I suppose there might be some doubt, but at the time we were obsessed with one another." He looked up and went on. "What's important now is that Nathan loves me as his father. I'm devoted to him and always will be. I hope this is obvious."

"Yes, I have no doubt about your commitment to your son. You're an excellent parent. I also think he looks like you. But go on. What became of Josephine?"

"Ah, Josie! She remained the same, my enigma. Soon after Nathan's birth, she resumed her old pattern of flirtations. I guess she tired of me. I found this very unsettling, for I never considered that either of us would be unfaithful. From the beginning of our marriage I gave up my days of living as a bachelor with a roving eye. I wanted a bona fide family, but our fights were horrendous. Even though I can hold my own, I'm not argumentative by nature." Unbeknownst to Clarissa, his thoughts flitted to Nellie for a moment. "The whole infernal mess became intolerable. Those days still haunt me."

He stared at his feet. The pain in his voice reached a tender spot in Clarissa's heart.

"What a terrible dilemma. Explain something to me. If you loved her and were willing to provide for her and your son, why would she send you away?"

Clarissa watched him struggle to own his part in this tragedy. She cleared her throat and he continued.

"I think she expected more of a social life than I could offer. I couldn't be with her all day every day. In her circles, men live off their fortunes and don't have professions they love. My dedication to surgery baffled her. Too often she attended events alone or declined them because I was with a patient. Also, I don't think she ever forgave me for not complying with her wishes to. . .end our unborn child's life."

"Perhaps this is why Nathan is with you now."

"You may be correct. Honestly, when I fled to America it never occurred to me to take a two-year-old away from his mother. I assumed she would see to his well-being. In those days she wouldn't allow me near Nathan."

"Do you still feel that you made a good decision to move to America?"

"Yes, I do. At first, I regretted the things I gave up, especially Nathan and my new medical practice in London. But now I have few regrets. With the exception of getting caught up in your Civil War, it's been what I needed: a new life in a new place." He looked over at her with a crooked smile, "Most of all, I am very relieved to have the Atlantic Ocean between me and Josephine. At least I hope that's far enough."

They continued to visit about their lives in Springdale. As their conversation wound down, he stared down the creek and shook his head in disbelief. "I can't believe I told you my outrageous history."

"You needed to tell someone about it. Thank you for choosing me."

"*Au contraire!* Correct me if I'm wrong, but don't I recall being rather forced into this confessional booth by the High Priestess of Springdale Gossip, the notable Widow Chambers?"

Her spontaneous laughter shattered the somber mood of their discussion. He continued in almost a whisper. "It's a relief to have told someone. You're a gracious listener. Thank you."

"Did you know the Bible not only encourages us to tell God our troubles and problems, but also to tell them to each other? That way we all share the load and help one another."

"Really?" he replied, but said nothing else.

"It's all in the Bible."

He cleared his throat and pulled on his boots. No more was said about the doctor's secrets. Each took their child by the hand and walked up the path to Clarissa's cottage. The bare trees of fall tatted their black lace against the remains of the brilliant sunset. Clarissa and Polly waved to Nathan and Adam as they walked away and disappeared into the evening shadows.

When she found herself staring after his receding silhouette, she lectured herself. "Mind your feelings now, Clarissa Francine."

Why was her determination never successful when it came to controlling her responses to Adam Norcutt?

Chapter 34

What's the matter with me? Sometimes when the doctor smiled directly at her, Clarissa struggled to speak. Or she found herself staring at him and worried that he might think she had a girlish crush on him.

"Which, of course, I do not have — not at all," she whispered as she pushed Polly's carriage into town. "From now on I'm only allowing myself feelings of respect for Dr. Adam Norcutt, which is a proper response to a sewing customer and the father of a piano student. He's a serious suitor for Miss Nellie's affections. His social life and that clinic are all he cares about. He's simply not my sort. There is no meeting ground for our lives except cordiality."

In an attempt to shore up her peace of mind, Clarissa ordered new sheet music by one of her favorite composers, Frederic Chopin. Devoting herself to her piano had long been a treasured balm for her life. Sometimes when her marriage to Elliot was at its worst, she would wrap beautiful music around her painful struggles. When the Chopin sheet music arrived, she set about learning it, a project which should keep her thoughts in check.

Two weeks later, when Adam planned an afternoon of riding with friends in the country, Clarissa agreed to look after Nathan. She took the now dog-eared Chopin sheet music along with her. Nathan had agreed she could play on his old piano, perhaps not the best instrument in the world, but at least she could practice on it. While Polly napped in her carriage and Nathan looked at his books, she sat down at the old piano. A steady rain began tapping at the windows and she lost herself in the music. When she played the last note, she looked up to find Adam leaning against the door jam and smiling at her.

"Dr. Norcutt!" Her hands jumped off the piano keys and onto her lap. "I didn't hear you come in. Aren't you home rather early?"

"Yes, one of the horses came up lame, so when the rain started we called it a day. We turned the hobbling horse over to Leon and headed home to dry out."

"I hope you'll forgive me for practicing while I'm here with Nathan."

"What's to forgive? Why would I object to a private concert like this? When I rode up and heard you playing, I came in quietly. I had no idea Dr. Logan's old piano could sound like this." Clarissa was speechless. "I've only heard you play the piano with the children." He hopped on one foot then the other as he pulled off his wet boots. "I must say your command of Chopin is amazing. It is Chopin, isn't it?"

Surprised he was familiar with the Polish composer, she agreed. "Yes, it is. Too bad he met such an untimely death."

"Yes, quite tragic. Consumption, wasn't it?"

"I believe so. Nevertheless he left us quite a legacy of delightful music. Whenever I want to challenge myself, he never fails me. You see, I can't have my students catching up with me."

"I doubt anyone in Springdale will challenge your ability for a very long time. Certainly not my son." He tossed his riding boots out onto the front porch.

"Why, thank you, Dr. Norcutt."

"Now that I've dripped all over Magnolia's clean floor, I'd best get out of these wet clothes." As he went in his stocking feet toward his bedroom, he called to her, "I appreciate the concert, Widow Chambers."

"Thank you, Dr. Norcutt."

She stared at his tall, muscular form as he walked away. His drenched shirt still clung to his shoulders and he left a trail of wet foot prints. *Oh, my*, Clarissa thought to herself. *I'm hopeless*. Her strategy for keeping her thoughts in check about this complex man was a complete failure. When she returned to Chopin, she kept making simple mistakes.

During another of Rosalie's absences, Clarissa was helping with Nathan when Adam came in from the clinic with a request.

Glory Be!

"Miss Clarissa, could you be sure that Nathan's Sunday clothes are ready? I forgot to ask Rosalie to take care of that before she left yesterday."

"Of course I can. Are you and Nathan having Sunday dinner at the hotel?"

"No, we're going to mass and then Sunday dinner at Miss Nellie's. If we aren't properly dressed, I'll get an earful about it."

Clarissa's curiosity got the best of her. "You know, for the life of me I don't understand why you attend church with Miss Desmond if you don't believe in God."

"That's a valid question and to be quite honest, I don't have a succinct answer. Here's how it works. Miss Desmond invites us to mass with her family. Her invitation automatically includes Sunday dinner. The two events are inseparable in her mind. Mrs. Murray's Sunday dinner is well worth an hour of sitting on an uncomfortable pew. And I'm sure you'll agree that going to church doesn't harm me, right?" He looked at her with a smirk and a raised eyebrow.

"But there is no worship on your part. Correct?"

"I can't say that I worship. But I wager every church in this country is sprinkled with reluctant Sunday worshippers."

"That's probably true, but I for one wouldn't sit through a church service every Sunday if I didn't believe in what was going on up at the altar."

"Let's let it go. After all, something good might rub off on me." He spun on his heel and went back to the clinic. She knew he was avoiding the discussion because she had him on the defensive. She doubted he'd ever lost a debate with a woman.

Later, when Adam told an elderly lady who was quite ill, "You'll be in my prayers," he could almost hear Clarissa accuse him of being a hypocrite.

"Miss Clarissa," he rehearsed his response under his breath, "what I said to my patient is the expected response around here. I'm not expressing my own personal beliefs."

"But are you being true to yourself if you say things like that?" was the answer he was sure he heard in his head. He muttered as he walked back into the house, "That Widow Chambers can sound just like a British barrister in a white wig."

From the kitchen where Clarissa was still ironing Nathan's Sunday suit, she called out to him.

"What did you say, sir? I couldn't hear you?"

"Never mind."

Chapter 35

On a Sunday afternoon Adam decided to exercise the horses on a footpath south of town. Before The War, countless barefoot slaves had worn the trail as they walked back and forth to the fields. Now the crumbling plantation homes stood like injured ghosts along the overgrown path making an interesting ride in the countryside. Adam and his friends often rode their horses out to inspect the ones that were being restored.

He found Nathan playing with his soldiers on the front porch.

"Nathan, let's take a ride south of town. You haven't ridden with me out that way in a long time. Put your soldiers back where they belong and let's go."

"All right, Papa, but I want to ride Fancy."

"I don't know, son. Fancy can be hard to control."

"I can do it, I know I can. Remember how well I did on Standard last week? Please, please!" He begged and Adam relented, for it was true—the boy was now quite competent at riding Standard.

"Be careful, son," he cautioned as he cinched up the girth on the mare's saddle. "Fancy responds to the reins quicker than Standard. Don't let her get away from you." He gave Nathan a lift up and handed him the reins.

"Papa, don't worry. She knows I have sugar cubes in my pockets. She'll behave."

The crisp, late fall weather was spectacular. Sunshine warmed their shoulders as they rode along the footpath and paused at one of the wasted plantations. The foreman, out planning his work for the coming week, walked over to explain the project. Adam dismounted to look at the architect's drawings. Nathan waited astride Fancy for the ride to continue.

Suddenly Fancy gave a whinny of alarm, reared and went into a full gallop. A fox in close pursuit of a rabbit had darted from the underbrush and between her hooves. Nathan barely stayed in the saddle as Adam dropped the foreman's drawings and scrambled to help his son. With Standard's mane tangled in his mouth, he gave the old horse full rein and cursed the day he purchased retired racing stock.

"I should've known this would happen." In the distance, he could hear Nathan's screams of alarm. "Hang on, son. Pull back on her reins. Pull hard!"

But Fancy was gone. The road ahead beckoned and Fancy was born to run. She barely felt the weight of Nathan in the saddle, much less his small fists on the reins. She intended to put some trail between herself and the animals that startled her.

With a sinking feeling in the pit of his stomach, Adam remembered what Nathan would encounter next if the runaway mare couldn't be stopped. The last time he rode Fancy out this path, she had cleared a fallen tree with a magnificent jump. He complimented himself that day on having such a fine, capable mare. But today was different—Nathan had never jumped anything on horseback. Adam's face contorted with fear as Fancy disappeared at a dead run around the turn. Standard was no match for her speed.

"Dear God, keep Nathan on that horse. Help Fancy clear that tree."

As he rounded the curve, Adam could see Fancy with an empty saddle trotting off to the side of the path. He kept Standard at a full gallop until they were close to the tree. But where was Nathan? The winded old horse slid to a stop as Adam pulled hard on the reins.

"Nathan? Where are you, son?" No answer.

When he rushed closer to the fallen tree, he saw Nathan sprawled on the other side. Fancy came over and nudged her owner as if to apologize, but he ignored her and clambered over the fallen tree. A crumpled Nathan lay on the footpath, his small form still. A quick check showed he wasn't breathing. While Adam frantically examined his deathly pale son, he continued his pleas to God.

"Almighty God, spare my son. He's all I have. Show me what to do to help him. Please, God, please hear my prayer!"

Nathan stirred. The breath was knocked out of him and he struggled between sobs to get it back. He tried to sit up, but Adam kept him flat on his back until his breathing returned to normal.

"Did you hit your head? Are you hurt anywhere?"

"My arm hurts." He felt his arm.

Adam saw a twisted lump above Nathan's wrist, and shook his head in sympathy. "Looks like your arm is broken."

"Broken?" Nathan asked in a little boy voice.

"Don't worry. I'll set it and put a splint on it when we get home. It'll hurt, but in a few weeks that arm will be as good as new. You'll have to keep it in a sling. Think you can you do that, my man?"

Nathan grimaced with pain and sobbed, "I'll try, Papa."

Waves of relief came over Adam, but he was still concerned about a possible head injury. He felt Nathan's head and neck—no problem there. Next he asked him to follow his finger while he made circles around his face. He kept him talking.

"How did you and Fancy end up on opposite sides of this tree?"

"I thought Fancy was going to jump over it, but I guess she decided it was too high. She stopped all of a sudden. I went over her head and landed here."

"This tree isn't too high for Fancy. I jumped her over it coming and going last week when I was out here by myself."

"Maybe God stopped her. I was praying He would."

"That could be," Adam heard himself say.

He stabilized Nathan's injured arm by wrapping it in his jacket. He fashioned a makeshift sling from his belt and some sticks he broke off the fallen tree, a trick he learned on the battlefields. Nathan continued to wince from the pain, but when Fancy nuzzled him, he sniffled and rubbed her nose.

"Don't feel bad, Fancy. Papa says my arm will be all right." With his good arm he gave her a sugar cube out of his pocket.

"Thank God, you're alive, son." Adam knew he meant it.

When they returned home, Adam took Nathan into the clinic and tended his injuries. The scrapes on his face and legs were easily cleaned and bandaged, but the ordeal of setting the broken arm was painful for both. Not until the fractured arm rested in a proper sling did Adam notice that his hands trembled.

He carried Nathan back to his bedroom and brought him a bowl of milquetoast, his British mother's never-fail remedy for any ill. He read stories to him, heard his prayers and tucked the bedclothes around him.

"Try to go to sleep, son. You were very brave today. It wasn't your fault that Fancy bolted."

That evening as Adam lay in bed, he could not clear his mind of the sight of his pale, unconscious son. No doubt he hurt Nathan in the painful process of setting his broken arm, but when Nathan said, "Papa, I'm a lucky bloke to have a good doctor for a father," he knew all was forgiven.

Despite the good outcome of the accident, Adam felt disgruntled and disturbed for another reason. He had surprised himself by praying when Nathan was in danger. He had always sneered at people who cried out to God only when they were in dire straits. In the surgical tents during the war, God and Mother were frequently called upon. Now he joined the ranks of those soldiers in agony. He could not disregard his need for God when Nathan's life was in the balance. Now he understood that sort of desperation.

"Hmmph," he muttered and punched his pillow into a more comfortable lump. In his heart, he knew he had witnessed something close to a miracle, one he begged God for. A potentially fatal event, one outside of his control, was somehow suspended. The remnants of the atheist within him rose to push aside any consideration that his spontaneous prayers to God might have been part of the miracle. But where was he to go with the gratitude he felt in his heart that Nathan, though injured, was alive?

But I did pray, didn't I?

Chapter 36

The next day Rosalie welcomed the Chambers as they entered the Norcutts' front door. Clarissa knelt down in the front hall to remove Polly's sweater and Nathan came in to stand beside them. Without looking up, Clarissa greeted him.

"Good morning, Master Nathan. How are you today?"

"Look, Miss Clarissa." He moved closer with a nudge to show her his swollen hand with the dark blue and purple bruises around each finger. "I can't play the piano today." He patted his sling in triumph. No one could ask him to play the piano in this condition, could they?

"Good Gracious! What happened, Nathan?"

"I fell off Fancy and broke my arm while Papa and I were riding yesterday."

"Are you hurt anywhere else?"

"No, ma'am, but my arm still hurts."

"I can see it must. Where was your father when you fell?"

"He was chasing me on Standard, but they couldn't catch us. Fancy spooked when a fox chased a rabbit between her legs."

"Really? Fancy must've been terrified!"

Adam, listening in the background, chuckled. "I think the rabbit lost the race yesterday, but we'll never know. Nathan will be all right, but he won't be able to play the piano today. In all the confusion, I forgot about his lesson."

"Don't worry about that. But poor Nathan!" She looked up at the doctor with concern.

"I'm sorry you came in for the lesson. Of course, I'll pay you just the same."

"The way his hand looks, I'm pretty sure he'll miss more than today's lesson."

"We'll wait and see about that. The break is right above his wrist, but his arm will be as good as new before you know it. He was a brave soldier while I set that break."

Clarissa winced. "I'll wager that hurt you almost as much as it did him."

"Right you are. I had a hard time falling asleep last night."

"Honestly, Dr. Norcutt, why would Fancy act up like that?"

"I'm to blame for the entire debacle. I let the lad ride Fancy on an open path before he was ready to control her in a bad spot. Honestly, the way she took off yesterday would've tested even my skills."

"Surely you aren't blaming yourself for his broken wrist?"

"I've never felt so responsible for anything in my entire life."

"Papa, tell her how God helped us."

"How God helped you?" Incredulous, Clarissa looked in Adam's direction. She waited for his usual caustic reply, but he turned toward the clinic. Over his shoulder he spoke to Nathan.

"You didn't finish your porridge, son. Go back to it before it's stone cold."

Hoping the doctor would return to explain Nathan's remark, Clarissa lingered over a cup of tea with Rosalie. She finally lost her patience and went to find him in the clinic.

"Dr. Norcutt, what did Nathan mean when he said God helped you yesterday?"

Adam leaned back against his examining table, folded his arms and stared at the floor. Too late, she realized how intrusive her question must seem. She turned to walk out of the room.

"I'll leave. Please forgive me. My curiosity got the best of my manners."

"I prayed to God yesterday." Adam didn't look up. She stopped and turned back to be sure she understood him. "I said," he glanced up and repeated himself, "I prayed to God yesterday."

"I heard what you said. I just I don't know how to reply."

"Well, it was no huge papal invocation, so don't start singing that 'Hallelujah Chorus' of yours. Simply said, Nathan and I agree that God spared him a possibly fatal injury." Feeling suddenly exposed and vulnerable, he didn't want to discuss his prayers. But he knew from past debates that Clarissa was not one to relent in a discussion about either of their beliefs.

"You aren't just saying this to agree with Nathan?"

"No." He slumped down onto a nearby bench. "You'll never know how earnestly I called out to God when I saw Fancy with an empty saddle. I knew Nathan had taken a bad fall and when I found him unconscious, I thought he might be dying. He looked so frail." Staring at the floor, he struggled to continue.

"What on earth did you do?"

"I kept praying. At first, I was afraid to touch him. When he moved a bit I knew he might be all right. When he started crying about his arm, I could see what the problem was."

"Was he terribly upset?"

"Yes, but all things considered I was very proud of him. I've had patients with massive head injuries or broken necks from being thrown headlong off a horse at polo matches or on battlefields. It can be a terrible accident."

"I'm so thankful that your prayers were answered."

"Me, too. Very thankful." He stared at her and she waited for him to continue. His blue eyes registered an intensity she'd never seen there before. "I've always thought I might re-evaluate religion in my old age—maybe become more solicitous toward God on my deathbed. It never occurred to me I would turn on a tuppence into a praying man."

"Why, bless your heart, Dr. Norcutt. I—I have to admire you. That's a profound comment." He went back to staring at his shoes until she broke the silence. "At least now you can attend Miss Nellie's church with a clear conscience."

"I can't say I was ever overcome with guilt as I sat waiting for my Sunday dinner."

He chuckled at his own audacity. Both were relieved that the tension of their conversation was broken. They could hear the children arguing back in the house. When Polly began to cry, Clarissa left to stop the argument.

"Thank you for blessing my heart, Widow Chambers," he called after her.

Chapter 37

Nathan's arm healed right on schedule. Rosalie still helped him with dressing and eating, but overall, he was a good patient. Within his circle of friends he became quite a hero. After all, he had been on a racehorse that ran away with him. They didn't envy the broken arm, but they did covet the ride that led up to it and all the attention he was enjoying.

On a Sunday morning, Clarissa sat at the piano to begin the prelude for the Trinity Community Church service. As she adjusted her music and played the first chord, she noticed some commotion at the back of the church.

"I'll be switched!" she whispered. "I never thought I'd see the day." Nathan and Adam were being seated in the congregation. When she looked up again, Adam smiled at her. She felt the color rising in her cheeks and smiled in return. Nathan waved to her and when she nodded to him, she missed a note. To cover her mistake she changed the key of the hymn and kept playing.

After church Clarissa stood outside with Ida and Sophie. With his broken arm slipping out of its sling, Nathan played with a friend. Adam was on the other side of the churchyard where the horses were tied up. He was talking with several men when he was struck below the knees. He looked down to see what hit him.

"Why, hello there, Little Girl." He picked up Polly who gave him a smile and a hug. He explained to the curious men, "Polly comes to my house with her mother when she teaches piano to my son, Nathan. We're old friends, aren't we, Polly?" She smiled and patted his cheek. "I'd better take you to your mother before you get hurt around these horses."

He excused himself from the circle of men. Meanwhile Clarissa was searching for Polly.

"I have Polly, Miss Clarissa," he called out.

"Pity's sake—how'd she end up with you?"

"She came over to say 'hello.' With this kind of greeting, I'll have to come back to your church." Oblivious to the stares of the others, they visited while Polly patted Adam's cheek.

"Seeing you and Nathan come in this morning caused me to miss a chord." She laughed and a spot of color developed on her neck.

"I thought you'd be surprised to see us, but I didn't mean to ruin the prelude. Just between you and me, I doubt anyone was the wiser."

"Aren't you supposed to be with Miss Nellie?"

"I declined her invitation today because Nathan and I are ready to attend church on our own. There's no Anglican church in Springdale, so here we are."

"But if you and Nathan change your Sunday routine, you may be in danger of starving."

"What I might be sacrificing crossed my mind. However, since the Lewises just invited us home for dinner with them, at least we won't go hungry today."

"You sound a bit like a hungry opportunist."

"I suppose you've correctly identified me. I've never been clever at covering my voracious appetites. Remember the chocolates?"

"Of course I do." She laughed and tried to end the conversation. "Well, please come back again. I do hope our pianist is more skillful the next time you pay us a visit."

"Me, too," he said with a mischievous wink. He handed Polly back to her and called to Nathan as he walked back to Fancy waiting with the rig.

Prudence Phillips nudged Aunt Mag. "Did you see that?"

"See what?"

"Our little widow making eyes at that Dr. Norcutt."

"Shame, Prudence! She's just being friendly to our visitor. I don't believe I saw you welcome the doctor."

"Well, neither did you."

When Clarissa went back to Sophie and Ida, they were also full of questions.

"What was that all about?" Ida asked.

"Why was Dr. Norcutt here?" Sophie wanted an answer, too.

Clarissa was hesitant. She had not been sworn to secrecy, but she did not want to spread tales about the doctor's recent prayers.

"Polly spotted him standing by the carriages and ran over to see him. She has become quite attached to Dr. Norcutt and his son."

"So I see," Ida said.

"Isn't Dr. Norcutt a Catholic?" Sophie asked.

"He attends mass with the Murrays, but he isn't Catholic."

"Oh?" Ida and Sophie chimed in unison.

"He's Anglican."

Both women nodded and the conversation stalled until Clarissa gave in. She could not resist telling her friends what had happened.

"Oh, all right. I think there's a reason for the Norcutts' visit, but you must not whisper this to a soul if I tell you."

"We won't!" they assured her.

"I learned when Dr. Norcutt was quarantined with us that he didn't believe in God. Since then we've had some heated discussions about my faith because he doesn't want me to influence his son with my beliefs. But he told me about a recent experience they had which made him reach out to God."

Sophie was shocked. "He talked with you about this?"

"Yes, he told me about it when he cancelled Nathan's piano lessons because of that broken arm. You see, Nathan was riding the doctor's mare when she bolted and ran off with him. When she balked at a fallen tree, the boy went over her head and landed on the other side of the tree. The doctor found him unconscious and prayed that God would spare his son's life. He had never prayed before. They both feel that God intervened because Nathan could have easily been killed. I don't know much else."

Her friends nodded as they absorbed this story. She hoped their curiosity was satisfied. But Sophie spoke up.

"Maybe Steven should call on him."

Clarissa shook her head. "Let's let this mustard seed of faith grow a bit. We may be trimming its branches before long."

"You're right. Let's not badger the poor gentleman. Doesn't look like he's going anywhere any time soon," Ida agreed.

"We could invite them over to the parsonage for Sunday dinner. That way he and Steven could get acquainted," Sophie suggested.

"Well, they're coming to dinner with us today," Ida bragged.

"If there's food involved, he'll be there," said Clarissa. "I found out he has quite an appetite when they stayed with me. He's especially fond of chocolate."

"Tom's waving at me. He must be starving. I'd better hurry home to stretch our dinner for the Norcutts."

"Don't worry about Master Nathan. Sometimes he hardly eats a thing."

Clarissa packed Polly and her music into the baby carriage. They strolled along with other church members until she and her daughter were the last ones on the path. She thought about Dr. Norcutt's blue eyes when he winked at her after church and shamed herself for allowing her thoughts to linger on such a thing. She also questioned whether she should have told her friends about Dr. Norcutt praying when Nathan was hurt.

"At least I didn't tell them everything."

Chapter 38

Clarissa's thoughts went back to a recent day when she was sweeping the fall leaves off her front porch. She looked up to see the Norcutts stopping at her hitching post.

"Is Nathan here for an extra piano lesson?" She laughed at Nathan's look of dismay. At her invitation they came in for some cookies and lemonade.

After Adam sent Nathan down to the creek to play, to Clarissa's amazement, he had asked her some questions about his recent experience with prayer.

"I've called on you today because I have some questions. Perhaps you can shed some light on what happened between me and God on the day of Nathan's fall."

"I'm not sure I can, but I'll try."

"Have you ever heard of an atheist changing his mind so suddenly?"

"Exactly what are you asking me?"

"Come, come! Haven't you heard stories like mine before? Is it normal for a sane, grown man to burst into prayer with no prior change of mind?" He was feeling increasingly ill at ease.

"Please remember, I was the minister's wife, not the minister."

"But you told me about those discussion groups at the parsonage. You must talk with other people. I assume they don't all argue with you like I have, do they?"

"No, I can't say that they do." She stopped herself from laughing out loud.

"So, what do people say when they convert?"

She hesitated to reply but was thrilled to hear him claim his new faith. She could tell he wanted a succinct answer.

"Everyone has their own experience when it comes to finding God. You see, Christianity is built on certain principles described in the Bible. The bedrock of them all is that God exists and can intervene in our lives, most notably when Christ died on the cross on our behalf. Based on your recent experience with God, I think you've passed that test of belief."

"Yes, go on."

Isn't he going to argue with me?

"A man of your intelligence will have many questions, but there are also many answers and plenty of gentlemen around Springdale who will help you find them. Why don't you call on Pastor Steven. . . ."

"Stop." He held up his hand. "Let me set your mind at ease. I no longer have a host of unsettled issues about the Christian faith."

"I'm so glad you've found someone to talk with about your concerns."

"I haven't talked to anyone but you and Nathan."

"But how. . . ."

"Widow Chambers, when we stayed here, what did you think I was doing all those long evenings in that little study of yours?" He pointed toward her study.

"I don't know, resting or reading your books?"

"Correct. What else?"

"Maybe writing in your journal?"

"That, too. But after I read all the books Willy brought over from my house, I started reading those rather moldy books in your study."

"You don't mean you read Elliot's old theology books?" Her hand flew to her mouth.

"With the exception of a few scribbled recipes in your kitchen, a music theory book and a book of poetry, I didn't find much other reading material around here."

"Gracious, you should've asked me for some other books. I have more back in my bedroom. You must've been terribly bored if you read through Elliot's stodgy old collection of sermons and theories. I meant to dispose of those ages ago."

"On the contrary, I found them quite interesting. I even made some notations about them in my journal. Lifelong questions I've harbored about Jesus, questions I was never allowed to ask as a boy, were answered as I read. So, in your makeshift infirmary, the information

I needed was practically on my pillow for the taking. I guess all that reading started me on a path I didn't know I was on. Hmm?" He raised an eyebrow and waited for her answer,

"I reckon so. Sometimes God works in almost devious ways to lure us to Himself. I must admit that devising a path for you through a typhoid epidemic, a widow's front room, Elliot's old library and Nathan's broken arm is a most ingenious plot on His part."

"Madam, I've never read in any of my medical journals that faith in God may be a possible outcome of suffering from typhoid." He teased an incredulous Clarissa. "Perhaps I should write for a medical journal on this outcome. Let's see, I'll be sure to note that the patient with typhoid may suffer from bouts of boredom which can be cured by reading 'stodgy old books of theology.'"

He slapped his knee and opened the front door to call out for Nathan. To Clarissa's surprise, the discussion ended without their customary argument over her faith and his atheism.

"So, we are no longer adversaries, Dr. Norcutt?" She walked with them out to her gate.

"No, dear lady, we are not."

Clarissa put her hands together near her heart and resisted the urge to hug him. She marveled how God put Elliot's library together with a British atheist.

Now walking back to her kitchen and reflecting on this conversation with the newest believer in Springdale, she was glad she had decided to keep it in the confines of her heart. Ida and Sophie did not need to know everything.

As she said her prayers that night, she was thankful. "Lord, You always find ways to flood us with Your grace. Thank You for the doctor's faith. Also, for giving me some pleasant thoughts about those old books of Elliot's. I reckon I won't throw them out after all."

Chapter 39

1869

On a chilly winter evening, Adam suffered with a bad cold. His patients had passed along to him their stuffy sinuses and dripping noses. He closed the clinic for two days and Miss Nellie pouted without her usual escort around town.

"Adam, you picked a fine time to be sick. Can't you take something for it? We have several parties and our calendar can't be changed at this point. Our hostesses will not be pleased if we don't show up." She stood on his front porch bundled in a woolen coat with a fur muff over her hands.

"I'm sorry to inconvenience you and your schedule, but I'm too sick to be sociable. I must stay home and take care of this miserable cold."

"Just get dressed and make the best of it. You won't drop over dead if you go out to dinner, will you? After all. . ."

"Nellie," he said, his patience wearing thin. "I'm not going. I'm doctor enough to know I shouldn't be out on a cold night for anyone's blasted party. You'll have to find someone else to go with you."

"Well, I never, Adam Norcutt. You're impossible." She spun around and left him at the door.

Tonight I'm too miserable to worry about Nellie's infernal social calendar.

Thankful for peace and quiet, he brewed a pot of tea laced with brandy and settled in front of his fireplace. A steaming kettle bubbled nearby. His miserable aching sinuses dominated everything in his world. Anticipating a long evening, Bonnie jumped into his lap.

"Bonnie, I hate catching whatever is going around. At least this time it's not typhoid."

He blew his nose, inched his chair closer to the fireplace and recalled the frigid English nights when his family gathered close to their huge fireplace to sing together. Now huddled close to his grate in America, the fire burned low. He should add another log, but the woodbin was empty. If he went outside to fill it, he risked getting chilled. Also, Bonnie would object to being evicted from his lap.

"I'll bring in more wood in the morning," he muttered and scratched Bonnie's ears.

He opened the old Bible he'd discovered in Dr. Logan's library. His curiosity about the Bible was stirred during a recent conversation with Rev. Steven, who like himself was an avid horseman. They often crossed paths at the livery stables while buying tack and supplies. Several days before he came down with his cold, they had ridden together into the countryside to exercise their horses. While navigating their way through some dense woods, Adam told Steven about his recent prayers for Nathan.

"Have you ever read the Bible, Doctor Norcutt?"

"Can't say I have. I was heartily opposed to its contents until recently."

"That's where I'd challenge you to apply yourself. You'll be surprised at how the Bible has a way of explaining itself."

"Really?"

"None of us would believe the Bible if it didn't make sense at some level. Being a Christian is all about faith, but that faith has to be based on something of substance."

"I guess I'd better take up your challenge and start reading." Adam dodged an overhanging branch.

"Do you own a Bible?"

"I believe Dr. Logan left one behind in his library. I'll dust it off and start reading."

When the road straightened in front of them, they let their horses go at a fast pace. Riding Fancy Petticoats at a full gallop always made Adam homesick for England. He missed the fox hunting that was a regular part of his life there, but this was the best he could do. If only he could find a local replacement for the baying of the hounds and the sound of the hunt master's horn.

When the horses were winded, the men turned them around and trotted back toward town. But before they parted company, Adam had one more question for Rev. Steven.

"How do my son and I go about joining your church?"

"It's fairly simple. You appear before the Elders and they ask you about your faith. Based on our conversation today, I'm certain they'll be satisfied with your answers. The next Sunday, I'll present you to the congregation as a new member."

"That's simple enough. What about Nathan?"

"He goes through the same process, but his questions will be tailored for a child's responses. There's one other important issue."

"What's that?"

"Are you and Nathan ready to be baptized?"

"That's a relief—I thought you might ask for a big contribution."

"Like your salvation, church membership costs you nothing. When the weather warms up, we'll have a church picnic down by the river. I'd be honored to baptize you two then."

"I'll tell Nathan. He's been asking me about this for weeks. I think you know he had all this figured out long before I did."

"The Elders meet this Friday evening. Shall we expect you?"

"By all means."

Still shivering in the chill of the late hour, Adam set his Bible reading aside and covered himself with the shawl he found on the arm of the chair. As he dozed, he dreamed of spring flowers and fresh grass. When he stirred, the hour was well past his bedtime. The fire in the grate burned low and the candles on the nearby table looked weary. When he tossed aside the shawl, he recognized it. Clarissa must have left it behind when she and Polly stopped by earlier with some chicken soup "to help with that bad cold of yours."

Reaching for Bonnie, he held her for a moment while she purred. "Bonnie, Miss Clarissa's shawl must've done it. That 'Fresh Meadows' perfume of hers had me longing for spring, a delightful diversion on a cold night, don't you agree?"

He thought about the young widow who supported her own little family, but never neglected others. The soup she brought by for his supper was a good example. However, he was a bit concerned about her because of her visit. Thankful for some company on a lonely afternoon, he had kept her talking at a safe distance in his front hallway.

"Are you and Polly staying busy these days?"

"Yes and no. Some days are too busy. Then, like today, I needed something to do, so I made soup for you."

"I'm fortunate to fall under your good graces."

"I have to stay busy, you know." *And try not to look at your blue eyes.*

When she suddenly cut her eyes away, he noticed.

"Is something wrong?"

"Not really, but I'm still having those terrible dreams I've told you about. I stay busy to keep from going over and over them during the daytime hours."

"Don't despair. It'll take you many good experiences to replace those bad memories."

"I know, but I want to stop thinking about Elliot. Why can't I just let him go? The good Lord knows I've tried. Like last night—he was back again in my dream as a huge aqua python slithering around the church and up onto the pulpit. I kept warning people to stay away from him because he was dangerous. Honestly, I think the man is haunting me."

"Remember my arguments with Josephine when I suffered nightmares at your house?"

"Of course I do." She looked up into his eyes again to find him smiling at her. "I keep forgetting that you've also struggled with bad memories. Forgive me for prying, but how long before you stopped ruminating on the past?"

"Longer than I expected. Thankfully, those memories no longer control me. I suppose I've finally forgiven Josie, but I had to do it over and over again for a long, long time."

"It helps to know someone else has dealt with similar struggles."

"Make no mistake, those difficult memories are still with me. I can't erase them, but now I can leave them in the past where they belong. They don't trouble my daily life anymore."

"It appears I can't do that yet. Come on, Polly, we'd better head for home."

"Wait," he stopped her. "Remember, your wounded heart can take longer to heal than any physical injury. Someday your unhappy marriage will be like a forgotten chapter in an old book that hasn't been dusted, much less read, in a long time."

"I'm counting on your diagnosis, Dr. Norcutt."

"Don't give up, Miss Clarissa. Time does help us heal."

"Meanwhile, I hope my soup helps your bad cold a bit."

"I'm sure it will. My thanks for your thoughtful visit."

Still shivering, he left the cold fireplace and put Dr. Logan's tattered Bible on the shelf. After returning Clarissa's shawl to the hall tree, he sent Bonnie outside. In the kitchen, he checked the widow's delicious soup and smiled—it would last him through tomorrow.

I wish I had a cure for struggles like hers. God knows, she deserves a better life.

Chapter 40

"Hey! Doc Norcutt! Get out here in a hurry!" Jacob Featherson eased his wagon team to a halt in front of the Springdale Clinic. "We need you out here. I got some folks all stove up."

He whistled through the space between his front teeth and his team pulled tight against their traces.

"Whoa up, girls. Settle down, I'se whistling for the doc."

He jumped down and tied his team at the hitching post. On the bed of his wagon were two badly injured men who didn't move. Three other men gritted their teeth as they stepped down from the wagon and several women were in tears.

"Now, hang on 'til Doc Norcutt gets out here." He whistled once more for Adam.

Adam blew his stuffy nose, grabbed a coat and hat and ran into the cold air. He rushed down the path and jumped onto the bed of the wagon.

"What in heaven's name happened?"

"Some drunks held up that stage on the other side of town. Them idjits ran the stage off the road. The trail was slushy because of that thaw yesterday and the big rig slid all over. The team was terrible spooked. Thought we'd never get them poor horses settled enough to tend to these folks."

Jacob pointed to the most seriously injured man. "This man has a bullet wound to the shoulder. The other fella, the driver, fell off the stage and has a bad gash there over his forehead. The sheriff asked me to bring them over here so's they can warm up and you can tend to them."

"Bring them inside out of the cold and I'll see what I can do. Help me carry this bloke with the shoulder wound."

When the injured travelers were inside the clinic, Adam assessed their injuries and needs. Some of the shivering travelers were only badly shaken, not injured.

"Jacob, could you take these folks who aren't hurt to The Excelsior where they can warm up and rest? See that they get something warm to drink. These other injuries are going to take me some time, but there's no need for everyone to wait here in the clinic."

"I sure can," he turned to the travelers. "If y'all don't need the doc's attention, come on with me. We'll get you settled at the hotel."

"Be sure someone brings their luggage over from that wreck," he shouted after the wagon. "And have Leon take a look at that stagecoach team. They must be hurt, too."

Now Adam concentrated on the task at hand. He had two seriously injured patients and others with painful superficial wounds. All needed immediate attention. He rushed into the house to enlist Rosalie's help.

"Oh, no, Dr. Norcutt, I can't do that. I passes clean out at the sight of blood."

"Magnolia?"

"No, suh, not me. If you got folks hurt bad, you needs Miss Clarissa." He looked at the ceiling in frustration. "She be a good nurse. She help Dr. Logan all the time during The War. She'll help out."

"I saw her walking toward town," Rosalie said. "I'll fetch her."

"Go find her—hurry! Magnolia, bring over some blankets for these folks. I don't want them to stay chilled."

Magnolia bustled out and came back with an armload of blankets. A few minutes later, Clarissa rushed into the clinic, handed Polly over to Magnolia and headed for the clinic.

"Miss Clarissa! Thank God Rosalie found you." Adam was visibly relieved. "Is this asking too much? Can you stand the sight of blood? People in pain?

"Please, don't worry. I helped Dr. Logan during The War. This won't be new to me."

"Good. I need your help with some poor blokes hurt this morning when the stage was held up. The worst is a shoulder with a serious bullet wound. Come along—you can have a look." He brought her to the wounded man who moaned with pain. Without faltering, she found scissors to cut the man's clothing away and spoke in soft tones to calm him. She stood close by while Adam gave him chloroform and prepared to remove the bullet. Before he began he turned to Clarissa.

"Is there anything you can't do?"

Find a decent husband. Get you out of my head. But she said nothing and handed him the instrument he needed.

"Well done, Nurse Chambers," he said when he had removed the bullet and stopped the man's bleeding. "Perhaps you should see how our patients in the waiting room are doing. Can you clean up any surface wounds and scratches? You'll know what to do, won't you?" He raised an eyebrow as she nodded. "I'll be in to stitch up that bad gash in a bit."

She took care of the travelers' scratches with iodine and bandages, and cleaned up the driver's scalp injury. She sent the ones who were able to walk on over to the Excelsior Hotel. While the others waited, she visited with them about their destinations.

Later, as Adam prepared to sew up the driver's jagged gash, he handed her his curved needle. "Here, you're a seamstress, why don't you sew up this one?"

"I hardly think so. Look, Dr. Norcutt, you've scared the poor man."

He winked at her and took his first stitch. When all the remaining passengers were cared for, Willy took them over to The Excelsior. The man with the bullet wound would stay at the clinic over night. Adam removed his soiled white coat and thanked Clarissa for her help.

"You were such a help in here today. Maybe I should hire you as my nurse."

"After The War Dr. Logan wanted me to stay on, but Elliot wouldn't hear of it. Anyway, right now I have all I can handle, so I must decline." She smoothed her hands over her bloodied apron. *If I said yes, I'd probably just watch you and not pay attention.*

"Let me know if you change your mind." Ominous thunder rattled all the supplies and bottles in the clinic. "Another storm's coming. Allow me to walk you and Polly home. I'll bring along my big umbrella."

As they walked, they chatted about their work of the afternoon. Black clouds boiled on the horizon as the storm came closer by the minute. While they stood at the doorway of her cottage, he praised her skills once again.

"Thank you, Dr. Norcutt, but I saw much worse during the war. That shoulder was a mess, but the man was in your good hands."

"I haven't seen a serious gunshot wound since The War, but how to manage it came back to me. I guess it's something I'll never forget. At least, I hope not."

"That poor man ended up in the only town for miles around with a skilled surgeon. I was privileged to help—and to watch you at work."

"On a day like this, I long for a proper surgery. Maybe someday Springdale will have a better clinic, but for now I'll get by. Thankfully, this doesn't happen very often anymore."

Clarissa was trying to persuade Polly to wave "bye-bye" to Adam when a huge clap of thunder shook the evening.

"Here comes our storm. You'd better hurry home. Watch out for patches of black ice along the way."

He paused on her front steps. "Might I tap your skills again for some of my Sunday clinics down at the river shanties?"

"I'll help when I can, but only when I don't have a Sunday caller." They laughed at the memory of her Sunday afternoons with Jacob. He waved over his shoulder and ran down the steps. When he was gone, she berated herself for agreeing to help with yet another of Dr. Norcutt's projects. *Will I never learn?*

Bent under his umbrella, Adam ran toward home. With rain coming at him sideways, he was soon soaked. Icy bits of hail and sleet pounded the path in front of him. He was shivering as he dried off at home and pulled on his nightshirt. Exhausted, he pulled extra blankets over himself and tried to warm up.

I hope my head cold doesn't come back with this storm.

Chapter 41

"Nathan, I need some advice."

"About what, Papa?"

"I need a way to thank Miss Clarissa for her help in the clinic yesterday. We know she loves music. Do you suppose she'd like to hear some opera singers who are coming to town?"

Nathan thought a moment. "No, sir. She'd rather have a picnic."

"That's what she likes to do with you and Polly. But don't you think a grown lady would enjoy an evening of music?"

"Don't opera people stand around and sing?"

"Yes, but the music will be wonderful."

"No, she'd rather go on a picnic."

"Tell you what, we'll let her decide."

Adam arranged one other detail before he talked to Clarissa.

"Nellie, may my new assistant join us in the Murray seats for the opera program?"

"You have an assistant? I'm so glad, Adam. Now you'll have more time for us."

"She's a volunteer, not an employee. Widow Chambers assisted me during a recent emergency at the clinic and I want to thank her somehow."

"Thank her? I hardly think that sitting with my family would be appropriate. I hope you haven't mentioned this to her."

Adam recognized the signs of the gathering storm of her anger. He was becoming entirely too familiar with them.

"No, of course not, Nellie. I wouldn't have presumed on you or your family like that."

"Good."

"Don't concern yourself for a moment, Nellie. I respect your feelings. I'll purchase tickets for the widow and myself in another area for the evening."

With a short intake of breath, she fidgeted with the diamond bar pin at her neck and tugged on her crocheted gloves. Her patience with Adam's demanding schedule had grown thin. She weighed the implications of allowing the young widow to sit with them against another evening without an escort.

"I suppose we could make an exception this once." She busied herself with invitations that had arrived in the mail. "But my parents and I won't tolerate hangers-on on a regular basis."

"She's hardly a 'hanger-on,' Nellie. She'll be our invited guest."

Thus, a place was reserved for Clarissa for her evening at the opera—if she would accept.

Nathan was wrong about Clarissa's response to Adam's idea. When invited to attend the concert or have a picnic, she chose the evening of music without hesitation.

"But Dr. Norcutt, you don't have to do this for me. I was glad I could help you." She said the perfunctory words, but Adam could see the way her eyes lighted at the prospect of an evening of music.

"The morning of that accident I was fortunate to have someone who was not only willing to help but competent."

"Of course I'll go, Dr. Norcutt—gladly."

At home that night, Clarissa wished Ida was there so she could share her delight. She hadn't attended a theater performance since before she and Elliot married. Such extravagances were never within the reach of his salary. The doctor's invitation was like a dream come true, except for one thing: What would she wear?

While she rocked Polly in the shadows of the evening, she tried to think of a solution. She knew the latest styles for she created them every day for her customers, but she had neither the time nor the money to make a suitable gown for herself. Perhaps she could re-style something she already owned.

The next day when she found nothing suitable in her wardrobe, she remembered a trunk in the attic. As sunlight filtered through the attic, she opened the trunk and found her wedding gown and going-away ensemble. A flood of sadness swallowed her as she looked at the symbols of her marriage and reckoned once again with what a failure it had been.

But the clothing was lovely. She held up the travelling outfit and considered the possibilities. Made of teal-blue watered silk with long sleeves and a high collar, it had been high fashion for a bride. The tucks on the bodice were the tiniest she had ever made. She remembered laboring over the covered buttons down the back and at the wrists.

"This just might work."

She brought the outfit down from the attic and spread it out on her sewing table. Over the next several evenings, she restyled the gown and smiled when the waist needed scant easing. The long sleeves became cap sleeves, and the high collared neckline was changed into a scooped bodice. In her remnant basket she found pieces of imported lace to trim the sleeves and the neckline. She crafted small silk rosettes to hold the lace in place. Extra fabric provided a wide ruffle around the hem of the gown. The matching cloak became her evening wrap. From a discarded long sleeve, she made a little evening bag with a gathered top and a tassel on the bottom. The day before the concert, she hung the dress in her bedroom and was pleased.

She brought the gown with her when she came to watch Nathan the afternoon before the concert. Rosalie was coming to stay with Nathan and Polly for the evening. With everything in place, she felt giddy with excitement.

After Clarissa served supper to everyone, she dressed for the evening. She was pleased with her gown, but her hair was another matter. She was still struggling with it when Magnolia knocked and came into the bedroom. When she saw Clarissa's dilemma she didn't hesitate.

"Miss Clarissa, you needs my help with that hair. Now don't put up a fuss, 'cuz I knows exactly what to do. I did this every day for the lady on my plantation. Just let me heat up your curling iron again."

By the time Magnolia was done, Rosalie had arrived and together the women admired Clarissa's hair. Her auburn curls were secured in all the right places and several trailed over her shoulders. Some leftover rosettes and strips of the teal blue silk were tucked in amongst the curls. Clarissa stared at her reflection in the mirror. She could not remember the last time she had looked in a mirror and been pleased.

"Magnolia, thank you," she said, pulling her into a heartfelt hug. "I guess I'm as ready as I'll ever be."

The sight wasn't wasted on Adam. When he saw Clarissa, he was almost speechless.

"My, my! Miss Clarissa? You're transformed. Where's that little widow who was here earlier? You know—the one with those irascible children in tow?"

"With a lot of help from Magnolia, I think I'm ready."

"You're just in time. The Murrays' coach is pulling up out front."

Springdale had never seen Clarissa Chambers dressed for a formal evening. Heads turned when the unusual pair took their seats. Adam, who never objected to escorting a pretty lady, basked in the stir caused by their arrival. When the rest of the Murray party came in, he secretly enjoyed Nellie's flustered response to this pretty intruder in her accustomed limelight. Seating herself on the other side of Adam, she was barely civil to their guest. Adam knew that the tiff over the starched cap and apron was settled, for on this evening nothing suggested Clarissa was a serving maid. The evidence was quite to the contrary.

Because Clarissa was familiar with the soloists' arias, she admired and appreciated their abilities. Closing her eyes, she anticipated each note. She endeared herself to the other Murray guests as she explained the libretto. Much to her surprise, before the evening was over, she had three orders for silk purses like hers. She never told them that hers was made from scraps. The ladies of Springdale were impressed even if the Widow Desmond was not.

After the concert, they stopped at the Norcutts' for Polly and also for Rosalie, who would stay the night with Clarissa. Adam rode along in the Murray rig back to the cottage. He and Rosalie carried Polly, her baby carriage, and their other belongings into the house.

While Rosalie settled Polly in bed, Clarissa walked to the door with Adam. Her ruffled silk gown whispered as she moved.

"Thank you so much, Dr. Norcutt. I'm sorry that poor man was shot for this to happen, but I had a wonderful time. The concert was delightful. This is an evening I'll never forget."

"Nor will I, Miss Clarissa."

Chapter 42

On a Friday afternoon in the early spring, Adam and Clarissa crossed paths at The Mercantile. While they paused to visit, Nathan helped Clarissa load her purchases into the baby carriage. Polly ran to Adam and jumped into his arms.

"How do you do, Little Girl? Would you and your mother like to ride with Nathan and me into the country tomorrow morning?"

Clarissa overheard his question. "What did he say, Nathan?"

Adam continued talking to Polly. "Perhaps we should ask your mother." He turned to Clarissa. "I'd like for you to have a look at some property I may purchase. I want someone who remembers this place before The War to see it."

"What a marvelous idea. I'm no expert on farm land, but a morning in the countryside sounds delightful—as long as Nathan will be along." She could see Nathan nodding out of the corner of her eye.

"I'll have Magnolia pack us a picnic, if that's all right?"

"That's fine with us, isn't it, Polly? Maybe we'll see some of the first spring flowers."

"Fancy will bring us by around ten. It'll be cold in the morning, so bundle up. The baby will need a warm jacket and cap."

"Is it your turn to dress us now?" She smiled as she tied on her bonnet.

Recalling the memory of her help with his wrinkled cravat, he adjusted his collar and laughed. "Is this still straight?"

The next day Adam arrived on time for the promised morning ride in the country. After tucking thick Scottish lap robes around the children, he and Clarissa settled on the front seat. The fields glistened with dew and the morning sunlight enveloped the budding trees in a pale green glow. Spring was barely underway but couldn't be ignored.

"I'm curious, Dr. Norcutt. You want to be a landowner?"

"I'm no farmer, but I'm looking for some grazing meadows to encourage Nathan's interest in horses. I pass by this run-down place on my way to the shanties and the other day I trespassed enough to have a look around. The remains of an old plantation house sit on a hill."

"I'm familiar with the place you're talking about. Those folks left before the Yankees marched through. After they heard their home was in shambles, they've never returned."

"That's why I'm looking at the property. The family you remember is selling the place and the banker told me about it before the carpetbaggers hear it's for sale. I don't want the entire plantation, but I've ordered a survey of a section that would suit my needs."

"So, you're putting down some roots in Springdale? You must like being our doctor."

"I do, I honestly do. I needed a new start and look at me now. I'm a country doctor in a place I never knew existed."

"What does Widow Desmond think of this property?"

"She hasn't seen it yet. I invited her to inspect it with the banker and me, but it was too chilly for her that day."

He gave Fancy more rein and urged her into a trot. Clarissa and the children huddled under their blankets to stay warm. Along the way she told him about different landmarks. When they arrived at the plantation, Nathan jumped down to open the gate. They tied Fancy to one of the huge trees near the house and set out to explore the property. When they stood on a rise overlooking the impressive scene before them, he tossed out a challenge to her.

"Tell me where you would build a new house."

"Hmm, there's not a bad place on this property. You couldn't make a mistake."

"So, please, pick the best site. I'm asking your opinion."

"What's your choice?"

"No, Miss Clarissa—absolutely not. Don't ferret out what I want so you can agree with me. That's too easy. Tell me where you think a house should go." He pointed his finger at the center of her forehead. "You."

"In that case, my answer may surprise you."

"Really?" He teased her with a nudge. "Go on, surprise me."

"I'd restore this old dear of a plantation home. It's lovely. Just look at it...."

"I'll wager it was a beauty in its day."

"Yes, it was, and still is. It's a pity to see it like this."

"I thought it was too far gone to restore."

Clarissa could tell he was taken by her idea. "Can we go in and look around?"

"Let's give it a try. Nathan, stay here on the porch with Polly while Miss Clarissa and I take a quick look inside."

"All right, Papa. Just don't take forever."

Adam leaned his shoulder against the weathered door until it creaked open. Dust clouds swirled in the draft of their entrance into the old home, but an atmosphere of hospitality still showed through its ramshackle condition. That many soldiers had abused the place was all too evident. Except for a few massive pieces of furniture too large to carry off, the house was empty. If anyone lived there now they would be camping in squalor.

Adam stood in the entry hall and looked around. "So you honestly think this place could be made livable?"

"Yes, I do. Even in this deplorable condition, it seems sturdy. I'm sure it was well built."

"I'm beginning to see what you're talking about. Tell me, how does a little widow know about such things?"

"Haven't you heard? Preacher's widows are omniscient."

"I'm learning new things every day, Widow Chambers."

She rubbed the wide plank flooring with her toe. "Look at the beautiful floors under this filth. All they need is a good cleaning and a coat of wax. Honestly, I think it would be a pity to tear this beauty down."

"Extraordinary. I've never considered restoring one of these old places. You're right, she's still a wonderful house." He walked through the front rooms. "The house faces south to catch the breeze, but I like the view to the east. Perhaps I could put new windows in that eastern wall—a perfect place to enjoy the sunrise along with my morning tea." He clasped his hands behind his back and rocked back and forth on his heels.

Glory Be!

"I can see you now, Doctor!" She stretched out her hands in a frame toward the blank wall.

They sat in the spring sunshine on the veranda while they enjoyed Magnolia's deviled eggs, ham and cheese sandwiches, and her famous bread and butter pickles. At the bottom of the basket they found cookies for the children and Adam's favorite chocolate cake. They licked their fingers to clean up the frosting.

"Magnolia spoils you, Dr. Norcutt. She puts too much frosting on the cakes she bakes for you. Don't devour the rest of this cake when you get home or you'll end up with a bad headache."

"Are you the doctor here?" He leaned against a large colonial column, one of several across the front of the home.

"No, but I remember the terrible headache you suffered after eating all those chocolates Miss Nellie brought you when you were so sick."

"Hmmm, I consumed a lot of those, didn't I?"

"Yes, and you didn't offer a one to Polly or me. Not even one to your own son. Honestly, your proper British manners were slipping."

"I'm a selfish man when it comes to my chocolates, so let's talk about something else. We all need a drink. The banker told me the well water is safe to drink. Shall we give it a try?" He rose and reached for Polly's hand.

"Wait a moment, Dr. Norcutt." She dusted off the paint flecks covering his shoulders. "That column you leaned against still had some old paint on it. Buyer beware, this place is attaching herself to you."

"Ah, perhaps you're right. At least my emergency valet was along to clean me up."

They walked to the well near the detached kitchen. Nathan let down the bucket and cranked it back up again. They drank the cool, clear water from their cupped hands. When a brisk wind started blowing across the fields, Clarissa shivered and buttoned her coat against the breeze. Adam pulled Polly's cap over her ears.

"We'd better head for town before we're chilled to the bone. I don't want anyone to catch a cold. I've seen enough of those for one season."

Nathan, whose lips were turning blue, insisted he wasn't cold, but Adam bundled everyone into the buggy and they started back to town.

Along the way, Clarissa spoke up. "Have you considered staying in town and bringing your horses out at the plantation? You could hire someone to live there and take care of them."

"But didn't you say the place is worth restoring?"

"Yes, but I'm trying to come up with a more economical option. To restore that place will take a huge effort and a peck or two of money. Perhaps I spoke out of turn."

"On the contrary, I asked for your honest opinion. Tell you what, if you ever need a flat in London, I'll give you my esteemed opinions on British housing."

The ride back to the cottage seemed brief. Adam helped Clarissa down from the buggy and carried Polly, who needed her nap, up to the front door. Clarissa encouraged her to say "thank you" for their outing, but she was too drowsy.

"Thank you for a lovely morning. Please tell Magnolia how delicious her picnic was."

He paused as he was leaving and pointed to some new spring plants that were pushing up through the soil. "Aren't those hollyhocks? Will you have any extra starts?"

"I will in a few weeks. I'll bring you some. When they bloom, I'll teach Nathan how to trap a bumble bee in the blossoms."

"Why, I remember doing that when I was in knickers—I'd forgotten all about it. As a matter of fact, your hollyhocks always remind me of our English gardens. I'll be sure a place is ready for them."

After the Norcutts left, Clarissa whispered as she settled Polly for her nap, "I hope Dr. Norcutt doesn't demolish that lovely old home. I wonder if Widow Desmond will like it? She may get her big plantation home after all, Little Girl."

The idea of restoring the old plantation consumed Adam. That night he made long lists of projects to make the crumbling place livable. At the top of the first list was "clean and wax wood floors." At the bottom of the last was "check balance in London bank account." As he sketched floor to ceiling windows for the east wall, he could almost taste the first sip of his morning tea while he enjoyed the view.

Within days he decided to buy the section of the plantation that included the plantation house. When he told Willy, he broke into his gap-toothed grin.

"Mr. Doctor, you done a good thing. I'se the field boss out yonder befo' The War. You won't never find no better grazing for your horses."

"Honest, Willy?"

"Yes sir, I knows that place like the back of my hand."

"Maybe you could help me out there?"

"Mr. Doctor, you just might be looking at the boss man for your new place—if you wants me." He grinned from ear to ear. "And Magnolia? I came out yonder as a strapping boy off a ship, but she popped up out yonder. She lived there her whole life before 'mancipation."

Adam couldn't believe his good fortune. As soon as the ink was dry on the deed to the property, he set up a place for Willy to live at the plantation. His new foreman knew all the right workmen to hire. In no time the project was underway and Adam was scratching things off his lists. Folks in Springdale began to ride out River Road to watch the progress of the latest plantation restoration project.

Chapter 43

A letter arrived from Adam's parents—they were on their way to visit Springdale. Because the letter had been delayed by a storm in the Atlantic, he didn't have much time to prepare for their arrival. Everyone in the household rose to the occasion. Magnolia went on a cleaning spree; Rosalie and her mother were enlisted to do some extra cooking and Willy came in from the plantation to clean up the yard. Adam planted Clarissa's hollyhock seedlings in the clinic flowerbeds.

Because Nathan remembered visiting London stables with his grandfather, he wanted his American horses to put on a show he could be proud of. He curried Fancy and Standard until their coats shone, straightened the tack room in the barn and spread fresh hay in the stalls. He gave Bonnie her own chore in the barn.

"Bonnie, I don't want any mice running around to frighten Grandmother Norcutt."

On a beautiful spring morning, while honey bees, dragon flies and butterflies were busy over the fields, the Norcutt men met the boat bringing their British family to Kentucky. After everyone was welcomed, Fancy took them through the hills along River Road toward Springdale. Along the way, Nathan pointed out the old plantation his father was buying, and the creek where the huge willows with their fresh spring branches swayed in the breeze.

"I like to play on that sand bar where I can line up my soldiers." At the corner of River Road and Prather Boulevard, he told them about Miss Clarissa's cottage where he and his father recovered from typhoid fever. Adam told more details of their stay at the widow's home.

"Widow Chambers is a good and gracious lady. She took excellent care of us when we were both quite ill. I'm sure you'll meet her during your visit."

He eased his parents into his life in America, for it was far different from what they had envisioned for him. How would they respond to his life in Springdale? Still, he was proud of his recent accomplishments and anticipated showing them around.

Willy helped them inside with their luggage. Not wasting a moment, Nathan pulled his grandparents through the kitchen where they paused to meet Magnolia. Their next stops were the backyard and barn where they met Standard, the respected older gentleman of the stable.

"This is Standard. He's been here for a long time. Papa rides Fancy and I ride Standard, but I was on Fancy when I fell and broke my arm." He showed them his arm. "Papa took care of it and now it's as good as new."

"My, my, Nathan, these fine horses are very well cared for. I do believe you have the best of everything here in Kentucky."

"Yes, Grandfather, I do. Oh, I almost forgot Bonnie. She's our barn cat, but she's in the house a lot." Bonnie wound her way through their feet until Grandmother Norcutt picked her up.

"Nathan, isn't this the cat you named when you were still in London?"

"Yes, ma'am, she's the one. She's a good mouser and supplies our neighborhood with kittens."

The elder Norcutts had an unspoken agenda. They had come to see America and to visit their son, but they wanted to see if their grandson had adjusted to life with his father. Any concerns were soon laid to rest. Even a casual observer could see that Nathan was flourishing in his new surroundings and that Adam relished his role as a father.

A dinner party with Nellie and her parents highlighted the grandparents' stay. To her relief, Clarissa's help was not requested. The dining room table sparkled with Mother Norcutt's china, tableware and sterling candlesticks. Magnolia's meal was flawless. To please Nellie, Adam requested fruit compote with whipped cream for dessert. After dinner, Magnolia served dainty cups of coffee in the parlor and then whispered to Adam.

"Mr. Doctor, I'd best be going. My ride home is waiting out back. I'll finish up in the kitchen first thing in the morning. If that be all right with you, sir?"

He nodded his agreement and slipped her pay out of his pocket and into her hand. After she left, Nellie spoke to Adam behind her fan.

"Surely you didn't let your maid leave early?"

"Don't worry, it's all right. Magnolia lives out by the river and her ride was waiting to take her home. She'll finish up tomorrow."

"But what if we need something?"

"Then I'll see to it."

With a set to her pretty chin she handed him her empty demitasse which he filled from the silver coffee pot on the serving tray. He remembered to add two sugar cubes.

She didn't say thank you.

The next morning, Adam walked into the kitchen to find Clarissa helping Magnolia.

"What brings you to our kitchen today, Widow Chambers? You aren't supposed to volunteer here anymore, remember?"

"Rosalie took sick with terrible. . .hmm. . .monthly pains and asked me to help today. I hope you don't mind."

"Not at all. While you're here, I'll introduce you to my parents."

Clarissa finished in the kitchen and went looking for Nathan who needed to dress for a visit to the old plantation with his grandparents. She found him playing with a new set of marbles his grandparents had brought him from England. Father Norcutt was giving instructions to Nathan who sat on the floor still in his nightshirt.

"Good morning, Master Nathan. This must be your grandfather?"

"Oh yes, Miss Clarissa. May I present my grandfather, Mr. Wyatt Norcutt." He never glanced up from his new marbles. The elderly gentleman rose to offer his hand.

"What a pleasure to meet you. Nathan and his father have told us so much about you."

Mrs. Norcutt came into the room and was also introduced by her grandson.

"This is Widow Chambers. She's my piano teacher and takes care of me when Rosalie can't be here."

As Clarissa chatted with the elder Norcutts, she found them equally as charming as their son. Nathan continued to concentrate on his marbles until Adam came in and called a halt.

Glory Be!

"Nathan, if you want to go with us to the plantation, you'd better get ready. Go with Miss Clarissa and get dressed for the day—Now."

"Yes, sir. Let me put away my marbles. Miss Clarissa, did you see my new glass shooter?"

He showed her the shimmering centerpiece of his new set and hurried to change. Clarissa lingered long enough to invite the grandparents to stop at her place for tea on their return from the plantation.

"We'll be there if possible. Adam tells us you serve the most marvelous tea," Grandmother Norcutt said.

"He is an avid tea-drinker and we haven't broken him of the habit here in America. Actually, I'm just as bad." They made plans to see her and Polly later in the day.

Adam gave his parents a grand tour of the old plantation and house that would be his home in a few months. Nathan showed off the lush meadows for their horses. The grandparents were pleased with what they saw.

"This is exceptional land, son. I have some strong advice and hope you'll pay attention."

Adam cringed as he anticipated stern parental criticism about his plans to buy the old dilapidated plantation. But he was wrong.

"I believe Springdale will grow out this direction, and the Almighty has only made so much of this lush property between town and the river. If it's available, I think you should purchase more land out here. Buy more, son, and I'll invest with you."

"Excellent idea, Father. If you're serious, I won't be hard to convince." He made a mental note to talk to the banker before his parents returned to England.

Because of a threatening thunderstorm, they cut short their day in the country. As they hurried home along River Road, Adam stopped long enough at Clarissa's for Nathan to run to the door and explain why they couldn't stay for tea. The cookies Nathan came back to the carriage with were devoured before they reached home ahead of the storm.

Chapter 44

One afternoon Father Norcutt found Adam in the clinic and asked if they could visit.

"Of course, Father, happy to do so. The clinic is empty right now, so let's move into the house. I'll ask Magnolia to bring us a spot of tea."

"Delightful. I want to discuss something with you."

Adam returned in a few moments with Magnolia who carried a silver tray full of refreshments. The men made small talk as they sipped their tea.

"You said you wanted to talk with me about something? What's on your mind? More property in America?" He stirred his tea.

"No, it's something else. I don't normally get involved in such things, but since we're leaving soon, I thought I'd speak my mind."

"Carry on." Adam waited for his father to continue. He knew something important was brewing for his father was a man of few words.

"I think perhaps you're missing something here in Springdale." Adam's eyes widened over his teacup and he nodded for his father to continue. "This friend of yours, Widow Chambers. Why wouldn't she make you an excellent match? She is a lovely woman and seems fond of Nathan. Her beautiful little girl needs a father. Have you considered marrying her?" The unspoken words *instead of Nellie Desmond* dangled between them.

"Hold your horses, Father. Miss Clarissa is a friend, but nothing indicates a marriage is in order. I'm all but engaged to Nellie Desmond, who, as I'm sure you've observed, is a refined young widow. We enjoy one another's company. She's considered quite a catch around here."

"Adam, I'm hesitant, but let me confide another observation. Your mother and I were uneasy around her parents. I can't put my finger on what troubles us, but be careful around them, my boy."

"Thank you for your observations." He looked away as he re-filled their tea cups.

"Son, think about Widow Chambers. We've noticed that she is quite attached to Nathan and probably to you as well."

"I realize that Nathan needs a mother and I probably need a wife. However, Miss Clarissa is not a likely match for me. First of all, she's more than a decade younger than I."

"Many fine marriages have survived age differences."

"But do you know she was a parson's wife?"

"Yes, she told me a bit about her life as a clergyman's wife. Why is that a problem?"

"Simply said, she hasn't had our sort of life." He gestured toward his father. "I can't imagine marrying someone so different."

"What's different, son? She has many wonderful qualities. Even though her father is a merchant, she's had a good education in books and music. She's a skilled seamstress and piano teacher. And you? You seem happily settled here with a simpler life. So, where's the difference?"

Adam brushed by his father's questions and asked one of his own. "When did you become so well-acquainted with Widow Chambers?"

"We visited with her when she filled in for Rosalie and after Nathan's piano lessons. I'm sorry we missed having tea with her."

"We'll try to stop by there sometime, Father. We have several things to do before you leave. I'll give your opinions some thought, but I'm in no hurry to marry anyone right now." He disliked being involved in a match-making scheme devised by his parents. He was fast exiting the conversation when the clinic bell rang.

"Excuse me, Father. Duty calls."

Indeed! I think I can trust my own instincts about choosing a wife.

With the British grandparents doting on Nathan, Clarissa's assistance was rarely needed. To utilize her time off, she gave her house a thorough cleaning and caught up on her sewing orders. Late one afternoon, she settled down with her teacup to read some unopened mail. Puzzling over a letter from Vermont, she opened it first because she knew no one from New England. Written in a beautiful, level script, it began with a cordial greeting. Nothing could have prepared her for the letter's contents:

Dear Mrs. Chambers,

I am writing to you on a matter concerning our son, George Gary, who was killed six months ago in prison. The other man acted in self-defense. We knew George assaulted a woman who bore his child; however, we were ignorant of other details until we found his trial documents.

I am writing because George's inheritance from his grandparents was kept in trust. Under the trust provisions, in the event of his death, his inheritance belongs to his wife and or children. Since the two of you were not married, the funds belong to Polly, his only child.

We have discreetly investigated you and your circumstances, and learned that you have high morals and a good reputation. Your involvement in your church was noted, as well as your talents as a piano teacher and seamstress.

Based on these assurances, enclosed are documents which make you administrator of a trust for Polly. George's inheritance, now hers, has been wired to the Springdale Bank. This account is to be used for your family's well-being until Polly is twenty-five when it becomes hers. The financial details are enclosed.

Allow us to express our dismay concerning our son, who was our beloved only child. We prayed diligently that being a soldier would curb his erratic behavior—to no avail. Now we pray that his inheritance will not only benefit his daughter, but also serve somehow as a vehicle of forgiveness between us all.

Her grandmother, Louisa, requests that a likeness of Polly, whom we're told resembles George, be sent if at all possible.
Yours truly,
Alexander P. Gary, Attorney at Law

Clarissa clutched the letter under her chin and forgot to breathe. Shuffling through the official pages, she came to the amount of funds that belonged to Polly. She counted all the zeros on the bottom line of the accounting sheet and exhaled. Thankfully Polly slept, for she

Glory Be!

needed solitude to absorb this news. She went outside to sit on her porch steps. The songs of the birds and the whisperings of the soft wind were lost on her. Wrapping her arms around her knees, she rocked back and forth and prayed for wisdom in the face of this turn of events. Her thoughts were in turmoil, but they all ended with: *Can any good thing come from George Gary?*

The next day Clarissa did three things. First, she and Polly visited the Springdale National Bank. She wouldn't believe anything in the letter until she inquired about Polly's account. The banker welcomed her.

"Yes, Mrs. Chambers, the news in your letter is rock solid. I've been expecting you." He pushed a small blue accounting booklet across his desk toward her. "This is for you and Polly. Pvt. Gary's inheritance is in trust for Polly with you as the administrator. Please stop by here any time you have questions about the arrangements."

Next, she hurried to the druggist, the owner of the only camera in town. He bought it from a bedraggled Confederate historian in need of cash for his return home after The War. After he took Polly's portrait, he suggested one of the two of them together.

"I hope these turn out well. You and Polly are the loveliest customers in my short career as a photographer."

On their third errand, she called on Ida and Tom. She had to tell someone about this amazing turn of events. She thought about telling Dr. Norcutt, but he was probably too busy to listen to her news about Polly's inheritance. She read the letter to them and asked Ida a question.

"Is your cottage still for sale?"

"Yes, some day."

"Please consider it sold. Whenever you're ready I'll buy it for Polly at a fair price."

The Lewises looked at each other, swallowed hard and agreed. Clarissa blanched when Tom tousled Polly's hair with a question.

"Well, Miss Curly Top, how does it feel to be the richest lady in town?" Then he whispered to Clarissa. "Words to the wise, little widow, keep this news to yourself. If it gets out it might change the way people treat you."

Glory Be!

Clarissa took his advice to heart and told no one else. She knew Tom was right. The last thing she wanted was for people to start treating her differently because of Polly's inheritance—or stir up more gossip about the Pvt. Gary chapter of her life. That evening she fussed at herself. *Why did you even tell Tom and Ida? Why couldn't you keep your big blessing to yourself?*

Several weeks later when Clarissa had an idea about Polly's inheritance, she asked the banker on the square for some business advice.

"May I use Polly's inheritance to expand my sewing business? Would this violate the trust provisions?"

"I see no problem. The trust documents say the funds can be used for the family's well-being. And any deficit can be replaced with the income you'll bring in."

"So, I am not misusing Polly's inheritance? Would these dear folks in Vermont think I was stealing from Polly?"

"Not at all, the documents state you're to use this fund to enhance your lives."

With her concerns laid to rest and some papers signed, Clarissa breathed a sigh of relief. The banker walked with her to the front of the bank.

"Widow Chambers, you are becoming an excellent businesswoman." He shook her hand. "Welcome to the world of downtown Springdale."

Right away she asked Tom Lewis to order an expensive line of French fabrics to be sold at The Mercantile. When the goods arrived, her business doubled. With imported stylish fabrics available, the fashionable ladies of Springdale flocked to her with orders—with the exception of Nellie Desmond, who preferred to order her clothes in Charleston or Atlanta.

Soon Clarissa made another decision. With the increase of her sewing customers, she was overwhelmed to find a cash surplus in her bank account. After returning the funds she had used from Polly's trust, she still had enough to order two new treadle sewing machines, one for herself and one for the helper she planned to hire in the near future.

Adam complimented Clarissa one day when they crossed paths. "I hear your expanded sewing business is a huge success. Looks like

Glory Be!

you were smart to turn down my offers to work for Nathan and me. To think you could've been Nathan's governess or my nurse."

"If I'd taken your offer my fingers wouldn't be so sore. I've worn out my thimble." They walked along together and visited until he turned toward his house.

Clarissa was thankful for the success of her expanded sewing business, but she was concerned about the increasing demands on her time and energy. Perhaps she should forgo her never ending chore: mending. The next day she began telling her customers that she was no longer in the clothing repair business.

She stopped by the Lewis Mercantile to share her new blessings with Ida.

"Remember two years ago? Who could have guessed how blessed my life would be? I have everything I need. I still long for marriage to a caring husband, but I guess that isn't in God's plan right now."

"We'll keep praying for that husband to show up for you. These things do happen, so don't lose faith. You'll make a wonderful wife for some nice young man."

That night she walked out under the brilliant starlight near her back door and prayed.

"Dear God, thank you for all these new blessings, especially for relieving my financial woes. I still pray You might send a gentleman into my life with whom I can have a good marriage. My only requirements are that he be a good father to Polly, a loving partner for me and a devoted son of Yours."

Chapter 45

Adam was disgusted. "She might as well have hired their priest and set the date."

A relentless Nellie was pressuring him to join her in the Murray family's move to Atlanta. At last she would have her wish for life away from Springdale. Her determination to bring Adam along on the move never wavered and his resistance grew.

"Nellie, I'm not moving to Atlanta."

"But you'll be left in this little ol' backwoods town without any opportunity for a life of substance." Her tone of voice annoyed him. She had run his social life for a long time, but somewhere he had to draw the line.

"Did you hear what I just said, Nellie? I have no interest in leaving Springdale. I like living here and since you've hinted at it, I'm certainly not interested in marriage. I want to manage my clinic and raise my son. Above all, I refuse to make a decision like this under pressure."

Their debate intensified over several days. The climax of their arguments took place on a warm afternoon as they stood facing one another on the clinic's front porch. Nellie's angry words were loud and delivered with all the petulance she could muster. With every window in the neighborhood open to catch the breeze, the sound of their angry voices couldn't be ignored. Lace curtains parted all along Prather Boulevard.

"Adam Norcutt. . .oh, excuse me. . .Dr. Norcutt. Where's your decency? You've just been leading me on with your fancy Red Coat manners and those tea time stories of yours, to say nothing about your war stories that drone on and on. Well, I'm done with you and that's that."

Glory Be!

When Adam held up his hand and refused to argue anymore she gathered up her silk skirts and flounced down the path, screaming as she went, "I hate you, Adam Norcutt."

She slammed the door of her carriage and urged her poker-faced driver to drive away. "Get me out of here! Now!"

Adam stood stock still, debated what to do, shrugged his shoulders and did nothing. Widow Desmond's southern accent and beauty, now colored with bitterness and criticism, were no longer fetching. A bit surprised at his lack of regret, he found her pompous exit rather comical. Above all, he felt relieved and somehow thankful. He turned away so she wouldn't see him smile.

Magnolia, who had heard every word of the argument on the front porch, dusted in the shadows of the parlor as Adam entered the house. She muttered to herself as she cleaned.

"I don't know about that Mr. Doctor. The nicest lady in town be here most every day and he don't pay her no mind. She be pretty, she be smart, and she be the best around these parts. But no ma'am, he don't see beyond the end of that handsome nose of his. I'm glad that Desmond woman left out. Yessiree-bob! I thought she might chew him up and spit him out."

"Magnolia, what the blazes are you saying?"

"Oh, Mr. Doctor!" Anguish and fear spread over her wide face. "I didn't know you were listening."

"I wasn't. I came in the front door and you were talking. What's this about something at the end of my nose?"

"Shut my mouth. It ain't my place."

"Please, I'm asking you a simple question. Might I have an answer?"

"Yessir." She hesitated, but took a deep breath. "Far's I can tell, almost at the end of your nose is the best lady in Springdale. She's good from the bone out and she's right here under your roof most days."

"Go on."

"She always sends things down to our shanties. She waves when we walk by her place. I been round her a long time now, and you don't find folks like her very often. Why, she's a grand lady and she's pretty as can be. Besides all that, she loves Mr. Jesus."

"You're speaking of Miss Clarissa—Correct?" He raised his hands in exasperation. "For heaven's sake, Magnolia, don't you realize how young she is? She must be ten or more years younger than I. She's Nathan's piano teacher. And—and—she was a preacher's wife."

"Yessir, I know all that. But wait." With caution, she picked up the pen on his desk. She dipped the pen into his silver inkwell and wrote on a piece of paper she found on his desk. When she finished, she blew on it and handed it to him.

"Look at that, Mr. Doctor. She done taught me to write my name. I be the onliest woman on the river who can do that. She even say she'll teach me to read right soon. It takes a mighty nice lady to teach the likes of me." She stood with her hands on her hips, a stance he had come to respect.

He was enjoying Magnolia's lecture and decided to find out more. "And what's this about Widow Desmond?"

"Lawd, help me!" She dropped her chin toward her ample bosom.

He folded his arms and waited.

"This still ain't my place, but I suppose I'll tell you what you wants to know." But she hesitated, still fearing to continue. "You don't know how things was befo' The War." Her hand trembled as she dusted a Staffordshire figurine for the second time.

"So—enlighten me."

"News always traveled between us darkies. We all knew the Murray plantation was a terrible place for any slave—man, woman or chile." She paused, gathered more courage and went on. "Now I know Miss Nellie's papa's a rich gentleman, but he can be downright cruel. He slapped our women around and buggy-whipped the men. Ever so often one of our women birthed a mixed baby, so we knowed what . . . ." She averted her eyes. The implication was clear.

"What else can you tell me?"

"You ast' about Miss Nellie? Sir, she be spoiled rotten. When my baby sister was sold over to Murrays' place to be her maid, that po' little girl cried every day. Beneath her fancy ways that lady's like one of them little green lizards changing itself all the time. You can't please her. I'm telling you gospel truth, sir, she be flat out mean. You don't be around a lady like that if you can get out her way."

"What on earth, Magnolia?" Adam was incredulous.

"Poor thing, I reckon she can't help having that Murray family meanness—she be one of them folks. She covers it up mighty fast around nice folks like you." She looked him straight in the eye and went on. "Master Nathan knows about this. Mmm-hmm, he knows."

"Knows what?"

"Ain't you seen how he hides by me or Miss Rosalie whenever Widow Desmond be on the place?"

"No, I haven't. Do you suppose he's afraid of her?"

"You watch. You'll see."

"But she's never harmed him. Most of the time she pays him little mind."

"Uh-huh!" She put her hands on her hips again. "That's the whole problem right there. She don't pay him no mind because she don't like him and he can tell."

Her eyes opened wide as she let her words settle in on Adam. He knew that it was most unusual, even improper, to discuss such things with his household help. But he also knew she loved his son and these were things he needed to know.

"Mr. Doctor, I only told you what you asked about. Please don't let me go. I promise, I only told you the truth."

"Don't you worry, Magnolia. I know you're honest and we need you around here."

"Well, then I gonna say just one more thing."

"Yes?"

"Don't you fret none about that pretty little piano teacher being young. The way she look at you, she ain't seeing them gray hairs of yours. No, siree, not for a skinny minute."

While Adam stared at her in disbelief, Magnolia picked up her dust cloth and waltzed out of the room. He walked over to the mirror and ran his hands though his thick hair. Did he have enough gray hairs to notice? But there they were, and not just a few.

Chapter 46

After Nathan fell asleep, Adam sat outside on the back steps of the clinic. He twirled a badminton racquet with a broken string between his long fingers and made a mental note to speak to his son about it.

In the total darkness of the evening, Magnolia's advice began to make some sense. She had lit a candle in the midst of his life and it was shining all over his relationship with Nellie, his past with Josephine, and his future in Springdale. Why would Nathan be afraid of Nellie? If Nellie ignores him, what's to fear? Is he afraid I might marry her? Do other women remind him of his mother?

Then it hit him. . *Josie and Nellie are alike. Why haven't I seen that before?*

He thought back on Nellie's tirade that afternoon. He knew their relationship was over when she ignored his remarks and barged ahead to keep talking about marriage.

"Wasn't I supposed to come to her on bended knee with a declaration of my love, a breathtaking ring in my pocket, and exciting plans for our future together? Isn't that the way these things happen? Is there an American custom about proposing marriage I'm oblivious to?"

He rubbed the back of his neck as he remembered the time he entered into a marriage he had not planned on. Even with the blessing that Nathan was to his life now, his marriage to Josephine started with a less than desirable beginning.

"No more uncomfortable engagements for me, thank you," he muttered into the darkness.

Magnolia's comments about Clarissa were more interesting and more pleasant to think about. He couldn't help but be amused at Magnolia's interference, but her remarks were curiously close to his father's. What was it about Widow Chambers that caused them to focus their attention on her?

He sifted back through his memories of Clarissa. They met in the fall of 1866 on his first day in Springdale. The next May he delivered Polly. Although they first became friends while he and Nathan had typhoid fever that next fall, their friendship grew when she became Nathan's piano teacher and substitute for Rosalie. When he thought about their age difference, he realized their friendship never faltered over their ages.

He mulled over more of his recollections: the flash of Clarissa's red Christmas sash in the snow light, her fondness for Nathan, her courage as a young widowed mother, her embarrassment while dancing with him on July 4th, her shyness when playfully kissed, her tact in shifting a crisis about starched uniforms into new dresses for Magnolia, the sight of her shimmering in her teal-blue gown, her perceptive advice to restore the plantation, the fluidity of her body and the intensity of her countenance as she played Chopin on a rainy day. And the lingering fragrance of her "Fresh Meadows" perfume.

The memories were endless. He took a deep breath and smiled into the darkness. Slapping the damaged racquet against his palm he went inside. When he turned down the counterpane on his bed he admonished himself out loud.

"How much prodding is it going to take, Old Chap?"

The next morning, Adam washed at the bowl and pitcher in his bedroom and dressed for his day in the clinic. He walked through the front hallway toward the clinic and stopped. He saw Polly and Clarissa through the beveled glass door; they were right on time for Nathan's piano lesson. They laughed about something and the morning sunshine surrounded them. Polly's ringlets glowed like a halo while Clarissa's trim silhouette appeared outlined in gold. Her dress of soft green twill enhanced her auburn hair and made her hazel eyes glow. She leaned toward Polly and kissed her cheek before opening the front door.

Under his breath he whispered, "Why not? Dear God in heaven, have I been so blind? Why not?"

As he opened his front door, sunshine and laughter poured inside.

"Why don't you lovely ladies come inside and tell me what's so funny?"

"Good morning, Doctor Norcutt. Polly is begging to play with Nathan's lead soldiers and I told her she might as well ask for the moon." She nuzzled Polly's cheek. "We both thought that was pretty funny."

Polly giggled and tucked her head under Clarissa's chin.

"Well, Little Girl, why don't we find Master Nathan? Maybe he'll share one of his soldiers with a sweet little girl like you." He took Polly up in his arms and whispered to Clarissa, "I'll tell him you're here for his lesson but that may only slow him down."

She liked for Adam to pay attention to Polly, for her fatherless daughter had an empty spot in her little heart. But she stopped herself. *Why ruin my day with thoughts like that?* She placed Nathan's new music on the piano and waited for him. In a moment, Polly toddled in with an old wooden soldier in her hand.

"Thank you, Dr. Norcutt," she called out to him. "Maybe that will keep her entertained while I try to teach Nathan something."

"Not exactly the lead soldier she wanted, but we negotiated a reasonable solution. Have Magnolia watch Polly for you. Good luck with the piano lesson."

Nathan dragged in after putting off his lesson as long as possible. He simply was not interested, and—if Clarissa was entirely honest— never had been. His mood continued until Clarissa was at her wits' end. When the lesson was over, she was so exasperated that she and Polly left without saying goodbye or noticing the sheet music left beside the piano.

Adam saw patients all morning, but before noon he found time to talk to Nathan about the damaged racquet.

"Last night I found a badminton racquet with a broken string on the back porch steps." Nathan did not respond. "You'll lose your privileges if you can't take better care of our equipment, son. I'll see if I can repair it, but it may be ruined. What do you have to say for yourself?"

"I didn't do it."

Adam gave him a puzzled look and accepted his answer. "I'll talk to Miss Clarissa and Rosalie about it. Maybe they know what happened. It didn't just break its own string. This kind of damage wouldn't happen by accident."

Adam asked Rosalie later in the day about the racquet.

"Master Nathan put his things away before I left. I never touch them racquets."

"Then, perhaps Master Nathan isn't telling me the truth."

"Oh, now he's in a peck of trouble, ain't he?"

"Correct, but I'll take care of it. Don't worry about it anymore."

When Adam confronted Nathan again, after a long silence, he confessed.

"I hid the racquet under my bed instead of putting it away when Rosalie left."

"How did it get outside?"

"I played with it after supper."

"This isn't like you, Nathan. I'm surprised at your behavior."

"Papa, I was going to put it away when it got dark, but then I broke the string. I guess I got scared." His voice started trembling.

"I understand, but that doesn't allow you to lie to me about this, does it?" Nathan shrugged his shoulders. "I hope you've learned not to lie to me or anyone else. However, to be sure you remember this lesson, I want you to bring me your marbles. You may have them back at the end of the week."

Nathan stalked back into his room. When he returned his face was red with fury.

"Here!" He threw the bag of marbles at his father and burst into tears. Marbles went everywhere and Adam erupted.

"Pick up your confounded marbles, Nathan! Bring them to me and go stand over there in that corner. Don't move a muscle for fifteen minutes. I mean what I say."

A crestfallen Nathan followed his father's instructions, but stood sniffling in the corner. Adam checked his pocket watch before he walked onto the front porch to bring his temper under control. As he leaned against the railing he saw Clarissa and Polly returning for her forgotten music.

"I'm back for the sheet music I left by the piano," she called out. "I hurried away because I lost my patience with Nathan's lack of interest."

"Your music is on the hall tree shelf." He sat on the top step with his elbows resting on his knees. "You shouldn't have left. You missed today's main event."

"What happened?"

"Nathan lied to me about ruining a badminton racquet."

"Surely he wouldn't lie to you?"

"That's not even the end of the story. Shall I tell you more?"

When she nodded, he told her about taking away Nathan's marbles as punishment.

"I think that was warranted."

"Wait, there's more. When he brought them to me, he threw them at me."

"Oh, no—this isn't like him at all."

"I stood him in the corner for fifteen minutes and I'm out here trying to get a grip on my temper. He's inside still crying. What's come over the lad? What have I done to make him misbehave and lie and throw things at me?"

"I can't think of a thing."

"In the past I've only reprimanded him when he's been out of line. But today when things kept escalating I knew I had to be firm."

"Will you tell him I know about this?"

"Before he confessed, I told him I'd ask you and Rosalie about the racquet and that did the trick. He didn't want to get you in trouble so he owned up to it."

"Perhaps he's feeling secure enough to risk being a bad boy."

Adam looked at her, surprised.

"He's probably been working overtime to be a good boy so you won't send him back to his mother. Now that he knows you are going to keep him and take care of him, it's safe to misbehave once in awhile."

"You mean, now that he's happy here with me, this is the thanks I get?"

"He's certainly fighting me over piano lessons, so it looks like Nathan is a normal boy. I think it's rather sweet."

"If that boy were a scoundrel, you'd defend him, wouldn't you?"

"And you wouldn't?"

"Yes, when I first brought him here, I would have," Adam agreed. "But I expect him to behave now that he knows what I expect of him."

"He's an exceptional boy, Dr. Norcutt. Don't ever doubt that. But there'll be a lot of scrapes between now and when he's grown. You'll both do just fine." Polly stirred and Clarissa reached over to rock the carriage.

Adam stood up to go back inside. "Nathan's time is up. Perhaps the three of us should talk together about this someday?"

"I promise to look very stern." She gathered up her music and tried to hide her smile about Adam's parenting struggle.

He waved to her and was again thankful for her friendship—but this time his gratitude lingered.

PART THREE

"The end is where we start from."
—T.S. Eliot

Chapter 47

The door of the Trinity Community Church flew open with a loud crash. Clarissa, practicing on the piano for the next Sunday's service, looked up to see Rosalie running up the center aisle.

"What's the matter Rosalie? You scared me nearly to death. Are you all right?"

"Miss Clarissa! You gotta come! Miss Ida's fainted over at the store and Mr. Tom can't wake her up. He's tried everything!"

"Oh, dear God, what's happened?" She banged the cover of the piano down and ran with Rosalie out of the church.

"Where's Nathan?"

"He's at home with Magnolia."

"Go back to the clinic for the doctor."

"They already fetched him."

"Then find Nathan. Don't let him follow his father. Go tell Mrs. Jackson I need for her to keep Polly a little longer."

"Yes'm."

When Clarissa ran up the steps into the Lewis Mercantile, people stood around in hushed clusters. Some held hands in a tight circle and prayed for Ida. Adam knelt beside her. She was as pale as a shadow. Tom stood nearby with a stricken look on his face. She hurried toward him and he shook his head when he saw her.

"Oh, no, Tom! She's going to be all right, isn't she?"

"We can't—bring her back." His shoulders shook with suppressed sobs. "Pray to God Doc can do something."

"What happened?"

"She cried out for me and clutched her bodice. She crumpled against the cracker barrels and fell to the floor before I could reach her. She hasn't moved since."

Glory Be!

They watched and waited for some word from Adam. When he stood to his feet in tears, the little audience knew what he would say before he spoke.

"There's nothing I can do for her. God bless her, she's gone. I can't find a pulse. Her heart just stopped and..."

He grabbed Tom in a rough embrace and walked arm in arm with him to the back of the store. They talked for a few moments, Tom nodded and Adam looked back at the shocked audience still in the store. No one moved.

"Clarissa, I'm going home with Tom. I'll send for the undertaker, but could you stay here with Ida until he comes? Tom won't leave unless you stay with her." He turned away from the others and whispered, "See if you can find something to cover her. Surely there's something around here that will do." His voice trailed off.

Clarissa nodded and went looking for a white tablecloth. She patted Ida's cheek before spreading the cloth over her. *Am I play acting? Surely this can't be happening? Not to Ida—not my best friend!*

Steven Jackson appeared out of nowhere at Tom's side.

"God help you, Tom, I've just heard. What a tragedy for you and all of us who love you and your family."

"My family! How will I tell the twins?" Waves of grief flowed over him.

"Where are they?" asked Adam.

"They're at the parsonage. Sophie's watching them because we expected a big shipment this morning and we knew they'd just be underfoot. Thank the good Lord they aren't here to see her like this."

Adam blew his nose and assessed the situation.

"Reverend, can you take the twins back home? You and I can be with Tom when he tells them about Ida. Clarissa, here's the store key to lock up after the undertaker comes. Tom, let's take you home." The men left the store through the back door, but not before Tom looked one last time at the white shroud covering his beloved.

The rest of the morning was a blur for Clarissa. As soon as the undertaker and his assistant left with Ida, she asked the shoppers to finish their purchases.

"If you can pay now, I'll take the money over to Mr. Tom."

Aunt Mag was the last to leave. She bought enough flour and yeast to make several batches of rolls and bread.

"I'm going home to start baking. I'll have lots of fresh bread over at Tom's by tomorrow morning. I'll cook up a basket of cookies for them young'uns, too."

"Thank you, Aunt Mag. We can always count on you."

Clarissa found a length of black cloth for a swath over the front door and put the "CLOSED" sign in the window. She knew that the community had already slipped into the mode reserved for funerals and grieving families. After she gathered up the money from the cash box and the key to the store, she locked up and hurried to the parsonage for Polly. When she saw Steven leaving ahead of her with Lester and Lydia, her face twisted with sobs.

Sophie greeted her with an understanding hug. "A father should never have to tell two such sweet children that their mother is gone, should he?"

"Of course not, Sophie, this is just awful. I'm in such a state. Ida was in perfect health. We were going for a walk this afternoon. How can this happen out of the blue?"

"You know I can't answer that, but I'll do whatever I can to help. We all will."

"What will I do without her? I'm so alone, and now this." She began to sob, and Sophie put her arm around her.

"Just let God comfort you, honey. You know He promises to bless us when we mourn."

"Unfortunately," Clarissa snapped, "I'm already well acquainted with God's abiding comfort in grief. I just don't know how much more I can stand to lose."

Sophie looked a little startled at the outburst, but the compassion in her eyes didn't waver. "We'll be here for you, Clarissa, and we must all be strong for Tom and those children. They're going to need our help."

The comment about Lester and Lydia cleared Clarissa's mind. She picked up Polly and her things to leave.

"I must take Tom's key and store money to him. The undertaker said he would have Ida back before dark and I need to be there

Glory Be!

when...when she comes home." She walked away from the parsonage and called over her shoulder to Sophie, "I'm sorry I lost my temper."

"Don't worry, I know you're upset."

As she pushed Polly's carriage along to the Lewis home, she remembered with a start that twice that morning the doctor had addressed her as "Clarissa," not "Miss Clarissa."

"Polly, should I start calling him by his first name? Adam? Would that be proper?"

When Clarissa arrived at the Lewis house, nothing seemed right. Tom struggled to console the twins. Out in the kitchen, Steven and Adam looked exasperated and out of place as they tried to boil water for tea. They glanced up with relief when Clarissa walked in, as if she might make things normal again. Without speaking to either she began setting out cups and saucers for tea. Ida's kitchen was nearly as familiar to her as her own.

"What should we do for Tom?" asked Steven.

"I don't know."

"Can you think of anything that would help the children?" asked Adam.

"Gentlemen, right now I'm doing the only thing I can think of. I've just lost my best friend, so please don't expect much of me."

"I'm sorry, forgive us," Adam said. "We don't mean to be unkind. We're all feeling a bit helpless. I failed her when she needed me most."

Steven stepped into the role he knew best. "Perhaps we should have a prayer together." The three friends held hands while Steven prayed. "Lord, we feel sad right now. Please, wrap Your loving arms around all of us. Especially help Tom with Lester and Lydia. Give us the wisdom we need to support this dear family. We thank you for Ida's exemplary life and for our Savior, Amen."

Adam's hand lingered for a moment with Clarissa's. *I wondered if she noticed.*

The friends puzzled over what to do next. Steven went in to Tom and the twins to offer whatever comfort he could. Clarissa and Adam stayed in the kitchen and tried to prepare for the mourners who would start calling soon.

"Dr. Norcutt, I think Ida stores some extra chairs in their barn. Maybe you could bring them in. I'm sure we'll need them when people start arriving."

"I'll see what I can find." Adam, grateful to have a chore, any chore, returned covered with straw, but with a dusty chair in each hand. "I found these in the hay mow. There are several more if we need them."

"Good! That's a big help. Here's a towel to wipe them off."

Tom came into the kitchen and glanced around as if looking for Ida. Clarissa put a cup of tea in his hand which he sipped before he spoke.

"Clarissa, we've set the funeral for tomorrow afternoon. Will you help us plan the service? You know Ida's favorite hymns, don't you?"

"Of course, I'll be there in just a moment. But what we can do for Lydia and Lester?"

"I honestly don't know. They're so upset. If Nathan could come over later, he and Lester could run around outside. I think that would be a big distraction. And right now Lydia is playing with Polly."

The day progressed as consoling friends and family members came to pay their respects to Tom and the children. A steady flow of food and refreshments helped everyone through the sad occasion. Clarissa kept things organized and tidy in the kitchen. Adam welcomed guests at the front door. When they were alone in the kitchen for a moment, she spoke to him.

"You know, this is our church's first funeral since Elliot's." Her voice trembled with emotion and shock. "All of a sudden I feel like the breath is knocked out of me." She leaned against the dry sink and covered her face with shaking hands.

"You've carried the day around here for Tom and all of us." He put a hand on her shoulder. "Why don't I escort you home to rest a bit? You've done your fair share today."

"You're right, I'd best do that. I feel a bit undone. Be sure Prudence Phillips keeps an eye on Polly—she should take a nap in the guest room. I'll come back for her later." Despite his insistence, Clarissa refused Adam's offer to walk home with her.

"All right, but stay home and rest." She agreed and disappeared out the kitchen door.

Back at home, she didn't rest but walked to the creek where she spread a quilt under the willows. She lay staring up into the willows for a long time. She alternately wept and laughed as she reminisced about her close friend, Ida. They were having their afternoon visit after all.

"I'll try to help your family, but how, I don't know. I'll muddle through somehow. If you were here you'd tell me exactly what to do, wouldn't you?" She smiled through her tears. "Oh, one other thing: What hymns do you want at your service tomorrow?"

When Clarissa returned to the Lewis house, fortunately Adam walked with her to Ida's casket, for when she saw the still, pale form of her best friend, her knees buckled. He caught her before she slipped to the floor and helped her to a chair. While several friends hovered nearby, he knelt beside her.

"Why didn't you stay at home as I asked?"

"I wanted to be here for Ida's homecoming."

He turned to the others in the room. "Widow Chambers will be fine. The shock of seeing Miss Ida laid out was a bit too much for her. She needs a moment to recover her composure." He turned back to Clarissa and whispered, "Now that you and your stubborn little heart are here, I'm going to ask Mrs. Phillips to bring you some food. You haven't eaten all day, have you?"

When she shook her head, he spoke to Prudence who hurried to carry out his suggestion.

"When you've eaten and feel better, I will escort you and Polly home. No arguing."

"All right, Dr. Norcutt," she said in a small voice. But not before she noted that she was once again "Mrs. Chambers" and "Widow Chambers," no longer simply Clarissa.

Clarissa's flawless music for Ida's service preceded Steven Jackson's memorial comments. Ida's stellar life was honored and witness was given to her faith. Within an hour, she was laid to rest. Her family and friends surrounded her graveside to pay their last respects. Fresh flowers from local gardens covered the mounded soil over her grave. Only yesterday she had cut flowers from her own garden to take to The Mercantile.

For days caring people offered their help with armloads of food for Tom and the twins. Aunt Mag's bread and cookies arrived at regular intervals. But when people had done their fair share in the mourning of Ida, the focus turned to Tom. Some things only he could do for his family and his business. After a week passed he returned to the store, but the memories of Ida's last moments there overwhelmed him and he walked away after an hour.

Tom's friends felt helpless as they watched him grieve and struggle with his heartbreak. Clarissa often invited the twins over to help with Polly, but after they baked dozens of cookies and several cakes, they were bored. One morning, she stopped by the store.

"Tom, I've run out of things to do with Lester and Lydia. I think they would enjoy assisting you here, don't you?"

"Naw, they'd just be in my way." He thought for a moment. "Nope, not a bit of help."

"You could give it a try, couldn't you? They really need to be with you right now. It would help if they could spend the day here with you."

"Not a good idea."

"So they'll stay home by themselves every day?"

"I guess so. They're too old for a governess and they have chores to do."

"Well, I know you'll find a way to take good care of them."

But the days went on, and Tom did nothing. Either the twins were with Clarissa or at home alone. Occasionally another mother would invite them over, but more often than not, the Lewis children were unsupervised. People began talking about "poor Tom" and "those poor children." He received ample advice from concerned friends.

"Why don't you send for that maiden aunt of yours over in Lexington?" But Tom had no spare room for her.

"Can't you hire someone to be with the children and help with the household chores?" But Tom feared a servant would steal him blind. Regardless of how much it might help him and his twins, he refused to consider suggestions. Clarissa asked him about one more possibility before she gave up trying to help.

"Tom, I'm a store keeper's daughter, so I know what you are dealing with. While you are busy running the store, your children expect their mother to be at home for them."

Tom growled a grumpy reply which she couldn't understand.

"I have one more solution for you to think about."

"What's that?" He stuck the stub of a pencil behind his ear.

"What if I come over to the store for a couple of weeks and teach the twins how to help you. What do you think?"

"That might work."

Chapter 48

Adam suffered in his own way over losing Ida. He knew he couldn't cure every ill, knowledge hard-earned over a career that spanned many years. However, he still he struggled with watching Ida's life disappear through his fingers. Often he wanted to talk about this with Clarissa, but she spent most days with Lester and Lydia at the Lewis Mercantile. Every time they saw one another, she hurried away to tend to some pressing chore. Always punctual for Nathan's piano lessons, she came and went with no time for visiting. Sometimes he found himself almost shy around her, a feeling he was not used to. He wrote in his journal:

"I'm so aware of her broken spirit, but I'm determined to win her affection—if she'll have me. I know I must care deeply and be cautious of her past wounds. Since losing Ida, she's been consumed with grief. She seems relieved of her sorrow by helping for hours at The Lewis Mercantile. I'll just have to be patient. At least she's not cringing away from me anymore."

His resolve to be patient did not prevent his wanting to be near her. He touched the back of her waist when opening a door for her, or held her elbow when assisting her with Polly's carriage. After helping her with her shawl, his hand lingered on her shoulder as he opened the front door with his other hand. He liked to watch her smile and wondered when he might kiss her or hold her in his arms. He never tired of her presence and her spontaneous, often humorous, responses to him. Above all, he enjoyed her company and her ways with their children.

Even though Clarissa knew from Magnolia that the doctor and Nellie had argued, she was unaware that Adam's relationship with Miss Nellie was over. They'd had lovers' spats in the past and she felt sure it was only a matter of time before they reconciled and announced their engagement. She never noticed Magnolia smiling when Adam was attentive to her. And she never heard her comment, "I do believe Mr. Doctor heard what I told to him."

The two weeks that Clarissa agreed to work with the twins at the Lewis Mercantile stretched into six weeks. She enjoyed having a destination every day, and being in a store again made her feel at home and secure. Her childhood memories of helping her father made her a good teacher for the twins. They started assisting Tom, and now he welcomed having them there with him. Not only did the children benefit, but Tom's outlook also brightened. The store's fabric sales expanded from her presence at the store, but the day came when she knew it was time to move on.

"Tom, being here for the twins has helped me adjust to losing Ida, but it's time for Polly and me to return to our normal routine."

He did not argue with her. "The Lewis Mercantile will certainly miss you."

With Tom's family coping well on their own, she knew she had done the right thing to train Lydia and Lester. It was her gift to Ida. But once again she was forced to face her compulsion to step in whenever she saw a need.

One afternoon as Clarissa finished with Nathan's lesson, Adam asked her and Polly to stay for supper. "Nathan and I are tired of eating alone, aren't we?"

The Norcutt men begged until the Chambers ladies stayed. After giving thanks for the food, Adam asked, "What shall we talk about? I'm tired of local gossip, American politics and news from Kentucky farmers."

"Why, Dr. Norcutt, are you pining for England?"

"No, but I'm ready for one of our interesting discussions. Can't you suggest a topic?"

"Hmmm, we can't argue about religion any more, can we? How about this: Do you think the freed slaves are ever going to be given any land from the government?"

"No one knows when or if that will happen. Constant speculation and a lot of rumors are circulating, but I fear most are a far cry from realistic. Many former slaves do nothing while they wait for that promised 'mule and forty acres.' A lot of expectations are going begging."

"I do feel for them. All they've known is plantation life and it's difficult for them to find another way of getting by. Even with the problems of slavery, most of our slaves were fed and given shelter."

Nathan launched himself into the midst of the conversation. "Miss Clarissa, did you own any slaves?"

"I'll tell you when you finish your vegetables."

Nathan devoured his vegetables as his father took another generous helping of pot roast from the platter in front of him.

"All right, I'm done."

"Good for you, Nathan. To answer your question, my grandparents in Georgia owned a large cotton plantation. When it came time to pick their cotton, they needed lots of help, so they owned a lot of slaves."

Adam spoke up. "On my trips to the shanties, I've seen many cripples due to the years they spent bent double in those cotton fields. They call their aches and pains 'the misery.' It's not exactly a medical term, but a perfect description of how they suffer."

"I still remember the slaves dragging those heavy sacks of cotton behind them. Even as a child, I could tell it was difficult work. But Nathan, do you know what? They sang praises to God as they worked. If you listen, you'll still hear freed folks singing while they work."

"When you were little, did you have your own slave?" He was still curious about slavery.

"No, my parents didn't own slaves. Earline, a wonderful maid, worked for our family and we loved her dearly. My father always paid wages to people who worked for us."

"Like Magnolia?"

"That's right. But Earline lived in a room on the backside of our house. She didn't come and go every day like Magnolia does."

Nathan's eyes narrowed as he thought about this. He blurted out another question.

"Papa, why can't Magnolia live here? Couldn't she use that room behind the kitchen?"

"Is this customary?" asked Adam. "Do women who work in town live on the premises?"

"Yes, many local families provide housing for their servants on their property."

"We'll have to give this some thought, son. And see what Magnolia thinks about it. But for now, I have another question for Miss Clarissa. What's your opinion about this President Grant? Do you think he can mold this divided country into a nation again? Can The South rally behind the general of the army that defeated it? People say that Andrew Johnson only half succeeded in this endeavor."

"At least President Johnson had his chance."

"I suppose he did. To follow an assassination must be a terrible way to become president."

"Indeed. Well, I need to go on home now, but Polly and I must invite you to supper at our house soon. I'd like to discuss the possibility of bringing a schoolmaster for Springdale. It's high time, don't you think?"

"Lovely idea! I agree we need a school here. Tutors and parents can only do so much."

"Sorry I can't linger. Tom asked me to come in tomorrow for one more day to help him organize some more new fabrics."

"How's he doing these days? Any better?"

"He's getting by. Now that he's letting the twins help him, he doesn't seem so sad. Honestly, he never talks much. Between you and me, he can be pretty grumpy."

"When I try to talk with him, he barely replies. We'll keep trying."

She clucked over the mess that Polly had made and excused herself from the table. Adam made sure that Nathan returned his napkin to his silver napkin ring. He smiled because Clarissa suggested another time for them to be together.

Perhaps my patience is starting to pay off.

Chapter 49

By the time Clarissa and Polly arrived at the Lewis Mercantile the next morning, Tom had unwrapped most of the large bundles of fabric.

"Morning," he said without looking up.

"Good morning," she replied as she tied on her apron. "It looks like you've already done everything."

"Couldn't sleep last night, so I came in before the shipment arrived."

"What's left to do?"

"Could you organize and catalog the new bolts?"

"Certainly." She went right to work and kept chatting with Tom. "My sewing customers will come to The Mercantile in droves when they hear about these. These fabrics are the best we've ever had. Don't you agree?"

Tom's comments were sparse. He nodded, muttered something occasionally, but never looked up. She created a window display for the new fabrics and made a sign to announce their arrival. Mid-morning, she made coffee over the old black stove in the back of the store. Tom stopped working long enough to sit by the stove with a tin cup of steaming coffee. Polly played with the discarded packing from the delivery of fabrics.

"You've been such a help around here, Clarissa. I haven't thanked you properly."

"I haven't felt neglected, Tom. I'm happy to help."

"I know, but to show my appreciation I'd like for you to join me for supper at the Excelsior this Saturday."

Her thoughts screeched to a halt. *Dinner? With Tom Lewis?*

"I. . .I suppose I can go along, but I'd have to bring Polly."

"We've thought of that. The twins will take care of Polly for the evening. It's their part in our thank you."

"How nice of the twins. If they're willing, of course I'll accept." When she finished with the fabrics, she and Polly hurried home. She needed time to absorb this unexpected invitation.

As Clarissa weeded her flowerbeds that afternoon, a weary Adam rode by. He was returning from a house call at the Feathersons where they were coping with measles. Clarissa waved him down and caught Fancy's bridle.

"How are the Feathersons doing?" She squinted against the bright afternoon sun. "Do you think Rosalie can avoid the measles?"

He removed his straw hat and wiped his brow. "Rosalie had the measles a long time ago, so she's immune, but Jacob's boys are very sick. I hope the worst is over."

"I dread these childhood diseases for Polly, but it's best to get them over with early in her life, isn't it?" Polly hung behind her mother's skirts and peeked around at Adam.

"Usually." He knew it was true, but he hated the thought of tiny Polly with the measles. He leaned down to greet her where she clung to Clarissa's skirts. When he straightened, he surveyed their work of the afternoon. "Your flowers are having a banner year."

"I hope so." She hesitated. "Could I ask you something?"

"Of course, what's on your mind?"

"Have you ever eaten at the Excelsior Hotel?"

"Oh, yes," he said with a sardonic smile. "Nathan and I eat there regularly due to my poor cooking skills."

"Tom Lewis has invited me there for supper this Saturday night. The twins have offered to watch Polly for the evening." Seeing his puzzled expression, she explained, "It's their thanks for my help at the store. I thought you'd like to know he's not so withdrawn anymore."

"After all, Ida's been gone three months. I'm glad he's getting out and about. By the way, The Excelsior's roast beef is my favorite." Fancy was restless to be underway. "Be sure to order it," he said over his shoulder as he left. "And wash up a bit."

She looked at her muddy hands and apron covered with grass stains and dirt. "I'll do that and I'll let you know if I like the beef," she called after him.

Adam went on his way into town, pleased that Clarissa stopped him to visit. He'd been thinking of her on his way home. If he weren't so weary, he would have welcomed a cup of tea. If Clarissa weren't covered with dirt, he felt sure she would have invited him in. As he curried and stabled Fancy for the night, he puzzled over Tom's dinner invitation to Clarissa.

What in tarnation is going on?

Over the next few days Clarissa fretted over having dinner with Tom Lewis. Her mind raced over and over the same details. She even talked out loud to herself.

"I know Tom is a widower and Ida is gone to glory, but this seems so strange. It's too soon after Ida's death, isn't it? I can almost hear Miss Prudence and Aunt Mag scolding me for having designs on the shopkeeper when Ida's not yet cold in her grave."

As Saturday evening neared, she calmed down enough to look forward to the evening. The restaurant at the Excelsior Hotel was not elegant, but it was the best that Springdale had to offer. She knew she would order the beef the doctor recommended.

Tom and the twins arrived on time. Clarissa gave a few instructions as Tom held the door open for her. "Just be sure she has her yellow blanket, and she'll go right to sleep."

Clarissa broke the silence as they made their way into town. "Lovely evening, don't you think?"

"Certainly is," remarked Tom, but then remained silent. He guided his horse and buggy over to the front of the Excelsior Hotel. Leon, who worked for the hotel in the evenings, held the horse's bridle while Tom assisted Clarissa from the buggy. She smoothed the skirt of her cotton sateen dress and straightened her bonnet. When they were seated at a table by the window, she noticed people staring at them. She hadn't anticipated being on display with Tom, and knew the event would be an item of gossip before church started the next day.

The waiter came over with the dining choices for the evening. Clarissa was delighted that roast beef was among them.

Glory Be!

"Dr. Norcutt told me their beef roast is delicious."

"Hmm."

"What will you order?"

"Not sure." After a long pause he decided on the chicken fricassee. Throughout the meal, Clarissa tried to engage him in some sort of conversation. She even tried being silent to see if he might talk to her. After he finished his dinner, he wiped his mouth with a flourish.

"Now — how about some dessert?"

He called the waiter over. Clarissa chose bread pudding with hard sauce and Tom selected apple pie. The waiter brought a small silver coffee pot to their table. She looked around the room, still trying to think of something else to talk about.

"Aren't you proud of your twins and their help around your store lately?"

"Yes, I am. Thank you for helping them learn the business." He launched into a boring monologue about his store which ended with, "I think The Lewis Mercantile has a bright future."

"You have every right to be pleased with your store. I'm sure it will continue to flourish."

"Yes, I must say I'm pleased. And I have some special plans for the future. For instance, I'd like to involve you more at the store."

Clarissa blinked. "You would?"

"Your fabrics have sold well. You could expand that department. Also, since you are no stranger to how a general store works, I would like to make you a partner in The Lewis Mercantile. You could assist me in running the store."

"Wait, Tom! You're asking me to become a partner in your store?"

"Yes, and if you care to invest I'll make you one of the owners. What do you think? Might you be interested?"

"I'm really floored, Tom. I don't know what to say."

"Don't feel pressured, Clarissa, but think about it. I've had some documents drawn up with our collaboration in mind."

He pushed a document in a blue paper cover toward her. She flipped through the legal papers without reading them.

"I'll consider this, but it'll take a lot of thought and prayer on my part before I can give you an answer." She slipped the papers onto her lap.

"There's one other thing, Clarissa." He cleared his throat. "Will you marry me?"

Her cup clattered onto its saucer.

She choked and whispered behind her napkin. "What on earth?" She looked around to be sure no one was listening before she spoke again. "You want us to be married?"

"Yes, I think you would be an excellent partner for me and mother for my family."

"But Ida—she just passed." She struggled to keep her voice low.

"I'm putting the past aside. I want to go on in life with you as my wife and mother of my twins."

"Good Gracious, Tom, I'm speechless. What about Polly?"

"Don't worry. You know me well enough to know I'll welcome Polly into my family."

She nodded and thought of another concern. "Forgive me, but what part does love play in your proposal?"

"We've known each other for years." He cleared his throat again. "Of course, we've not been. . .romantically involved. . .but surely affection will grow between us. Don't you agree?"

"I can't answer that question, Tom. I never dreamed that you'd propose to me."

"I asked you to be a partner in the store before I proposed so you'd know I have respect and admiration for you. Please think about this. After all, you need a husband and I need a wife."

"I'm overwhelmed, Tom, and completely surprised." Both ill at ease, they finished their coffee quickly. Tom called for Leon to bring his buggy around. The trip back to Clarissa's was wrapped in silence. She couldn't put words together for polite conversation.

At home, Lydia greeted Clarissa at the front door. "I put Polly to bed sound asleep!" Both she and Lester beamed as though they had superintended a miracle.

"Did you enjoy your dinner, Miss Clarissa?" asked Lester.

"Yes, my roast beef was delicious and your father enjoyed his meal, as well. Didn't you, Tom?" Tom nodded. "Thank you for minding Polly. This evening was a rare treat."

She could tell they knew nothing about their father's true agenda for the evening. Tom sent the children to the buggy and lingered by the door. She wondered if he might kiss her good night. After all, he just asked her to marry him. Instead, he took her hand and bowed over it. As he released it, he brushed it with his moustache. His lips never touched her hand.

"Thank you for a wonderful dinner, Tom. I have a lot to think about."

When the door closed, she went to her bedroom and threw herself onto the bed. She stared at the ceiling for a long time.

What am I supposed to do now, Lord?

Chapter 50

"Why are those silly mockingbirds still singing in the middle of the night? They don't know when to quit." Clarissa rubbed her eyes and saw a faint wisp of daylight coming through the curtains. Sunday morning had dawned and she still wore her best dress. When the memory of Tom's proposal came to mind, she sat bolt upright.

My stars! Did that really happen or was I dreaming?

Since Polly still slept, she took a cup of coffee outside to sit by the spring. Perhaps watching the sunrise would help her sort out this bizarre turn of events. With her back to the old shed and its memories, she thought over Tom's surprising proposal. Details swarmed into her head. Tom's business opportunities as well his offer of marriage had come as a complete shock, but how should she answer him?

She knew she needed God's wisdom. "Dear Lord, I can't imagine being married to Tom Lewis. Is he Your answer to my prayers? Can he possibly be ready to marry so soon after Ida's death? Is this simply about missing a woman in his bed? Can I be the mother of thirteen year-old twins? What would it be like to be a wife again? What about his business proposals? God, I'm in a quandary and need Your guidance."

When Polly called for her, she went inside. She was dreading the day because the news of her dinner with Tom at the Excelsior was probably already spreading like wildfire in Springdale. What if anyone had overheard his marriage proposal? She decided to hold her head high, go to church and play the piano. After all, nothing improper happened between her and Tom at the Excelsior or anywhere else. Nevertheless, she felt uneasy.

Clarissa and Polly were not sharing their usual Sunday dinner at the Jacksons. Sophie had worked all week to prepare a sumptuous meal for a group of visiting preachers and their wives. A bit edgy to play in front of their visitors, Clarissa hoped her music would do Pastor Steven's sermon justice.

When she and Polly arrived at church, Adam and Nathan were already seated. He motioned to her and spoke in a loud whisper.

"May I talk with you a moment?" Putting her music in place, she went over to them. "Might you go out to the shanties with me this afternoon? I am treating several children and you would be a big help. You're so good with the little ones." Unbeknownst to her, he had arranged to see only children with this invitation in mind.

"Of course I can. Shall I bring Polly along? Perhaps I could find someone to mind her."

"Why don't I bring Nathan and Magnolia to your place when I call for you? They can spend the afternoon together." Another part of his plan.

"Sounds like a perfect solution, but tell Nathan the creek is off limits today. Magnolia worries about the children playing around the water."

"I'll do that. Be ready at two o'clock."

The church service continued and the congregation behaved well for the visiting dignitaries. Everyone sang at the top of their lungs, said enthusiastic "amens," and put large offering envelopes in the box by the door. Once Clarissa embarrassed herself by starting off on the wrong hymn, but she recovered quickly and managed a smooth transition. Tom's proposal had intruded into her thoughts and distracted her.

After church, Tom came over to her but except for a cordial greeting, he stood silent. She longed to chat with a friend, but Ida was gone to heaven and Sophie had rushed home to tend to her guests. She felt trapped by Tom and his silence until the twins began to visit with her.

Adam guided his rig over and called out. "I'll pick you up around two. All right?"

"I'll be ready, Dr. Norcutt." She explained Adam's request to Tom.

"I'm going with the good doctor over to the shanties this afternoon. Some children need his attention and he's asked for my help."

"Should he be working on the Lord's Day? Should you?" He stared over her head without meeting her gaze.

"I think the doctor's work today comes under the 'ox in a ditch' category, don't you? During the week he's too busy at the clinic to go to the river, so almost every Sunday afternoon he tries to go."

"I see."

She could tell Tom was opposed to Adam's good will if it involved working on a Sunday. They would have to discuss Adam's charitable doctoring some time soon. Surely Tom wouldn't oppose helping these poor folk who had no other medical care, would he?

"May I take you home?" asked Tom.

"No, but thank you, Tom. Today I have Polly's carriage, so we'll walk home."

On the way home, she smiled.

How nice for a gentleman, possibly my future husband, to offer to escort me home.

Clarissa was waiting on the front porch for Adam to arrive with Nathan and Magnolia well before two o'clock. She sat with a pencil and paper to list the reasons for and against accepting Tom's proposal. The longer she pondered this possible miracle of God's provision, the more she could see no reason to reject Tom Lewis. As she listed reasons why she should say "yes," her list kept growing.

Reasons to Accept Tom's offer:
1. He is a Christian gentleman with no obvious faults.
2. His looks are pleasant and clean cut.
3. He assures me that affection between us will grow.
4. He will be a good provider.
5. He will accept Polly as his daughter.
6. We both need a spouse.
7. He will make me a business partner, perhaps part owner at the store.
8. I've known him for years.

Reasons to Reject Tom's offer:
1. It's too soon after Ida's death.
2. I'm not in love with him.
3. I can't be sure affection will grow between us.

Glory Be!

Tom had always been the nice man married to her best friend. She knew Ida adored him, but could she come to love him? Could this be one of those marriages of convenience that developed the kind of love and passion she longed for? They would have to pray about it and work on it. She had a comfortable feeling about having a husband of Tom's caliber. She drew a deep breath.

"I think I'll accept his proposal."

When she saw the doctor's wagon coming around the corner, she added one other notation to her list: Not very talkative.

Magnolia, delighted to have an afternoon with nothing to do but watch the children, hurried up the path. Nathan ran ahead of her. Clarissa kept telling her what to do for Polly until Adam became impatient.

"Come along, Miss Clarissa. We must go. Magnolia knows what to do."

She hurried to the wagon and they were on their way. As they chatted, she decided to tell him about Tom's proposal. She couldn't hold her secret any longer.

"Want to know the real reason Tom took me to dinner last night?"

"I suppose so. What happened?"

"After our dessert, he asked me to marry him."

She waited for his reaction, but he said nothing. After clenching his jaw several times, he put Fancy into a fast pace and concentrated on the road ahead. Going at such a high speed, they skidded around one of the hills.

"My soul! Slow down, Dr. Norcutt. You could've killed us!"

"Hang on. We're late."

When they arrived at the shanties, he climbed into the back of the wagon and handed his supplies to her. They struggled to set up a wooden folding table, but it kept collapsing.

"This blasted table. Forget it. We'll work from the back of the wagon." He swore under his breath.

"Wait, surely we can make it work. Try again." This time the old table held firm.

"Are you always such a saint?"

"Hardly. You know me better than that."

When he smiled at her reply, she avoided his blue eyes and began organizing the line of parents and children. He showed her what to do to assist him and the work of the afternoon began. He frequently dropped instruments or reached for the wrong medicine.

"Dr. Norcutt, are you all right?" She retrieved a jar of salve he knocked off the table.

"I'm fine." But he still seemed out of sorts.

Clarissa kept busy helping to calm the children who were terrified in spite of her reassurances. Because the sun was getting lower on the horizon, Adam had to shut everything down while mothers with sick children still waited in line. After making sure that no child was seriously ill, he assured them he would return the next Sunday. The supplies and the old table were loaded into the back of the wagon.

"I hope you'll go slower on our way home." She gave the bow on her bonnet an extra tug.

"Sorry, but we must keep up the pace to be home before dark."

Fancy moved right along, but this time Adam slowed her down on the curves. Spring was in full sway but they concentrated on the road rushing along rather than the lovely spring panorama. They talked a bit about the children he treated during the afternoon. One little girl had screamed in fear until Clarissa held her and sang to her while Adam painted her sore throat. By the time she was back in her mother's arms, she smiled and waved goodbye to them.

"Clarissa, you have an amazing gift with children."

"Thank you, but you're the one with the healing gifts they need. However, I do love to see their tears turn into smiles." After a moment, she changed the subject. "You haven't said anything about Tom's proposal."

"I haven't any comments."

"Really? Why not?"

"I don't want to spoil your excitement. You must be very happy."

"Yes, I am." *I'm sure I am*, Clarissa told herself. *Of course I am.*

He grimaced and shook his head.

"Doctor Norcutt? What is it? I want to know."

After a slight hesitation, he asked, "Do you really want to know what I think?" She turned to face him. "I think you'll make a big mistake if you marry Tom Lewis."

"Why do you have any doubts at all?" *This man is so audacious. How dare he be so opinionated?* Her voice rose. "He's a nice Christian gentleman who wants to take care of Polly and me. He's going to make me a partner and maybe an owner in the Mercantile. We've known and respected one another for years. I think we can be happy together."

"So, your mind is made up? You've already promised to marry him? *Fait accompli?*" He felt his heart was in a vise with no hope of release.

"I haven't given him my answer, but I see no reason to turn him down. I've prayed for a Christian husband and now it looks like I'll have one."

"Tom just asked you last night. Aren't you rushing into this decision? Shouldn't you wait until he's grieved Ida's death? He can't be over losing her, can he?"

"We talked about all that over our coffee last night. He says he's ready to move forward into the next chapter of his life. Fortunately for me, he's including us in that chapter."

"Have you told him about your difficulties with Elliot?"

"No, why on earth should I?"

"He needs to understand you and your responses to—things."

"Honestly, you're worse than Prudence Phillips and Aunt Mag all rolled up together."

"What does that mean, madam?"

"I expect them to be critical and fault finding, but I thought you'd be happy for God's provision in my life. Don't you want me to marry and have a normal family?"

"More than you know." He all but growled as he slowed the rig down to a stop at her hitching post.

"I don't need any more lectures, thank you very much."

She tried to hide her disappointment over his reactions. He said nothing more and helped her down from the wagon. She hurried up the walk to tell Nathan and Magnolia that the doctor was waiting on them.

She had already thought of every drawback Adam mentioned. Even though she recoiled at his intrusive comments, something within her heart heard a warning. The doctor's opinions caused her to reconsider

Tom's proposal. As she prepared for bed that night, she read over her list and prayed about what to do as she brushed out her hair.

"Heavenly Father, I think it's probably best to live with my decision a few days before talking to Tom. Please guide my heart and thinking about Tom's proposal. I only want Your best for Polly and me."

On their ride back to town Adam hid his foul mood from Nathan and Magnolia, but inside he was fuming. When he led Fancy into the barn, he found the stalls had not been cleaned. As he shoveled away the manure and spread clean hay, he expressed his disgust to Fancy.

"You can be sure I'll speak to Willy about this. What a mess to come home to."

He gave Fancy some oats for her hard work of the afternoon and started unloading the wagon. When he came to the old table, he threw it onto the trash heap where it splintered apart with a loud crash.

"Lucky for you it's only the table, Tom." To further vent his anger, he gave the splintered table a couple of swift kicks. Bonnie scampered for safety into the shadows of the barn.

As he walked toward the house he remembered that Sunday was Willy's day off and he had no one but himself to blame for the dirty stalls. What else could go wrong with this afternoon he had so carefully planned?

That evening after Nathan was asleep, he puttered around in the clinic until there was nothing to do but go to bed. He paused in the foyer and remembered how lovely Clarissa and Polly had looked standing there in the sunlight a few short months ago.

Dear God, what am I supposed to do now?

Chapter 51

Adam sank deeper into his quandary about Clarissa. His feelings for her only deepened as he thought about Tom's proposal. He tried to convince himself not to care, but she was now too fully entwined in his feelings to dismiss. He berated himself for falling in love with someone whose fragile heart might reject him, but how could he have known about Tom's competition for her heart? His slow and patient approach had backfired.

If she was so positive Tom was God's answer to her prayers, how could he question that decision? He couldn't compete with the Almighty. She had prayed for a marriage to a decent man who would care for her and Polly and oddly enough, Tom fit her criteria. Case closed. However, his mind would not leave this case alone. Endless questions swirled between his heart and his mind:

Is this what jealousy feels like? I can't compete if a marriage to Tom is God-ordained, can I? How can I argue with that sort of conviction? Why do I want to deck Tom whenever I think of him on a honeymoon with Clarissa? Does she honestly want to marry a man who can barely converse? Should I tell her of my own intentions? Maybe I'd feel better if I did.

On the next Saturday morning Adam decided he would rather say everything wrong than keep his feelings to himself. He could not watch Clarissa marry Tom Lewis without telling her how he felt. He sent Nathan to the Jacksons' house for the morning and closed the clinic.

Walking along the same trek he had covered on his second day in Springdale, he thought about the contrast of this visit to Clarissa's house with that first one. No longer was she the little widow who would do his mending, but now he hoped she would become the love of his life. Nervous as a schoolboy clutching a handmade valentine, he walked to Clarissa's cottage and knocked on the door.

Dear God, here we go. In his heart he felt God's affirmation: "Take Courage."

"Good morning, Clarissa. Might I interest you in a bit of a walk down by the creek?" He saw pleased surprise in her eyes. He gestured toward the willows in the distance where glimmers of sunlight hovered over the creek. "This lovely morning is too glorious to waste inside."

"Oh, pshaw, Polly just went to sleep. I guess I can't go."

"What if I carry her along with us? We'll put her on a blanket in the shade and keep her in sight."

"Wonderful idea, I doubt she'll stir if we move her. She's been very fussy today." Her thick, auburn hair was still loose around her shoulders, but she didn't keep the doctor waiting to pin it up. After she grabbed Polly's yellow blanket, she dabbed her throat with "Fresh Meadows" perfume. With one last look in her oval mirror she whispered,

Hmm—now I'm 'Clarissa' again?

When Adam put Polly down on her blanket near the creek, the breeze ruffled her curls but she never stirred. They walked among the willows whose long, green fronds shaded them from the warm sunshine. The tiny flowers of Clarissa's dress matched the lush display of wildflowers along the creek banks. Metallic dragonflies on gossamer wings flitted back and forth across the creek.

"Just look at those beautiful insects, Doctor. They have no idea how breathtaking they are, do they?"

"No, they don't and there's no way to tell them, is there?"

"I suppose not. It's really sad, isn't it?"

"What is?"

"It's a pity they'll never know we appreciate their beauty."

After they meandered a short distance down the creek bank, Adam stopped and cut some long willow branches with his pocketknife. He tied them into a crude circle which he placed on Clarissa's hair, the first step in his carefully planned scenario. Even though he had rehearsed what he wanted to say to her, he felt he was fumbling his way into this conversation.

Glory Be!

"Clarissa, you're like these dragonflies. You don't realize how lovely you are."

"Thanks to your magic potion for my skin problems, I do look a bit better." She adjusted her willow crown and smiled up at him.

"No, you have something more. You have an inner beauty that my skills can't improve."

"Why, you flatter me, Dr. Norcutt." She flushed under his unexpected compliments.

"I've asked you to walk with me this morning for a reason." He stuffed his hands into his pockets as they walked along.

"Really?" She sensed he struggled for words.

"Yes. Have you given Tom an answer to his proposal?"

"Not yet. But as I told you, I plan to accept."

"And there is no possibility I can dissuade you?"

"I've prayed about this. A nice gentleman of staunch faith and impeccable reputation has asked for my hand in marriage. God seems to have put this all together for us and I see no reason to turn him down."

"No reason at all?"

"None."

"Forgive me, Clarissa, he's such a rigid, stuffed shirt. I don't see how..."

She interrupted him. "Please, no more lectures."

"I can't seem to let go of my concerns about this, Clarissa. The most serious is this—you don't love him."

His voice had an exasperated tone that puzzled her, but she held her tongue. *When did he become an authority on my emotions? I refuse to argue about this decision. After all, Tom didn't propose to Adam Norcutt, he proposed to me.*

He skipped some smooth stones across the gentle current of the stream. Throwing another rock at a tree, he hit it dead center.

"This all boils down to one thing in my thinking, Clarissa. You and Tom don't have the kind of loving relationship I hoped you'd find in a new marriage." He brushed a strand of hair away from her eyes and waited for her to argue with him. She broke the discomfort of the silence between them.

"So, lecture finished?"

"My dear, if you can't see the folly of this for yourself, I have nothing left to say." The distance between them chilled despite the warmth of the day. "However, I do have one more concern." He kept tossing rocks at nothing in particular. "I don't want to lose your friendship."

"Oh, Dr. Norcutt, you dear man. Tom and I will always be close to you and your family. I'll always be your friend. Please never doubt that."

Then, he knew. He refused to be the future Mrs. Lewis's "dear man." He wanted more of her than her friendship. In his mind's eye he saw a shuttlecock emblazoned with the face of Tom Lewis coming over the badminton net at the perfect angle for a magnificent slam.

Take the shot, Old Chap!

"Clarissa, we've shared many secrets, haven't we?"

"I must admit we've learned to trust one another's confidence." Sunlight glinted off the golden specks in her hazel eyes as she smiled up at him.

"Yes, of course." He tossed aside the remaining rocks in his hand. "But I've one more secret to confide."

Clarissa laughed. Her lighthearted response was in contrast to his mood.

"Please, don't laugh. Just listen."

"Certainly, Dr. Norcutt. Forgive me. I'm only laughing that you have yet another secret."

"Yes, I have another secret and you are right in the middle of it, my dear."

"Wait? I'm in a secret of yours? I don't recall. . . ." *My dear?*

He reached between them and took her hands. "Of course you don't. I've kept this from you for months, a decision I now regret. However, in light of your plans for a dubious marriage to Tom, I must tell you or I'll never forgive myself."

"Yes?" *Quit staring at his blue eyes, Clarissa Francine.* "What is it, for heaven's sake? Is Nathan all right?"

"It's not about Nathan. It's about me." He swallowed and took a deep breath. "You want to know the real reason I don't want you to marry Tom Lewis? I've fallen in love with you."

Her hands flew to her temples. Squeezing her eyes shut, she backed up. She felt buffeted in the silence between them until Adam filled the void.

"I know this seems sudden to you, but I've felt this way for some time. I was ready to tell you, but then Ida died and you were consumed with grief. You're always helping Tom at the store or tending his children." He knew he was babbling, but the words still poured out. "And now, all of a sudden, you are thinking of marrying the man."

She jerked off the makeshift crown and walked down the sandbar. Adam followed.

"Aren't you going to talk to me? Clarissa?"

"Dr. Norcutt, I don't know what to say. I love Nathan, that's no secret. You and I have become friends, but. . . ."

He stopped her mid-sentence. "Clarissa, stop. Your friendship is a treasure, but this isn't about being your friend. It's about being hopelessly in love with you. Just when I was ready to tell you, here comes Tom, who has somehow persuaded you to marry him even though you don't love him. You're breaking my heart and you don't even know it. This is why I had to tell you."

He spat out the last few words and spun away from her. When he turned to face her, deep emotions etched every line in his face. He smoothed his side burns and continued.

"I've been frantic all week trying to think of ways to divert your well-ordered plans to marry the man."

"You wouldn't be playing with my heart, would you?"

"I'd never do anything to hurt you, Clarissa. I'm completely serious about my love for you."

"But you and Miss Nellie are almost engaged. Aren't you?"

"We ended our relationship some time ago. Surely you heard about that."

"Magnolia told me you'd had a row but I thought you would. . . ."

"No! I haven't even seen her in weeks. No more Nellie Desmond for me. Not now, not ever."

When she continued to wander down the creek bed, he followed along and reached for her shoulder. He turned her to face him and found her cheeks glistening with tears.

"Please, don't cry. I couldn't let you marry Tom without telling you that I love you with all my heart. There, I've come straight out with it. Please tell me you could love me, too."

He rested his hands on her shoulders. She was mesmerized by the look in his eyes as he drew her to him and kissed her. His kiss was full of both tenderness and passion, unlike any kiss she had known before. Stunned, she pulled away from him.

"You're kissing me, Dr. Norcutt. . ."

He smiled. "I know that, Clarissa." He drew her close again. This time she sobbed and melted into his embrace. She returned his kisses as a new wave of emotion welled up with feelings for him, feelings she had denied too long.

"Dearest Clary, I'm so afraid of losing you. I had to tell you." He held her closer. "I can't, I won't let you go. Not even to a good man like Tom."

She looked up at him. "Is this really happening? I'm so confused."

He wiped her tears with his handkerchief. "I was hoping and praying you would be. To have you reconsider your decision was my prayer as I walked to your place. Today I'm officially tossing down my gauntlet in the duel for your affections."

Now oblivious to the darting dragon flies, they walked down the sandbar and back again. Her simple responses charmed him. He knew he was treading on treasured ground, for each time she trusted him with a piece of her heart, they were forming a strong bridge over their painful losses from the past.

Clarissa fidgeted with her willow crown as she tried to absorb what Adam was telling her. "Is this why you wanted to go for a walk?"

"Yes, I fear you have uncovered my nefarious intentions."

"How long have you had these feelings?"

"For a long time. I've been hoping and praying to find someone like you, even before I left London. When I thought I had finally found the right one to share my home and my heart, Tom cut in front of me and diverted the progress of my honorable intentions. I was appalled when you said you planned to marry him. As far back as that day Nathan threw his marbles at me, I knew I was falling in love with you."

"That long ago?"

"Yes, but then Ida died and you were inconsolable."

After Polly woke up, Adam helped her find some flat rocks she could stack up and knock over again and again. When she asked for something to eat, they made their way back toward the house. They came to the fence by the backyard and when he held the gate open, Clarissa put her hand on his arm.

"I suppose I must reconsider my answer to Tom now."

Adam smiled at her. "I think you should turn him down. You shouldn't enjoy my affection and return my kisses while you keep another poor bloke on his aching, bended knee, should you? Are you turning into a duplicitous vixen?" His eyes twinkled as he teased her.

"Heavens, no. But I was so sure of my decision until now."

"Follow your heart, Clarissa. God has given us more love for one another in this very moment than you and Tom could conjure up in a lifetime. Oh, sorry! You said 'no more lectures.' But I do have other means of persuasion."

Before she could move through the gate, he pulled her close with another kiss that left her breathless. Polly jumped up and down and demanded to be included.

"All right, Little Girl, we have hugs and kisses for you, too." He lifted the giggling toddler into their arms and they covered her cheeks with kisses. When they reached Clarissa's cottage, she invited him to come in.

"Polly and I have simple meals on the weekends, but you're welcome to join us."

"I'll say 'yes' to that, but I have one request and one reservation."

"Oh?"

"First of all, I'd like you to call me 'Adam.'"

"All right, Adam, I'll try. And your reservation would be?"

"I must know the exact location of that iron skillet of yours because I may want to kiss you again."

Chapter 52

Her lips still warm with Adam's parting kiss, Clarissa collapsed into her wicker rocker. She glanced around her home which seemed like a strange, new place. Within the space of a morning her life as a widow had crumpled. And what about Tom and the plans she was so sure God had put in place for a future with him? Now those were in disarray as well. Polly began to cry.

"Come here, sweetheart. I hope you aren't coming down with something." The toddler crawled into her arms where she fell asleep. But Clarissa needed to talk to someone. Never had she missed Ida more.

After Polly's nap, they walked to the parsonage where they found Sophie cutting flowers.

"Hello there, you two," Sophie pushed the stems of the colorful flowers into a bucket of water. "What brings you over here so late in the day?"

Clarissa acted nonchalant, but when Sophie took a closer look at her, she knew this was no social call.

"Clary? What's happened?"

"I'm sorry to come by so late in the day, but I've had quite a shock."

"Don't mind the time of day. Are you all right?"

"I think I am, Sophie. This is a good thing—at least I hope it is." She paused a moment to catch her breath and gather her thoughts.

"Dr. Norcutt called on us this morning and—" she paused again. "Oh, my stars, Sophie, you won't believe this." She put her hand on her chest and kept gulping for air. "He told me he's in love with me!" Red spots erupted up and down her neck.

"This is great news, Clary! Calm down, dear. It's high time you get serious about one another."

"What on earth are you talking about? How can you say that? Until recently, he's been all but engaged to Nellie Desmond."

"Haven't you heard? Miss Nellie and her parents are moving to Atlanta and he refused to move with them."

"Magnolia told me about their terrible argument at the clinic, but I assumed they would patch things up. They seem so perfect for each other."

"Oh, I disagree with you about that. I think Adam Norcutt has had his eye on you for a long time."

"Don't be ridiculous. When Dr. Logan left Springdale, he told Dr. Norcutt to look after me because I was pregnant. That's why he's been attentive. Nothing else has been going on, nothing at all."

"If you're honest with yourself, you've been sweet on him, too."

"I can't believe you would say that."

"So—am I right?"

"If you count a silly, sort of schoolgirl crush, then 'yes.' But honestly, until today I never dreamed he had any affection for me at all."

"I know you didn't, but for a long time he's had a gleam in his eye whenever you're around. Now you be careful, I wouldn't want him to draw you close only to break your heart."

"I know. I don't need that again."

"Come sit on the porch where it's cooler. We'll talk some more." They settled down with glasses of cool water from Sophie's cellar. "Let's think about this. First of all, you're sure he wasn't simply expressing his love for you as a friend?"

"I don't think so—not from the way he kissed me. More than once." She patted her heart and blushed. "He says he fell in love with me before Ida passed, but put off telling me until I recovered from losing her."

"Oh, dear, I see what you mean. Well then," she cleared her throat, "let's think of some other things. Do you think he would love Polly as his own daughter?"

"I don't need to think at all about my answer to that question. He and Polly have their own sort of camaraderie. Haven't you noticed how he calls her 'Little Girl?' And I've never seen a more devoted father than he is to Nathan. No doubt he'd be a wonderful father for any child."

"I do have some worries about your diverse backgrounds. He's been such a sophisticated man of the world, we all know this. So, is he ready for a Christian wife and homemaker, not a fancy socialite?"

"He always seemed comfortable at my place when he and Nathan were quarantined there. As for his wanting a Christian home, I've seen that mustard seed of his faith put down deep roots in his life. He may not have all the details figured out, but who does? His faith is real and growing. He talks about it openly. And why on earth would he claim to love me if he isn't interested in a Christian wife? After all the debates we've had over these past two years, he knows what I believe and that I won't compromise my convictions."

"Yes, we've all watched his amazing change from atheist to Christian. You're right, Christ has done a miraculous work in his heart. That seed of faith finally found fertile ground in his heart. But what if he decides to return to high society? Maybe someday he'll decide to leave this simpler life behind."

"He'll just have to take me with him. I can gussie up if I have to. I know how to make all those elegant clothes, so I can make them for myself. To be quite honest, Sophie, I've had more schooling and finishing than some of the finest ladies in Springdale. But from what he says, I don't think he misses that life."

"Nevertheless, no one is perfect. Marriages are built on trust. Can you trust him?"

"Awhile back he told me that when the right man came along I would know if he was trustworthy. I certainly didn't dream he would be that one. Anyway, he didn't propose, he just declared his love."

"I'm telling you, I think you'd better get ready to make a wedding gown. That doctor's been biding his time for you all along. You've been so determined not to fall in love with him that you couldn't see it." Sophie had won the argument and they both knew it.

"I'd better go home. I'm fortunate to have a friend who is such a good listener."

"I wouldn't miss a story as good as this one."

"To make my news a stitch better, I'll tell you one last thing. I've had a marriage proposal and until today I planned to accept it."

"What? Who on earth?"

"Tom Lewis."

"You can't be serious. So soon after Ida's death?"

"That's what I thought. But he assures me that he is ready to move on with me as his wife."

"Did you really consider marrying him?"

"I've asked God for a long time to send Polly and me a Christian man who could be a good husband and father. That's Tom in a nutshell, so when he proposed, I thought he must be God's answer."

"But you don't love him, do you?"

"I've known him a long time and think the world of him. But to be quite honest, it's been hard to imagine being married to him. I decided that God would supply the missing feelings—when necessary." They giggled at the preposterous scene Clarissa hinted at.

"Now you listen to me. You know that verse that says God will give us more than we can ask for or think of? You'd better claim it!"

Clarissa jumped to her feet.

"Glory be! Of course I know that verse—it's in Ephesians. For Adam Norcutt to fall in love with me is far beyond anything I've ever dreamed of, much less asked God for."

"I don't think God is finished with your love life yet. In my opinion you should scratch Tom Lewis off your list of possibilities. Honestly now, which of these men could you truly love as your husband?"

"Right, that's the question I must answer. I have a lot more excitement and joy in my heart when I think about loving Adam Norcutt. Sophie, I feel so safe with him. I can picture him as my husband and Polly's father so much better than Tom. Now promise you won't tell anyone about all this."

"I won't tell a soul. But when you and the doctor are together, it's no secret."

Clarissa wrestled late into the night over the change in her determination to marry Tom Lewis. Adam hadn't proposed, but neither could she accept Tom's proposal if she was in love with someone else. Sitting by the glow of a single candle, she wrote:

Dear Tom,
  I have prayerfully considered your proposal of marriage and feel I must decline. Despite your many fine qualities and our friendship

over the years, I am unwilling to marry a man for whom I have no loving affection. I also must decline your offer to become involved at the Lewis Mercantile. Please know that I will always consider you a friend.
Clarissa

As she dressed for bed and said her prayers, she wondered if she had done the right thing.

"Lord, if rejecting Tom's proposal is going against the grain of Your plan, please stop me. I can't believe what happened today with Dr. Norcutt. I mean, *Adam*. But if You aren't in these events, please show me Your path."

At the Springdale Clinic, Adam complimented himself on his morning mission and Clarissa's response to it. Before supper, he and Nathan rode horses and later played checkers until the boy started yawning. Adam sent him off to bed and welcomed the long, quiet evening.

Settling down on the back porch, he mulled over the prospect of bringing a wife and a daughter into his life. If he ever married again, he wanted a wife who would love him and enjoy having a happy home and family with him. After Clarissa's responses to him that morning and knowing her for two years, he felt sure she would be that kind of a partner.

He thought about housing, schooling, and the expenses of a larger family. He tried to imagine a life with Clarissa under his own roof. His next thought brought his plans to an abrupt halt.

What if she rejects me? What if she won't marry me?

He had made the grand assumption that her responses to him that morning were tantamount to a marriage contract. The more he thought about it, the more determined he became to secure her hand in marriage. He was going to enjoy pursuing Widow Chambers. This time, he would not hold back as before.

When Sunday morning dawned, Adam was up early and made sure Nathan was awake. After they finished breakfast, they dressed for church.

"How would you like to ride out and offer to escort Miss Clarissa and Mistress Polly to church? Shall we surprise them?"

"Yes sir, they like surprises."

"Most girls do, don't they—if they're the right kind. You comb your hair while I hitch Fancy to the buggy."

Soon they were on their way. Adam eased Fancy and the rig up to the hitching post at Clarissa's cottage.

"Go to the door, son. See if they'll go along with our surprise."

Polly's carriage stood ready for the Chambers' walk to church and their customary Sunday dinner at the parsonage. When Clarissa opened the door to find Nathan smiling at her, she accepted their offer with a glowing smile.

"Of course we'll go with you, Nathan. How nice of you come out here to offer. We'll be ready in a moment."

"Good." He waved to his father.

Adam came onto the porch and called to Clarissa. "We're loading these things in Polly's carriage into my rig."

"Thank you, but don't spill my butter beans." She rushed to put the last pins in her hair and scoop up her sheet music. Her heart pounded so hard she cautioned it not to burst through her bodice. *Just calm down.*

Adam stole a kiss and then another as he helped her into the carriage. Clarissa's heart soared, but she made herself turn to him sternly. She was sure he could see the gleam in her eye, but something had to be said. *Didn't it?*

"None of that, sir," she whispered. "You must behave. I haven't even turned down Tom's proposal yet."

Adam smiled and winked, but made no further attempts to touch her.

Adam anticipated people's stares when he and Widow Chambers entered the church house together and was not disappointed. More curiosity followed when Clarissa finished at the piano and went to sit with Dr. Norcutt and their children. But she was careful to sit with Nathan and Polly between them.

After church she sought out Tom as he was hitching up the Lewis carriage. It seemed a bit callous to respond to his proposal in the churchyard, but she knew she must do it immediately. She squared her shoulders as she greeted him.

"I—I'm sorry, Tom, but I must turn down your proposal. It means a great deal that you would ask, but I don't think we'd suit." She handed him the note.

Tom nodded and shoved the note in his pocket. "All right, then." He turned away to deal with something on his horse's harness.

Clarissa waited beside him for an instant. *Right. Reason number four: not very talkative.*

"Well," she said, trying to sound bright and casual. "You'll be at lunch at the parsonage, won't you? I'll see you there."

He nodded but did not respond. She noticed him watching her step into the Norcutt rig. She cringed inwardly, but there was no help for it. She knew she loved Adam, and she wasn't going to hide it. Tom would find someone else soon enough.

On the way to the parsonage, Adam asked quietly, "All taken care of?"

Clarissa nodded.

"So I can kiss you freely now?"

"Not in front of the children, Doctor." She tried to sound serious, but she had a hard time not giggling like a fourteen-year-old. When he reached over to hold her hand, she made no protest. The children weren't paying attention anyway. She was sure of it.

Before they served up Sunday dinner, Sophie and Clarissa visited out in the parsonage kitchen. First there were whispers, then lots of smothered laughter, then more whispers and more laughter. Tom and Steven were oblivious to what was happening. Only Adam had any idea what might be going on in the kitchen. When the women joined the men for dinner, Clarissa looked embarrassed and self-conscious. Adam restrained himself from announcing to everyone how pretty she was when flustered.

After dinner Pastor Steven pushed his chair back from the table. "I enjoy Sunday dinner with you friends because at least this is one place where folks won't be criticizing my sermon today—at least I hope not. Or should I leave the room?"

"We've used a good deal of restraint, Pastor," teased Adam. "To your credit, your sermon today on Romans 8 gave me some good food for thought. Now I'll have something to think on as I go about my week. Today's sermon made high marks. Keep that arrow in your quiver."

"I'll register any complaints I have in the offering plate, Padre," groused Tom.

Sophie began clearing the table. Clarissa went to help her. When she returned to the dining room, she noticed Adam watching her with a besotted look on his handsome face.

She gave him a sly wink and a tiny smile.

Chapter 53

After Adam declared his love for Clarissa, their days went by in happy sequence. She basked in his loving attention while he marveled that this relationship had become such a delight when it had come so close to not happening at all. One lazy evening as they sat on the back porch watching their children play in the twilight, Adam took her hand in both of his and leaned toward her.

"Tell me what went on in that pretty little head of yours before I talked to you down on the sand bar. Be honest. Were you surprised?"

Clarissa hesitated. She balked at telling him how she had tried to suppress her feelings for him, but she did not want to evade his direct question.

"I'm not very good at this, Adam." He nodded for her to continue. "You did surprise me." She looked away. "I don't know how to say this, but I've always been drawn to you."

He raised an eyebrow and pointed to himself. "Drawn to me?"

"It was improper, but I've thought you were—are—a very appealing gentleman." She concentrated on the meadow before them. Little beads of perspiration broke out on her upper lip. A splotch of red erupted on her neck.

"Don't be shy. I want to know how you felt."

"You mustn't think that I was vying for your affections."

"Clarissa, I didn't. I was unaware of your interests."

"Not interests, I had no interests." She sighed in exasperation. "I'm not making myself clear. I was determined not to be 'interested.' I knew my place in your world and the gulf between us." She stamped her foot. "Surely you know that?"

Instead of sharing her feelings, she was making herself miserable and this was the last thing either of them wanted. She was relieved when Adam dropped the subject and helped her to her feet. As she turned to walk toward the children, he took her wrist and pulled her with him into the shadowy dining room.

"Come in here with me, pretty lady."

Clarissa gasped and pulled away in terror. *Pretty lady. . . pretty lady.* She could smell Pvt. Gary's breath and the dank, dark air of the shed. "No!" she whispered in a hoarse croak and stumbled toward the kitchen. Magnolia watched in wide-eyed silence as Adam followed her, asking, "Clarissa, darling, what's the matter?"

When she saw them staring at her, she ran sobbing out onto the back porch.

"Magnolia, see if you can help her."

Magnolia rushed out and the screen door slammed behind her. Nathan reached for the door but Adam stopped him.

"But Papa, what's the matter with Miss Clarissa?"

"Wait here, son. Magnolia is taking care of her."

As Clarissa leaned against the railing of the back porch, she gasped for air. Magnolia hovered over her.

"Miss Clarissa? Honey, cain't you breathe?"

Clarissa tried to speak, but shook her head. Perspiration soaked her clothing while she gasped for air. Magnolia motioned for Adam to bring a wet cloth.

He spoke to Nathan as he poured cool water on a kitchen towel. "Son, I think I know what's happening. Our Clarissa will be all right, but I need to take her into the clinic. Why don't you and Polly go to your room and play with your blocks? Magnolia will be with you in a few minutes." Nathan nodded and led Polly away.

"Magnolia, keep an eye on the children for us. I'll tend to Miss Clarissa now."

"Yes, Mr. Doctor. Will she be all right?"

"Don't worry. She'll be herself in a few moments."

He sat by Clarissa and wiped her face with the cool cloth. She still struggled to breathe.

"Listen to me, Clary. Cup your hands around your mouth and nose. Now breathe into them. Take all the time you need. Don't be afraid, I'm right here with you." He stayed close beside her. "In and out, in and out," he paced her breathing. "You aren't ill, are you?"

She shook her head.

"Did I do something to upset you?" She nodded and began to gasp again. "But what did I do? Did I hurt you?" She shook her head.

"Clarissa," his voice was gentle but firm. "Tell me what this is all about." He paused for her explanation. When still there was no answer, he took her in his arms. "What upset you? Something did, so tell me—please, tell me."

"You did upset me," she struggled to inhale, "but I can't really blame you."

"Widow Chambers, you aren't making sense."

"It's what that soldier did."

"What soldier?"

"P-private Gary."

"You are upset with *me* because of what he did to you?"

"No. Well, yes."

"What the. . .?" When he was obviously irritated, she found a stronger voice.

"When that soldier took me by the wrist and pulled me into that old, dark shed, he said the same thing, exactly the same words, that you said to me a moment ago."

The horror of what she was telling him began to register.

"I know it was coincidence, but it was like you were re-enacting that nightmare. You even called me the same name, 'P—Pretty lady.'" She shivered at the horrible memories. "You pulled me by the wrist into a dark place like he did."

"Oh, sweetheart, no wonder." He wiped her tears as she collapsed with relief against him. She began to calm down, but still wept.

"I felt like everything was happening again and I was trapped and helpless. It was horrible."

"But I wouldn't harm you in any way."

"Of course you wouldn't, but all those bad memories took over. I guess I lost control."

"Do you have these memories often? Like this?

"Never like this before. I've never been too upset to breathe."

"What brings these memories to mind?"

"I can't predict when they will come back. But when they do I try to block them out before I get too upset. Whenever I see that awful shed out back, I look away and think about something else. That soldier still shows up in my dreams. Sometimes he is all mixed up with Elliot. In the worst dreams, Elliot steals Polly from me and gives her to Pvt. Gary."

"I grieve those horrible memories with you, Clary. I'm so sorry."

"I'm so sorry I dragged you into this. After all, you didn't even live here when it happened."

"Now that I know why my words upset you, I understand. But I only wanted to kiss you in the privacy of the dining room to show you my love, not to frighten you."

They continued talking and by the time the children wandered into the clinic, Clarissa had dried her tears. When Polly ran from the clinic toward the parlor, Clarissa hurried after her. She turned and whispered, "Thank you," then blew Adam a kiss which he caught mid-air and held over his heart.

He checked his ledger for the next day and put a large "X" through the morning.

Chapter 54

Early in the morning, Adam and Nathan arrived unannounced at Clarissa's cottage in an open cart drawn by Standard. Fancy was saddled and tied in back of the cart which held Willy and some other workmen. Adam, stripped to his undershirt, jumped down with Nathan. They waved when Clarissa and Polly walked out onto the front porch.

"Adam? What on earth are you two up to this time?"

"These men have come along to help me with a chore. If you'll give Nathan some porridge, we'll be about our business."

"Of course, but what chore are you talking about?"

"Don't worry. You'll understand soon enough."

The gruff tone in his voice and his look of fierce determination startled her. She was puzzled, but took the children inside. She was spooning up Nathan's porridge when she heard loud noises coming from her backyard.

"What on earth is happening out there, Nathan?"

"Let's go out and see."

She rushed to the kitchen door to see Adam and his helpers tearing down the old shed. Her belongings stored in the shed now sat in the wagon. When a pile of debris stood in place of the old shed, he came over to the kitchen door where she stood watching.

"These men will take your things to the farm to store them, if that's all right?" She was speechless, but nodded her agreement.

He turned to the workmen. "Willy, tie Fancy out front for me, then go out to the plantation with this load. Come by the clinic later to pick up your pay." As the cart moved out River Road toward the plantation, the sounds of the men singing lingered in the morning air.

Adam opened the screen door and beckoned for her.

"I need you now." He reached for his shirt and pulled it on. "The rest of this chore is up to you."

They walked together to the mound of splintered, rotten wood. He reached for a handful of dry moss and kindling which he set on fire with a flint. In a moment he held out several burning sticks to Clarissa.

"Now, my precious Clarissa Francine, burn this infernal place down."

She nodded. Her cheeks were wet with tears, but she was composed and determined as she held the flame under the pile of rubble. Together, they watched the fire lick beneath the remains of the old shed and her horrific memories.

"Think, Clarissa. Is there anything else you should add to this pyre?"

She was quiet for only a moment before she ran into the house and returned with her marriage license and the old love letters from Elliot in one hand. In the other hand she held the torn clothing from her last violent encounter with George Gary. With a shudder she threw everything onto the blaze.

"Good riddance," she whispered.

"Louder," prompted Adam.

"Good riddance," she declared in a stronger voice.

"Again."

"Good Riddance! Forever!" She shouted the words and looked toward heaven through her tears. For a long time they stood close together as they watched the pain from her past turn to ashes. He held her until her sobs subsided.

"I couldn't get here fast enough this morning. I wanted to destroy this miserable shed and all the ghosts inside it. Does this help at all?"

"Yes, it does, a great deal. I've needed to do something about that shed, but I didn't know what." In a few moments she looked up at him, "What about your memories?"

"Make no mistake, my wounds have taken years to heal. Before I left London, I agonized for a year over my failed marriage. I had terrible times of remorse whenever I had any quiet moments in Lexington. My worst moment was when I threw my wedding ring overboard during a ranging storm on my voyage back to London."

"But you rescued Nathan out of all that neglect."

"Yes, thank God for that."

"Isn't it interesting, Adam? Without our difficulties, we'd both be childless. Now, our little ones bring us so much joy, don't they?"

Adam nodded. They were silent as they absorbed the magnitude of what they lived through in the past two and a half years. "You know, Clarissa, I suspect that God in His goodness brought us this far so He could bring us together."

"He's been good to us, hasn't He?"

"I hope Tom will forgive me. Not only have I wrecked his marriage plans, but now I've demolished his shed. I'll have Willy build him a new one if he objects. But I won't give you back."

Her next comment puzzled him.

"You won't have to answer to Tom about the shed."

"Why not?"

"This place belongs to Mistress Polly Chambers."

"You mean even our Little Girl has a secret?" He held her at arm's length. "I thought there were no more secrets between us?"

"This property will soon be in her name. Come on inside and I'll explain. Your tea cup is waiting for you and there's some oatmeal—I mean *porridge*—left over if you're hungry."

After washing himself off with cold water at the spring, he came inside. While he devoured a large bowl of steaming oatmeal covered with cream and maple sugar, she told him about Polly's inheritance from George Gary. They spent the rest of the morning sipping tea and talking about the current blessings of their lives.

Wisps of smoke still curled over the place where the shed once stood. The smoldering coals glowed as a diminishing memorial to Clarissa's memories. When they went outside, he pointed toward the creek. The willows in the distance had moved through the smoke and into the view that had been blocked by the unsightly building. A peaceful scene now rested in its place.

"From now on, when you look this way, remember those willows witnessed the beginning of our love story. Can you do that?"

"Yes, it will always be our special place. Thank you for this lovely gift."

"Gift?"

"Yes, this new panorama in my backyard."

"You're most welcome." He leaned down to kiss her. "I should go into town now. I still have a clinic to run. When I rushed out here, I forgot to leave a note on the door."

"Why don't I keep Nathan here for the day? We'll walk back with him in time for his supper."

"Good idea. If you'll join us, I'll have Magnolia set a place for you and Polly."

Clarissa stood on the front porch and waved good-bye as Adam mounted Fancy. She went inside to tidy up the kitchen and finish dressing. She put on a clean apron, pinned up her hair and dabbed her throat with "Fresh Meadows" perfume. With a grainy twist she put the stopper back into the cut glass bottle and smiled.

"Clarissa Francine," she spoke to her reflection in the mirror, "I think you've found God's answer to your prayers. Adam claims to love you and I think he really means it. He said some day I'd know, and I do. I know without a doubt I can trust Adam Norcutt and his love."

Chapter 55

Two weeks later oppressive heat and stifling temperatures hovered over Springdale. Hoping for a cooling breeze, Adam and Clarissa strolled in the shade of the huge oak trees in his back yard. The children played with Bonnie's latest litter of kittens. When Adam told Polly she could have one, she picked out a tiny calico kitten and named her 'Kitty Kay.' They watched the children play with the kittens until Polly needed her nap.

"Nathan, you two go inside out of this heat, and ask Rosalie to put Polly down for her nap. I'll be in later to play some checkers with you."

Polly was despondent when Adam made her leave Kitty-Kay outside with Bonnie. The screen door slammed as the children went inside and their parents continued walking.

"By the way, Clary, when I was at the bank yesterday, I heard that Tom Lewis is close to financial ruin and may lose his store."

"Why, I had no idea. He told me recently how successful he's been. He never mentioned money problems in all the hours I worked there."

"Sometimes men have a hard time admitting these things."

Clarissa was silent and looked into the distance. She began to frown and fidget.

"Is something the matter?"

"Do you suppose this is why Tom urged me to buy the cottage for Polly? Ida always told me there was no rush."

"I think he's selling everything of value—with the exception of Lester and Lydia."

Clarissa turned away.

"What's the matter?"

She walked ahead, then turned back.

"Think about it, Adam. Other than you and the banker, Tom is the only person who knows about Polly's fortune. I read the letter to him and Ida the day after it arrived. When he asked me to invest in the store, he gave me some documents to look at. I only glanced at them, but I remember seeing the word 'collateral.' Is this why he proposed so soon after Ida's death?"

"Wait a minute. You think Tom was after Polly's money to save his financial neck?"

"Maybe. Oh, Adam, if that was his motivation, I was headed for another loveless marriage."

"Well, at least you've found your instincts about men who don't have your best interests at heart."

"But I can't be angry with him. I've been friends with him too long to hold it against him. He loves those twins and that store is everything to him. I can't blame him for doing everything he can to save it. Do you think there's a way we can help him?"

Adam shook his head. "We would just embarrass him. He's a proud man. He's moving to Tuscaloosa where his brother has a store. I think we have to let the poor bloke go."

"Ida is turning over in her grave. She'd be mortified."

"Yes, but I also think she is cheering for you. I know I am."

They walked arm and arm down the fence row and Adam began talking about more pleasant things.

"Even before I came here, I was determined to find a life with peace and trust in it."

"You've made real progress in finding what you came for, haven't you?"

"Yes, and you've been a good example for me to watch. Even with all the difficulties you've faced, you glow with such peace within."

"You're only seeing how God blesses me in the midst of it all. You know how I've struggled. I'm no expert on life."

"You are in my eyes. You and Polly have quietly seeped into every part of my life. Remember when I was first quarantined at your house?"

"How could I forget? I thought you were dying. I felt so helpless."

"As I came to that first morning, I felt safe for the first time since The War. I fought waking up because I wanted to stay there, wherever it was."

"And then God answered my prayers. Your fever broke."

"I can still go back there to the fragrance of your perfume and the softness of your hair tangled in my fingers. God knows, I want to go back there with you and stay." He held her at arms length. "I want the way it felt with the four of us living together. Will you create a family with me, Clarissa?"

"You know I will." She smiled. "But this time I want you healthy."

"Nathan and I need you and love you so much."

"And I love you with my whole heart."

He kissed her softly, much like she had seen him kiss the children.

"Clarissa, my Clarissa," he stopped and looked at her. "You'll be my Clarissa, won't you? Will you marry me?" He bent down on one knee. "Please say 'yes.'"

Her arms circled his neck and she placed her forehead on his.

"Yes! A thousand times, yes."

He stood to kiss her, but this time not at all like he kissed the children. She pulled away, laughing.

"I should have said 'maybe' or 'I'll think about it,' so we could prolong this moment. I don't want it to ever end."

"Then I suggest we go to the sand bar, then move to your front porch, then come back here to my back yard, then ride out to the plantation. Let's find ways to prolong this moment for a lifetime. I'll keep asking you as long as your answer is 'Yes.' Can I count on that?"

"Yes, Adam, I want to be right beside you wherever that is."

Reaching around, he pulled the combs and pins from her hair. As she shook it free, it cascaded around both of them. As in his memories, it was soft and silky. He breathed in the fragrance of her perfume, another welcome memory. A brisk breeze came from out of nowhere and caught them in the auburn web of her hair.

"I still don't see how you can change so fast. You were all but engaged to Miss Nellie."

"Will you quit worrying about that?" He caught her hair in his hands and tugged on it. "I was never in love with Nellie Desmond. Not ever. I wasn't even tempted to move to Atlanta. My place is here, in Springdale, with you and Nathan and Polly."

"But one day I'm your friend and the next I'm engaged to you?"

"Blame it all on Magnolia."

"Magnolia?"

"Ask her. She'll be happy tell you all about how it happened." Then he remembered. "Uh-oh, I forgot—checkers with Nathan. Somehow you've distracted me."

They walked arm in arm through the yard toward the back porch.

"I love you, Clarissa. You can depend on my love. It isn't going to vanish." He wanted to reassure her that his love was and always would be constant.

"Do you mind reassuring me of that for the rest of my life?"

"Not at all, as long as you stay right here by my side."

Chapter 56

After Adam asked Magnolia to watch Polly and Nathan, he invited Clarissa to go with him to see his secret project at the plantation. The hot, humid air had continued to languish over the hills of Kentucky. Even the underbrush along the roadside wilted for lack of rain. The breeze they felt riding into the countryside was a welcome relief from the oppressive heat.

As they neared the plantation Adam leaned toward her. "Do you still like surprises? I have one for you if you'll close your eyes."

"Of course, but don't tell me you painted the house red." She squeezed her eyes shut.

"No, nothing like that." He laughed and guided Fancy to the entrance of the plantation. "Whoa, Fancy, stop right here. All set?" She nodded. "Tilt your chin up and open your eyes."

Clarissa looked up and gasped. At the entrance was a new gate topped with the name of the plantation: FRESH MEADOWS FARM. Underneath was the owners' name: NORCUTTS.

"Oh, Dr. Norcutt, it's perfect!" She brought herself up short. "Did I just call you 'Dr. Norcutt?'" He nodded. "Adam, Adam, Adam. You'll have to be patient with me."

"What's really going to take some patience is convincing Nathan to call you 'Mother,' and persuading Polly to call me 'Papa.'"

"I think Polly will call you whatever Nathan does. You're the only father she's ever known. You've been with her since the night she was born. Isn't that a God-given coincidence?"

He agreed. Knowing that Polly would be his daughter always made him smile. They had already discussed adopting one another's children. He felt sure that Josephine wouldn't refuse to relinquish her rights to Nathan. Or would she? Someday soon he must find out.

Glory Be!

"Adam, when can we tell Nathan? He's going to figure things out on his own if we don't tell him."

"Let's set our wedding date first. He'll be unbearable unless he has something definite to look forward to." He guided the buggy to a halt in front of the plantation house.

"Afternoon, Miss Clarissa." Willy came around the corner of the house.

"Hello, Willy. Let me guess. Did you have something to do with that beautiful new gate?"

"No'm. Not all of it. I built the wood part, but the blacksmith from town forged the iron work."

"It's perfect. From now on, everyone will know that the Norcutts live here." Willy took Fancy's reins and led her into the shade.

Adam and Clarissa walked into the plantation house. Clarissa stopped in the foyer, amazed. Even though some projects were still ahead, the place no longer looked abandoned. She had no idea so much progress had been made. She spun around on the newly polished floor.

"It's beautiful, Adam. It's even better than I imagined. When will you move in?"

"Soon. Nathan's room is finished and my—I mean, *our* bedroom is next on my agenda. Choose the wall covering you want for that room and we're done."

"You want me to make the choice?"

"Of course, why not? You'll be mistress here, Clarissa. I plan to turn many decisions over to you. Wall coverings, carpet, furniture—all of that will be up to you."

Clarissa tried to absorb the changes that were happening so quickly. Suddenly she was nearly dizzy with joy. She made another spin around in the foyer, and Adam caught her around the waist so they could waltz together.

"We must dance often, Clary." He held her closer. "You know, I first noticed how pretty you are while dancing with you and the children at that Fourth of July festival. Your beautiful smile that day changed you from a shy widow into a beautiful lady. Two other little souls were squeezed between us as we danced, but they didn't obstruct my view."

"As I recall, I thought about you that night, too."

"Wait." He paused mid-step. "Thoughts about your doctor? Tell me about this."

"You were smiling at me when Miss Nellie cut in. Let's just say I remember that day, too." They spun around another time or two.

"Come over by my new windows. I have another surprise for you."

He held her hand and led her toward the mid-morning light as it streamed over them. They stood in front of the huge windows and looked eastward over Fresh Meadows Farm. In the distance, a few geese flew south toward the river, an indication that perhaps cooler weather was on the way.

Adam raised Clarissa's hand to his lips, then reached into his watch pocket and pulled out an heirloom ring. He held it toward her in the sunlight.

"Adam? Is this really for me?"

"Yes, it's been in my family for years. It's yours now if you like it."

Clarissa choked back salty tears and nodded. "It's beautiful," she whispered. "I'm speechless."

He reached for her hand and slipped the ring onto her finger. She stared at the glittering ring, far more elaborate than any she'd ever dreamed of owning.

"My parents brought this with them when they came to visit. They knew I'd eventually marry over here."

"Why didn't they give it to you for Josephine?"

"They didn't approve of my choice. Now, let's make some plans. What if we marry here in front of my new windows on Thanksgiving Day? The house will be finished by then."

"Why that day?"

"Because I'm so thankful for you."

"I like the part about being thankful. It's a perfect wedding day for us."

"One more thing. For our wedding, could you wear that beautiful gown you wore to the concert? I'll never forget the sight of you that evening."

Clarissa shook her head. "No, I made it out of part of my trousseau from my other life. I'll make something even more beautiful to begin our new life together."

"Then I suppose I must retire that cravat from my first marriage."

"I think you should keep it. I'm rather fond of it."

"Why on earth would you like that cravat?

"It prompted the first kiss you ever gave me."

"Ah, that's right. As I recall, you didn't resist my amorous advances that night."

"No, but weren't you out of line to kiss a grieving young widow?"

"Downright scandalous! And to think I defended your virtue at the church house when your reputation was challenged."

"I know what I'll do. I'll make a new one for you from the same silk I use to make my wedding gown. I hope I can find a blue silk brocade to match your eyes."

"I've never heard of a bride's wedding dress matching her groom's eyes."

"Now you have." She held his face in her hands and looked into his blue eyes with no need look away or hold back her feelings.

Chapter 57

As Fancy took them back toward town, Clarissa had a question for Adam. "Since we've decided on a wedding date, shouldn't we tell Nathan when we get home?" She moved her hand so the sunlight caught her ring at the best angle.

"Good idea! I suspect he will be a very happy boy."

Clarissa wasn't so sure. "I worry about taking on this role in his life. He probably doesn't remember what it's like to have a mother."

"Don't sell yourself short. You said I'm the closest thing to a father that Polly knows, and the same is true of you and Nathan. You watch his reaction—you won't be disappointed."

Adam stopped the buggy at the parsonage and went to the door for Nathan. Sophie came out on the porch, waved to Clarissa and spoke a moment with Adam.

He called out, "Sophie is inviting us in for supper. What do you think?"

"Can Magnolia mind Polly this late?"

"She told me not to rush home. Come on in, I'm sure it's all right."

The friends gathered around the table for supper, a meal stretched to include unexpected guests. Clarissa kept her new ring in her lap out of sight; however, when the women were out in the kitchen cleaning up the supper dishes, Sophie glowered at her.

"How long do you intend to hide that ring on your finger? I saw it the minute you walked in this house. Now let me see it and tell me everything."

"Adam gave it to me this afternoon, but I accepted his proposal a few days ago. We haven't told anyone because the children don't know yet." She held her hand out for Sophie, who pulled her closer to the light from the kitchen window.

281

"It's spectacular, but if this were the ugliest ring in Kentucky, I'd still be happy for you."

Adam called out to the kitchen. "Come on. We have some important things to tend to at home this evening."

"What things, Papa?" asked Nathan.

"Don't be so curious, son. We'll tell you at home."

As they left the kitchen, Clarissa whispered to Sophie. "We've settled on Thanksgiving Day for our wedding date. I hope Steven is available. I can't wait to tell the children tonight. I still can't believe this is happening."

"What did I tell you? Honestly, I thought you two would never figure out this romance."

Fancy tossed her head and pulled the Norcutt carriage away from the hitching post. Clarissa waved to Sophie who wiped her eyes with her apron.

"Too many chopped onions," she replied when Steven asked her why she was crying.

As soon as Nathan learned something important was afoot, he was beside himself. He fidgeted and wiggled all the way home. As soon as they walked in the front door, Polly absorbed Nathan's excitement and spun around to make her little skirts stand out in a circle.

Under the guise of saying prayers with Nathan, Adam guided the beginnings of his new family back to his son's bedroom. Even though it was bedtime, both children were still wound up with excitement. After Nathan changed into his night shirt, he clambered around on the bed and under the pillows to play with Polly.

"We'll never get them calmed down, Clary."

"Probably not--not tonight!" Her own excitement matched Nathan's.

"Shall I just go ahead and tell them?"

"Yes, dear—there's no turning back now."

"Tell us what, Papa? What?"

Adam took Clarissa's hand and a deep breath. "Nathan and Polly, we have some good news. We have decided to be married and. . ."

"Hooray! Hooray!" Nathan shouted. He jumped up and down and kept hitting the bed with his pillow. Polly joined in by bouncing around and squealing. Her blond pigtails flew upright with excitement. Errant feathers floated above the new family.

"Whoaaaa!" Adam tried to calm things down, but there was no holding Nathan back.

"Hooray! I knew it, Papa. I knew it!"

Clarissa was curious. "Nathan? Did you overhear our plans to marry?"

"I didn't." A smug look covered his face. "I just knew."

Adam recalled a similar conversation in London when Nathan said he "just knew" his father was coming back to London for him.

"Hold your horses, son. Is this another one of the things you asked God for?"

"Yes," Nathan shouted. He took a huge leap and landed flat on his back with his arms spread out over the pillows. "Yes, I did."

Adam shook his head in disbelief. "I should've known."

Clarissa spoke up. "Adam? Should've known what?"

Adam gave Nathan a nod of encouragement. "Go on, son, tell us."

"I started praying we could be a family when Papa and I stayed with you."

Adam and Clarissa stared at him and then at one another.

"We barely knew Clarissa then. Why would you pray for that?"

"I don't know, Papa. I guess I liked it when all of us were together."

"Well, I'll be," Adam stammered.

"Why did you think I should marry your father?" Clarissa asked.

Nathan thought for a moment. "First of all, you like being with us and taking care of us. And Papa and I smile more when you're here."

"I'm sorry it took us so long to catch up with that prayer of yours." Adam reached over to smooth down Nathan's tousled hair.

Clarissa showed him the ring Adam had given her that afternoon. "An engagement ring means that we've promised ourselves to one another for the rest of our lives. You and Polly are a part of that promise. From now on we'll all be one family."

"Don't you want to hear about our wedding plans?" Adam asked.

Nathan nodded and listened to the details. As predicted, he had question after question. Polly kept jumping on the bed until Adam caught her and held her still.

"Calm down now, Little Girl."

The last rays of the sunset formed golden streaks and crimson shadows over the hills as Springdale was caught in the dusk. A peaceful calm settled over the family scene in the home adjacent to the Norcutt Clinic. Adam looked down at Polly who was almost asleep in his arms.

"Look at us, Clary. Why did it take me forever to figure all this out?"

"Sweetheart, I'm just thankful we both came to our senses. I loved you a long time before I knew it. I guess that doesn't make much sense."

"It makes perfect sense. I understand because I can echo the same sentiment."

They gathered their children into their arms and Adam kissed her as they all hugged.

When Nathan said his prayers, they were very brief. "Dear Heavenly Father, now I lay me down to sleep. Thank you for my new mum. Oh, and for my new sister." Together they all said, "Amen."

Polly slept on Adam's shoulder, but Nathan was still wide awake as his new family stood to leave. Clarissa straightened out the bed and tucked him in.

"Go to sleep now, son," said Adam. "Tomorrow we'll talk about the plans for our family as much as you want."

They extinguished the candle by his bed and Nathan burrowed down under the covers. As the rest of the Norcutts walked down the hall, they heard another muffled, "Hooray!"

In her quarters, Magnolia said to no one in particular,

"I think they's celebrating some mighty big news in yonder. I'se been expecting this for a month of Sundays. Yessireebob! I feel just like them children. Lawdy, Lawdy, it's high time we had us a broom jumpin' around here."

Discussion Questions

1. When was Clarissa Chambers wounded in the past? How?
2. When was Adam Norcutt wounded in the past? How?
3. Do these past wounds create any difficulty in their present lives? In what ways?
4. Do Adam and Clarissa come to a resolution of their past struggles? If so, how?
5. What pivotal incidents help Clarissa and Adam find stability?
6. What is the significance of the scene prior to Adam's giving Clarissa her engagement ring?
7. How does faith enter into the healing of Clarissa and Adam?
8. How do the following points of discussion surface in *Glory Be!*? Forgiveness, Trauma, Stress, Prayer, Worship Woundedness, Humor, Faith, Nightmares, Intolerance, Friends, Activities, Choices, Patterns.
9. Using modern terms, identify Clarissa and Adam's situations, conditions and personalities. What might be current solutions for their struggles?
10. What positive steps did Clarissa and Adam take to recover from their difficulties? What particular healing incidents stand out in your mind? Would their solutions be helpful today?
11. What significant roles do Nathan and Polly play in *Glory Be!*?
12. What symbolism, if any, flows throughout the story?
13. How do you relate to Clarissa and Adam? With which parts of their story do you most identify? Which was the most difficult? Which brought you joy?
14. Did you gain any wisdom or insight from reading *Glory Be!*?
15. To whom might you recommend *Glory Be!*? Why?

Acknowledgements

Cheers to my daughters Brenda Morris, Barbara Nelson, Mary McKee and their husbands, who have stood by me with their wisdom and humor. Thanks for all the times you read and re-read countless raw editions of *Glory Be!* My grandchildren and extended family helped with hugs and smiles along the way.

I'm also thankful for Leta Fae Arnold, Susan Clark, Linda Crocker, Alexandra Depuhl, Cheri Endean, Heather Gemmen, Susan Hamm, Gloria Hook, Charlynn Johns, Susan Klein, Dixie Lawson, Linda Lesniewski, DiAnn Mills, Peggy Nyquist, Golden Keyes Parsons, Julie Patrick, Trudy Richardson, Dorothy Satten, Kelly Stern, Les Stobbe, Lillian Tate, Priscilla Tate, Kathy Tolan, Anne Waldie, Anne Worth, my writers' group, along with friends, co-workers and neighbors too numerous to list. You all make me thankful to God for this adventure.

A Special Note to Readers

If you struggle with problems similar to those in this story, please seek professional help. The mental health field has many supportive solutions not available to Clarissa and Adam in the nineteenth century. Trained therapists, physicians, and pastors, as well as many community services can help you begin a renewed path in life. God bless you in your journey.

"Behold, I make all things new."
—Jesus

Revelation 21:5 NIV

Martha B. Hook
5202 Cloverdale
Tyler TX 75703

mhookdal@sbcglobal.net
www.marthahook.com

Stories you'll like about people you'll love.